INTELLIGENT SYSTEMS

The Unprecedented Opportunity

Horwood Artificial Intelligence Series
Series Editor: John Campbell

Machine Intelligence (Vols 8—10)
Editor-in-Chief: Donald Michie

Computer Game-Playing
Editor: Max Bramer

Implications of Computer Intelligence
M. Yazdani and A. Narayanan

Automatic Natural Language Parsing
K. Sparck Jones and Y. Wilks

INTELLIGENT SYSTEMS

The Unprecedented Opportunity

Edited by

J. E. HAYES
Research Associate
University of Edinburgh

DONALD MICHIE
Professor of Machine Intelligence
University of Edinburgh

ELLIS HORWOOD LIMITED
Publishers · Chichester

Halsted Press: a division of
JOHN WILEY & SONS
New York · Brisbane · Chichester · Toronto

First published in 1983 by
ELLIS HORWOOD LIMITED
Market Cross House, Cooper Street, Chichester, West Sussex, PO19 1EB, England

The Publisher's colophon is reproduced from James Gillison's drawing of the ancient Market Cross, Chichester.

Distributors:

Australia, New Zealand, South-east Asia:
Jacaranda-Wiley Ltd., Jacaranda Press,
JOHN WILEY & SONS INC.,
G.P.O. Box 859, Brisbane, Queensland 40001, Australia

Canada:
JOHN WILEY & SONS CANADA LIMITED
22 Worcester Road, Rexdale, Ontario, Canada.

Europe, Africa:
JOHN WILEY & SONS LIMITED
Baffins Lane, Chichester, West Sussex, England.

North and South America and the rest of the world:
Halsted Press: a division of
JOHN WILEY & SONS
605 Third Avenue, New York, N.Y. 10016, U.S.A.

British Library Cataloguing in Publication Data
Intelligent Systems. –
(Horwood artificial intelligence series)
1. Artificial intelligence-Congresses
I. Hayes, J.E. II. Michie, Donald
001.53'5   Q335

Library of Congress Card No. 83–12715

ISBN 0-85312-646-1 (Ellis Horwood Limited)
ISBN 0-470-27501-4 (Halsted Press)

Printed in Great Britain by R.J. Acford, Chichester.

COPYRIGHT NOTICE —
All Rights Reserved. No part of this publication may be reproduced, stored in a retrieval system, or transmitted, in any form or by any means, electronic, mechanical, photocopying, recording or otherwise, without the permission of Ellis Horwood Limited, Market Cross House, Coooper Street, Chichester, West Sussex, England.

Contents

Foreward
John Pascoe

Preface
Jean Hayes and Donald Michie

Contributors

Acknowledgements

PART I **Knowledge-based Reasoning Systems**
1. The calculus of reasoning
   J.C. Shepherdson

2. Logical reasoning in machines
   J. A. Robinson

3. Knowledge engineering: the applied side
   E. A. Feigenbaum

4. A prototype knowledge refinery
   D. Michie

PART II **Engineering Tomorrow's World**
5. Seeing machines
   M. J. B. Duff

6. Walking machines
   R. McGhee

7. Computers in medical biotechnology
   W. F. Bodmer FRS

8. Technology and the universities
   D. B. Thomas

9. Robots of the future
   E. C. Joseph

INTERMISSION **The Population and Other Explosions**

10. Make room! Make room!
    H. Harrison

PART III **Impact on Life and Work**

11. The emerging challenge
    I. Lloyd MP

12. Training for multi-career lives
    P. Virgo

13. The future of work
    Sir Ieuan Maddock FRS

Author Index

Subject Index

Foreword

This book is an edited collection of the papers given at the annual Press Seminar organised by the Computer Systems operations of Sperry Limited. Each year senior journalists are invited to the company's International Management Centre at St Paul-de-Vence, near Nice, to hear presentations by leaders from industry, the sciences and the political arena. The seminar is now well established as a forum where subjects covering almost any facet of human development can be discussed, and it may be asked why Sperry, a pioneer and leader in the design, development and manufacture of computer systems, should sponsor such an event. The answer is simple. We believe that large multinationals, as well as being important elements of the commercial and industrial sectors where they operate, should also take a wider interest in these communities.

Sperry endeavours to make this contribution and in the UK two examples may be taken to illustrate this policy. First there is the sponsorship of the British Computer Society annual lecture. With Sperry support the society is now developing this event as one of its most important presentations to the computer community each year.

The second example is the seminar of which this book is a record. The theme title was *The Next Ten Years* and Professor Donald Michie of Edinburgh University was invited to be the independent chairman of the meeting, to select the speakers and to devise the programme. This brought together scientists, academicians and politicians who spoke on artificial intelligence, expert systems, and the future of work, education and medicine. Some of the financial and political aspects of the technological age were also discussed.

Sperry is the company which listens. At this seminar, as at those in former years and at those still to come, we listened to the distinguished speakers and to the journalists who were our guests, and learned. We hope they too benefited from this exercise in communication, and that a much wider audience will now also benefit through the pages of this book.

John Pascoe
Sperry
London

Preface

The question motivating this book is believed by some to be the most consequential ever posed. From the industrial revolution mankind gained a race of willing slaves — tireless and mindless machines. Today's information revolution is now set to populate our factories and homes with intelligent systems. The social change will be profound. The promise of augmentation for human life overstretches our powers to imagine or predict.

For five days as guests of Sperry Limited, research workers on intelligent systems joined with leaders of industrial and political life in contributing to a debate with invited representatives from the senior ranks of science journalism. The results, based on verbatim transcripts, are assembled in the thirteen chapters which follow.

Jean Hayes
Donald Michie

Contributors

Lord Balfour of Burleigh, Clackmannan, UK

Lord Balfour, who succeeded to the title in 1967, trained as an engineer and after war service with the Royal Navy, joined English Electric in 1951. He remained with the company for the next fourteen years, seven of them spent in India. From 1966-1968 he was Director and General Manager of Napier and Sons and from 1971-1980 he was Chairman of the Scottish Arts Council. Since 1968 he has been a Director of the Bank of Scotland, and of the Scottish Investment Trust since 1971. He is a Fellow of the Institute of Electrical Engineers.

W. F. Bodmer, FRS, Imperial Cancer Research Fund, UK

Walter F. Bodmer is a graduate of Cambridge University. His major research interests have been in molecular genetics, somatic cell genetics and the HLA system, now coupled with various applications of these areas more directly to cancer research. After graduating in mathematics he obtained a PhD in population genetics under the late Sir Ronald Fisher, and was a Fellow of Clare College, Cambridge from 1958 to 1961 as well as a Demonstrator in the Department of Genetics. In 1961 he went to Stanford University, California, to work with Joshua Lederberg, ending up as Professor in the Genetics Department in the Medical School before he went to Oxford in 1970 as Professor of Genetics. In 1974 he was elected to Fellowship of the Royal Society. He joined the Imperial Cancer Research Fund as Director of Research in 1979.

M. J. B. Duff, University College, UK

Dr Michael J. B. Duff is a Reader in Physics in the Department of Physics and Astronomy at University College London, where he heads the Image Processing Group. He is a Fellow of the Institution of Electrical Engineers and Honorary Secretary of the British Pattern Recognition Association, which he founded in 1967. Dr Duff's research interests have centred around parallel processing techniques applied to image analysis and his research group has been responsible for the development of the CLIP series of image processors. He has published over fifty papers on these and related topics and has organised and lectured at many international conferences and workshops promoting understanding in this field.

E. A. Feigenbaum, Stanford University, USA

Edward Feigenbaum is Professor of Computer Science at the Computer Science Department, Stanford University. He is Senior Principal Investigator of the work of the Heuristic Programming Project at Stanford, and has been Chairman of the Computer Science Department and Director of the Computer Center at Stanford University. He has served on the National Science Foundation Computer Science Advisory Board, and other governmental committees concerned with Computer Science. He is the co-editor of the recent encyclopaedia, *The Handbook of Artificial Intelligence*, and of *Computers and Thought*, also co-author of the *Applications of Artificial Intelligence in Organic Chemistry: the DENDRAL Program*, all published by McGraw Hill. In 1980-81, he participated in the founding of Teknowledge Inc., specialising in knowledge engineering, and IntelliGenetics, specialising in expert systems applications for genetic engineering. He received his BS from Carnegie-Mellon University in 1956 and his PhD from the same school in 1959.

Harry Harrison, Co Wicklow, Republic of Ireland

Harry Harrison was born in Stamford, Connecticut, grew up in New York City and was drafted into the United States Army when he reached his eighteenth birthday. After a short term in college and a longer one in art school he spent the next years in New York as an artist, art director and editor, finally as a freelance writer. He is the author of 30 novels, has published five collections of his short stories, four juvenile books, and edited countless anthologies. His books have been translated into 21 languages. He received the Nebula Award for his novel *Make Room! Make Room!* made into the film *Soylent Green*.

E. C. Joseph, Anticipatory Sciences Incorporated, USA

Earl C. Joseph, born in St Paul, Minnesota, obtained a degree in mathematics from the University of Minnesota in 1951. With Sperry Univac as a computer scientist and a staff futurist for the past 20 years, he is now President of Anticipatory Sciences Incorporated. He is a founder, current Director and past President of the Minnesota Futurists (a chapter of the

World Future Society), member of the IEEE, American Association for the Advancement of Science, DPMA, Robotics Section of SME, Society for General Systems Research and its Minnesota chapter co-founder . He is Editor and one of the founders of the journal *Futurics*, Advising Editor for the *Journal of Cultural and Educational Futures*, and editor of the newsletters *Future Trends* and *System Trends*. In addition he is an adjunct professor and visiting lecturer at the University of Minnesota.

Ian Lloyd MP (Havant & Waterloo), UK

Ian Lloyd was educated at Michaelhouse, (Natal), Witwatersrand University and King's College (MA, MSc). He is a Fellow of the Royal Statistical Society and has been an MP (now for Havant and Waterloo) since 1964. In October 1970 Mr Lloyd was appointed a member of the House of Commons Select Committee on Science and Technology and took an active part in the works of Sub-Committee 'A' on the Computer Industry. He was Chairman of the Sub-Committee on Technological Innovation and a member of the Japan Sub-Committee which visited Japan in February 1977. After the General Election of 1979 Mr Lloyd was elected Chairman of the Select Committee on Energy. Shortly before that election he also organised and chaired a Conservative working party on Information Technology, and later brought about the formation of the All-Party Committee on Information Technology. This Committee became the Parliamentary Information Technology Commitee in January 1981. Mr Lloyd is its current Chairman.

R. McGhee, Ohio State University, USA

Robert McGhee is Professor of Electrical Engineering and Director of the Digital Systems Laboratory at Ohio State University, Columbus, Ohio. He received his BS degree in Engineering Physics from the Unviersity of Michigan in 1952 and the MS and PhD degrees in Electrical Engineering from the University of Southern California in 1957 and 1963 respectively.

Before entering academic life in 1963 Dr. McGhee served in the US Army Ordnance Corps as a Guided Missiles Maintenance Officer and subsequently worked on missiles guidance problems with the Hughes Aircraft Company, Culver City, California. His current research interests include robotics, biomechanics, computer graphics, and machine intelligence.

Sir Ieuan Maddock, FRS, UK

Ieuan Maddock (Kt 1975, CB 1968, OBE 1953) was educated at Gowerton

Grammar School, Glamorgan and the University of Wales. The senior government posts he has held include Assistant Director of the Atomic Weapons Research Establishment (1965), Controller (Industrial Technology, Ministry of Technology (1961-1971)), Chief Scientist DTI (1971-1974) and DoI (1974-1977. He was Director of the National Physical Laboratory from 1976-1977. From 1977-1979 he was Secretary for the British Association for the Advancement of Science and Principal of St Edmund Hall, Oxford, between 1979 and 1982. He has Honorary DSc's from Wales (1978) and Bath (1978) and has contributed papers to various technical and scientific journals. In 1967 he was elected to the Royal Society. Sir Ieuan is currently Deputy Director of International General Electric, USA.

D. Michie, University of Edinburgh, UK

Donald Michie is a Fellow of the British Computer Society and of the Royal Society of Edinburgh, and holds the degrees of MA, DPhil and DSc from Oxford University for studies in the Biological Sciences. His interest in the possibility of programming human knowledge and intelligence into machines was stimulated during the war when he joined the Bletchley code-breaking establishment at Bletchley Park. After pursuing a post-war career in experimental genetics and immunology he returned to machine intelligence in the early 1960s. In 1967 he was elected to a Personal Chair of Machine Intelligence in the University of Edinburgh. He is editor-in-chief of the Machine Intelligence series and is the author of books and papers on this subject.

W. R. Read, Sperry Ltd, UK

Bill Read is Vice President and General Manager of the Computer Systems operations of Sperry Ltd. He took up this appointment in July 1981 when the UK subsidiary became a separate operating region reporting directly to the International Division based at the Computer Systems worldwide headquarters at Blue Bell, Pennsylvania. Read had previously been Managing Director of the UK region for eight years and under his guidance a 400% growth in business was achieved. He joined Sperry in 1969 but his experience of the computer industry goes back nearly thirty years to the beginning of business data processing in the UK.

J. A. Robinson, Syracuse University, USA

J. A. Robinson received his BA in Classics from Corpus Christi College, Cambridge in 1952. The following year he gained an MA in Philosophy from the University of Oregon, and in 1956 a PhD in Philosophy from Princeton University. After a period with E.I. du Pont de Nemours and Company as an operations research engineer he spent a year at the University of Pittsburgh as a Postdoctoral Fellow. In 1961 he joined the faculty of Rice University and was Professor of Computer Science from 1963 to 1967. Since 1967 he has held the posts of Distinguished University Professor of Logic and Computer Science at Syracuse University, and Visiting Research Fellow at the University of Edinburgh. Research since 1960 has been mainly on the theoretical design and practical implementation of mechanical deduction procedures. In 1963 he devised the "resolution" principle and has recently published a book on this work entitled *Logic, Form and Function* (Edinburgh University Press, 1978).

J. C. Shepherdson, University of Bristol, UK

J. C. Shepherdson, MA, ScD, is the H.O. Wills Professor of Mathematics at the University of Bristol. Born in 1926, he studied mathematics at Trinity College Cambridge from 1943-45. He was Assistant Experimental Officer at the National Physical Laboratory in 1946. He was subsequently appointed Assistant Lecturer, Lecturer, Reader and then Professor at the University of Bristol. From 1953-54 he was a Member of the Institute for Advanced Study, Princeton, Visiting Associate Professor 1958-59 at the University of California Berkeley, and Visiting Professor there from 1966-67. His research interests are mathematical logic and theory of computation.

D. B. Thomas, Rutherford Appleton Laboratory, UK

David B Thomas was educated at the University of Manchester, obtaining an Honours BSc in Physics in 1952 and from the University of Cambridge a PhD for work in fluid mechanics in 1956. After a period in UK industry working as a systems engineer on guided weapons which included a one-year's attachment to the Instrumentation Laboratory, MIT, he moved to Imperial College London in 1959 to engage in instrumentation for high energy physics experiments involving a large hydrogen bubble chamber. He transferred with this project to CERN, Geneva in 1963. In 1966 he returned to Rutherford Laboratory continuing to work on such cryogenic systems, both bubblechambers and polarised targets. Appointed Head of Applied Physics Division in 1973, he is currently Associate Director, Engineering, and is particularly involved in the work at Rutherford Appleton Laboratory in information technology.

P. A. Virgo, National Computing Centre, UK

Phillip Virgo was educated at Dulwich College, Peterhouse, Cambridge (BA 1968, MA 1971) and the London Graduate Business School (MSc 1973). After graduating from Cambridge with a degree in History, he joined the Microwave and Line Division of Standard Telephones and Cables, moving to ICL in 1969. After eight years with ICL as Analyst, Project Manager, Consultant, Comptroller and Business Planning Manager he joined the Wellcome Foundation as a Corporate Planner. In 1982 he joined the National Computing Centre as Technology Assessment Services Manager, and has been active since 1973 in policy studies, political education and liaison. He is author and co-author of numerous studies on the political and social issues posed by fundamental technology change.

Acknowledgements

Thanks are due to Laura Tatham and Wordpro Business Services Ltd and to Brian West and Verbatim Graphics Limited for their expertise and helpfulness in all matters concerned with the production of camera-ready copy. Most of all, we would like to thank Sperry Ltd for making the Conference, and hence the book, possible.

PART I

Knowledge-based Reasoning Systems

1

The Calculus of Reasoning

J. C. Shepherdson
University of Bristol

Introduction

Alan Robinson discusses elsewhere in this book the current state of the art of programming machines to perform logical and mathematical reasoning. I shall here fill in the background and give a very brief survey of the history of this endeavour and of the inescapable limitations it is subject to.

This is not something of importance only to logicians and mathematicians, for expert systems, sophisticated data bases and simple robots need to perform elementary logical reasoning. If condition A implies symptom B and a patient does not have symptom B then he does not have condition A, an example of

$(A \rightarrow B) \rightarrow (\text{not } B \rightarrow \text{not } A)$.

If all trains from Bristol to London stop at Bath then the 10.20 from Bristol to London stops at Bath, an example of

$(\forall x)(Px) \rightarrow P(a)$

(For all x, P(x) implies P(a)).

A robot picking up parts might have to work out that if A was under B and B was under C then A was under C, so that in order to pick up A, C would have to be removed first. It might derive this from a statement that the relation of being under was transitive:

$(\forall x,y,z)\ (xUy\ \&\ yUz \rightarrow xUz)$

(For all x,y,z, x is under y and y is under z implies x is under z).

I have deliberately chosen trivial examples of logical reasoning here involving only one step because I do not want to spend time explaining them. One can easily convince oneself that everyday reasoning of this kind, when written out in full, could involve dozens of steps. Proofs of theorems in pure mathematics are of a much higher order of complexity; a recent proof of a theorem on finite simple groups occupies a whole issue of the Pacific Journal of Mathematics, 365 pages. And that was concisely written; it was intelligible only to experts in group theory. If one were to write it out in elementary logical steps — which no one would ever dream of doing — it would have millions of steps. Such proofs are of direct interest only to pure mathematicians, but proving the correctness of mathematical statements is basically the same as proving the correctness of computer programs. And all of us are at the mercy of computer programs; we rely on them to work out our bank balance correctly, to protect the aeroplanes we travel in from collision and to protect us from nuclear holocaust. We are told that the American programs for mediating the response to supposed nuclear attacks have made several mistakes, fortunately harmless. We could all sleep more easily in our beds if we knew that it had been proved that the programs at least did what they were intended to do.

Early history

So this attempt to automate reasoning is worth pursuing. The actual mechanisation of the procedure only became practicable with the invention of the electronic computer. But for a long time before that attempts had been made to formalise logical inferences and mathematical proofs so that they could be checked by following simple rules, like the rules of arithmetic, requiring no understanding of the meaning of the statements involved, depending only on their form. Looking back one can see that the Greek philosophers and mathematicians over 2,000 years ago had set this endeavour firmly on its way. Aristotle correctly classified all valid forms of syllogism e.g.

$$\text{all } A \text{ is } C$$
$$\text{no } B \text{ is } C$$
$$\therefore \text{ no } B \text{ is } A$$

and Euclid derived all his results in plane and solid geometry from five postulates. At that time the aim of reducing reasoning to formal rules had not been formulated; it was a question only of analysing the nature of logical inference and mathematical proof and presenting them in a way which could be checked by experts in the field e.g., Aristotle (Organon I, 12) says: "One should therefore not discuss geometry amongst those who are not geometers, for in such a company an unsound argument will pass unnoticed". And although these were large steps they did not take us far along the road. Aristotelian syllogisms are a small part of logic; and Euclid assumed without proof certain intuitively obvious geometric facts. It was not until this century that a complete formalisation of Euclidean geometry was given, and it needs many more axioms than Euclid gave.

Certainly most Greeks would have abhorred the aim of mechanising logic and geometry. Donald Michie has given me a nice quotation from Plutarch's life of Marcellus:

". . . Eudoxus and Archytas. . . in solving the problem of finding two mean proportional lines (i.e. duplicating the cube). . . had recourse to mechanical arrangements. But Plato was incensed at this, and inveighed against them as corruptors and destroyers of the pure excellence of geometry."

Liebniz's dream

A thousand years later, when the first calculating machines had been invented, by Pascal and Leibniz, the aim of mechanising reasoning, at least reducing it to a formal calculus, was clearly stated by Leibniz. In 1677 in the preface to *The General Sciences* he wrote:

"If one could find characteristics or signs appropriate for expressing all our thoughts as clearly and exactly as arithmetic expresses numbers or analytic geometry expresses lines, we could in all subjects, in so far as they are amenable to reasoning, accomplish what is done in arithmetic and geometry.

For all enquiries which depend on reasoning would be performed by the transposition of characters and by a kind of calculus, which would immediately facilitate the discovery of beautiful results. For we should not have to break our head, as much as is necessary today, and yet we should be sure of accomplishing everything the given facts allow.

Moreover we should be able to convince the world of what we had found or concluded since it would be easy to verify the calculation, either by doing it over again or by trying tests similar to that of casting out nines in arithmetic. And if someone doubted my results I should say to him: 'Let us calculate Sir,' and taking pen and ink we should soon settle the question."

His full programme would have embraced not only pure and applied mathematics but also grammar, law, politics, physiology, theology, the art of discovery etc. He was rather optimistic about the time it would take:

> "I think that a few selected men could finish the matter in five years. It would take them only two however, to work out by an infallible calculus the doctrines most useful for life, those of morality and metaphysics."

Peano, Frege, Russell, Gödel, Church, Turing

In fact it was more than 200 years before the study of formal logic and the analysis of the foundations of mathematics had been advanced, by the work of Peano, Frege and others, to the point where formal logic appeared to be adequate for all reasoning in pure mathematics. Unfortunately Bertrand Russell discovered that Frege's system was inconsistent. He showed that you could define the class R of all classes which are not members of themselves, which gives a flat contradiction: R belongs to itself if and only if it does not belong to itself. Russell, Whitehead, Zermelo, Fraenkel and others devised systems which were still adequate to develop all mathematics and avoided this and all other known paradoxes. In the 1920s many mathematicians, particularly Hilbert and his school, tried to prove that these systems were

(a) *complete* i.e. all true mathematical results could be proved in them
(b) *consistent* or *correct* i.e. no false results could be proved.

In other words that they enabled one to prove the whole truth of mathematics, and nothing but the truth.

Unfortunately in the 1930s the work of Gödel, Church and Turing showed that these results were doomed to failure, that there could not exist any logical system whose proofs could be checked mechanically which was both consistent and complete even for a small fragment of mathematics, namely the arithmetic of whole numbers 1,2,3,. . .

So Leibniz's dream of reducing all reasoning in natural, social and moral sciences to calculation was at last shown to be as wildly absurd as most people would have expected. You cannot even do it for arithmetic.

Unsolvability of halting problem

It would take a whole course of lectures to go through these results and more than one even to state precisely what they are. But I think it is possible, now that most people are familiar with computers and computer programs, to give a convincing argument that there are mathematical problems which no computer program can solve. I will explain as I go what I have to assume about programs. The reader who is familiar with a programming language such as BASIC or FORTRAN or ALGOL can identify "program" with "program in his favourite language" (though it must be admitted that the following argument as it stands works only for ALGOL or LISP and would require minor modifications for most other languages. Users of these will probably realise what modifications need be made).

For the present you need to know that a program is a sequence of symbols – letters, numerals etc. – which can be fed into a computer, for example:

Goldbach test Fortran

```
          integer i,m,n
          n = 4
1         n = n + 2
          i = 1
2         if (i*2.ge.n) go to 5
          i = i + 2
          m = 1
3         m = m + 1
          if (mod (i,m).eq.0) go to 2
          if (m*m.lt.i) go to 3
          m = 1
4         m = n + 1
          if (mod (n–i,m).eq.0) go to 2
          if (m*m.lt.n–i) go to 4
          go to 1
5         print "GOLDBACH WAS WRONG"
          stop
          end
```

This is a FORTRAN program which goes through the even numbers greater than 4 checking each one to see whether it is the sum of two prime numbers (numbers with no factors apart from themselves and unity); if it is, it goes on to the next; if it is not, it stops and prints out

GOLDBACH WAS WRONG

because in 1742 Goldbach conjectured that every even number greater than two was the sum of two primes, a conjecture which has so far resisted all attempts at proof or refutation.

8   KNOWLEDGE-BASED REASONING SYSTEMS

This program does not require any data, but many programs do; for example a program to work out income tax needs an input of salary, expenses etc. Such a program would produce a numerical output giving the tax due. In particular there are programs which give answers, "Yes" or "No" to questions about the data e.g. "Is a tax refund due?" or "Is this number a prime number?".

Now it is crucial to this argument that a program itself, being merely a sequence of symbols of a particular kind, can be used as input data and that it is possible to write programs which answer questions about programs. We could all write programs to answer simple questions about programs such as "how many instructions does it have?" or "does it have any 'read' instructions?". In fact very complicated syntactic questions about programs can be decided mechanically in this way, i.e. you can write programs to do it. An ALGOL compiler, for example, is a program which translates an ALGOL program into machine language; but before it can do that it must first check that what it has been given is a valid ALGOL program, i.e. satisfies the many complex interconnected grammatical rules which define the programming language ALGOL.

What is at first surprising is that virtually no semantic questions about programs can be decided mechanically. By *semantic* I mean questions which concern the input-output behaviour of a program, what the program *does*, as opposed to syntactic questions like the ones mentioned above which are concerned only with what the program is, regarded simply as a string of symbols. I shall show this for one of the simpler semantic properties, namely *whether a program halts or not*. One certainly hopes that one has written a program which does eventually halt on any input data you intend to give it; if it does not, then you will need to be very rich to keep it going. However every programmer makes mistakes and can inadvertently write a sequence of instructions which, on certain types of data which were not anticipated, goes into an endless loop. As mentioned earlier, it would be extremely valuable to check mechanically that a program does what it is supposed to do. A much nearer goal would be to check mechanically that a program will halt. But we shall show that even this cannot be done.

The question we shall consider is:

"Does program P halt when run on itself?"

i.e. given itself as data. Most programs would of course halt straightaway when presented with themselves as data. A program to predict the inflation rate from certain economic policies would get a nasty shock when given itself as input instead of a row of figures and would probably respond with an error message. An ALGOL program to check whether a given program was a valid

ALGOL program would halt on itself and say "Yes". A program such as the Goldbach program shown above would ignore the data anyway and might or might not halt.

Suppose we had a program P_0 for deciding this question, i.e. a program P_0 such that

If P halts when run on P, then P_0 when run on P halts
and prints 'Yes'.
If P does not halt when run on P, then P_0 when run on P halts
and prints 'No'.

I shall assume also that P_0 only prints 'Yes' or 'No' at the end of its deliberations.

Now modify P_0, so that instead of printing 'Yes' it goes into an endless loop: e.g. if instruction 295 of P_0 was

$$295. \text{ Print 'Yes'}$$

replace this by

$$295. \text{ Go to } 295$$

Let us call the modified program P_1. Then

If P halts when run on P then P_1 does not halt when run on P.
If P does not halt when run on P then P_1 does halt when run on P
Now take $P = P_1$ i.e. run P_1 on itself. We have
If P_1 halts when run on P_1 then P_1 does not halt when run on P_1.
If P_1 does not halt when run on P_1 then P_1 does halt when run on P_1.

A flat contradiction. Conclusion – there cannot be any such program P_0 which decides, given a program P, whether P halts when run on itself.

This is a very cunning self-referential argument. Essentially it amounts to saying that we cannot have a program which determines whether programs will halt, because if we had, we could construct a program which would try and find out what it was going to do itself, and then do the opposite, which is obviously impossible. One's first reaction is to say that this question of finding out whether a program will halt when run on itself as data is completely artificial and remote from any naturally occurring problems of mathematics or computer science. But with a little extra work one can show that the problem of deciding whether a program halts on any given data or on no data are similarly incapable of being decided by a program. In the last 20 years the same has been done for some problems which mathematicians have actually been trying to solve for decades, e.g. the word problem for groups, the solvability of diophantine equations.

The question we considered above is not as useless as it appears. If we did have a program P_o, which would tell us whether an arbitrarily given program P halted when run on itself we could use it to test the Goldbach program above. If it answered 'No', it would have proved the Goldbach hypothesis, that every even number greater than 4 is the sum of two odd primes, which human mathematicians have been unsuccessfully trying to do for over 200 years.

One's second reaction is that perhaps one can decide these questions mechanically but only in a more powerful language. It is quite plausible that to decide whether programs written in Language 1 halt you need a more powerful Language 2, to decide whether programs in Language 2 halt you need a more powerful Language 3, and so on ad infinitum.

In fact, the actual situation is quite the opposite: virtually all conceivable programming languages, from the most sophisticated down to machine languages, are equivalent in the sense that, with suitable coding of input and output, they can all solve exactly the same set of problems.

Probably the most convincing demonstration of this is still Turing's 1936 analysis of the nature of computation. He was thinking of human computation because it was before the invention of the electronic computer (in which Turing himself played an important role), but the same considerations apply to both. If you break it up into its atomic acts, he says, a computation consists of a sequence of moves, each of which is either to change the symbol printed on or stored in some basic cell; or to move to some neighbouring cell; or to read the symbol stored in some cell and to let one's next move depend on what that is. This is all under the control of some finite program telling you what to do next.

Turing then pointed out that although all this could take place in some two-dimensional space like a sheet of paper, or three-dimensional space, and although you might be able to scan more than one cell at a time, it could equally well be done by the simplest possible device of this kind (now called a Turing machine). This is simply a one-dimensional array of squares, each of which is either blank (0) or marked (1); one square at a time is scanned, and the symbol there can be read and altered; the read/write head can move one square left or right at a time.

Scanned square

| ... | 0 | 1 | 1 | 1 | 0 | 0 | 0 | 0 | ... |

TURING MACHINE

BASIC COMMANDS

Print 0
Print 1
Move (one square) right
Move (one square) left
If 0 (is the scanned symbol) go to
(instruction number) i; if 1 go to j.

A simple program:
1. Move right,
2. If 0 go to 3; if 1 go to 1
3. Print 1.

This sends
↓
0 1 1 ... (n times) ... 1 0 0 ...
into
↓
0 1 1 ... (n+1 times) ... 1 0 0 ...

i.e., it increases by 1 the number of 1's, between the reading head and the next 0 to the right.

Clearly even the most rudimentary language or machine is capable, given the ability to extend its memory indefinitely, of simulating such a device and, hence, in virtue of Turing's analysis, of simulating any conceivable kind of computing device.

So there is no escape via a hierarchy of stronger and stronger languages or machines. These questions, about halting of programs, about solving equations in integers, etc., really cannot be settled by any uniform mechanical method.

Mechanisation of reasoning

One very important question of this kind concerns logic itself. The most elementary kind of logic is propositional logic, the logic of "and", "or", "not"; next comes first order predicate logic which includes the notions "all" and "some" or "there exists" and inferences like:

$(\exists x)(\forall y) P(x,y) \rightarrow (\forall y)(\exists x) P(x,y)$
"If, for some x, P(x,y) is true for all y, then, for each y there is some x for which P(x,y) is true."

Church and Turing independently showed in 1935 that the problem of deciding whether a given statement of first order predicate logic, like the one above, is a valid theorem (i.e., true for all possible choices of domain of individuals for the x,y to range over, and for all possible relations $P(x,y)$ between such individuals) is, like the halting problem, one for which there is demonstrably no mechanical method. You cannot write, for example, an ALGOL program which when such a formula is input as data will output "valid" if it is valid, "invalid" if it is not.

So Leibniz's dream was a wildly unreal one; even within the limited precise domain of mathematics and logic, it is demonstrably impossible to mechanise reasoning completely. Many people have argued that this, and related results of Gödel, show that human beings have reasoning powers which machines can never have. It seems quite obvious to me, and I think it is fairly generally agreed now, that they show nothing of the kind. These theoretical limitations apply to both men and machines when they say that neither can have a deterministic, purely routine, infallible way of testing the validity of statements or logic.

This is not exactly a surprising result; I am sure that most mathematicians have believed for hundreds of years that mathematics is a bottomless well which can never be exhausted, because it deals with a genuinely infinite subject matter. No statement about all numbers, like Goldbach's hypothesis, can be proved simply by checking out a large number of cases. If you find that all even numbers less than ten billion billion are the sum of two primes, you do not know whether ten billion billion plus two is. To prove Goldbach's hypothesis (if it is provable) will require a profound analysis of number theory.

It is a reassuring result to those who are afraid that computers will take over all the interesting intellectual tasks, replacing human skill, originality and creativity by dull high speed calculations. It tells us this cannot happen, even in the precise formal domain of logic and mathematics which is one of the most accessible to mechanisation. It tells us there is no uniform systematic method of deciding the truth or falsity of statements of logic and mathematics.

However many mathematicians, whether human or mechanical, are working on a hard mathematical problem, there is no guarantee of their success. There is always room for a new idea, always hope that a new insight or bold intuition will lead to success, always a need for creative intelligence. Perhaps one day either by means of hardware, or software or bio-engineering, we shall produce machines or creatures which are much more powerful mathematicians than humans. Even that will not put human mathematicians out of a job. There are plenty of mathematicians like myself who are third rate even by current human standards and find satisfying and useful things to do. The impact of computers on mathematics will not be to supplant human mathematicians but to increase the rate at which we dip into the bottomless well.

Surely this will be true in other intellectual fields, too. AI and expert systems will increase the range of things we can do and the rate at which we can do them rather than leave humans with no job. They will remove the dull chores of trivial repetitive reasoning and allow us to concentrate on the more exciting things forever beyond the range of systematisation. It is interesting to note that even though Leibniz had the most exaggerated dreams of the possibility of mechanising all intellectual endeavours, he also thought of this as an aid to human intelligence rather than a replacement of it. Indeed, he may be said to have invented the concept of a "people-amplifier" when he said ". . . when the project is accomplished. . .[men] will have an instrument which will exalt reason no less than what the Telescope does to perfect our vision".

From the point of view of mechanising everyday reasoning, that first order predicate logic cannot be completely mechanised is not too disturbing, for one can express within it very hard mathematical problems which mathematicians have been trying to solve for tens and hundreds of years.

We would not expect much help from machines on these, except in those cases, of which there are now quite a few, where the problem can be reduced by a human mathematician to a very large number of special cases. A notable recent success for computer-aided mathematics is Appel and Haken's proof in 1976 of the hundred-year-old four-colour conjecture, that every plane map can be coloured with four colours. The published proof involves 35 pages of text, 566 pages of diagrams and the results of a computer check that each of 1834 configurations have a certain property, each of which took up to six minutes on a large fast computer (IBM 370/168) and would have taken hundreds of thousands of hours by hand.

In any case, hard problems like this are rare; human mathematicians have been more and more successful at solving the vast majority of problems which have arisen. And there is nothing in the results I have quoted to lead one to reject one of the main claims of cybernetics, that *every precisely described human behaviour can be simulated on a computer.*

We know there is no hope of finding a way of programming computers to carry out all reasoning, but there is no reason why we should not try and get them to do *some*, by analysing precisely what humans do and simulating it, or improving on that by making appropriate use of the computer's much greater speed and accuracy for repetitive operations.

The first actual machine for doing logic appears to be Jevons' logical piano constructed in 1869. It dealt only with propositional logic, the logic of "and", "or", "not", "implies". In principle the mechanisation of this is trivial; there is only a finite number of possible combinations of "true" or "false" for the component propositions and you can try all of them out and see whether the whole proposition always comes out true. For example:

A	B	A and B	not (A and B)	$\underline{\text{not (A and B) or B}}$ not (A and B) or B
T	T	T	F	T
T	F	F	T	T
F	T	F	T	T
F	F	F	T	T

But notice that although this is very easy it could take a long time; if instead of two components, A,B, there were n, then there would be 2^n lines in this truth table, and the number of steps would be some multiple of this. Exponential growth like this soon takes you beyond the range not merely of present day computers but of any computation which could be carried out within the time and space bounds of the known universe.

1 year	$= 3 \times 10^7 = 2^{25}$ seconds
human life time	$= 2 \times 10^9 = 2^{31}$ seconds
age of universe (3×10^{10} years)	$= 10^{18} = 2^{60}$ seconds
number of hydrogen atoms in universe	$= 10^{79} = 2^{262}$
present day computer, operations per second	$= 10^8$
theoretical limit	$= 10^{15}$?

If you had just 30 component propositions and you filled in T's and F's in the table by hand at the rate of 1 per second it would take 1,000 years to complete it. If you had had a computer operating at the theoretical limit in speed since the universe began it would not yet have worked out the truth table for a proposition with 110 components.

That is daunting; but there are two hopeful lines of escape. The first is that perhaps there are more efficient ways of testing for validity than the obvious one of trying out all possible combinations of true and false. Quite a lot of effort has been devoted to this because it is also closely related to problems of logical design of computer and other switching circuits, for example, minimisation. There are methods which perform much better for small inputs of particular forms. But no one has found a method which is substantially better for all values of n. And recent work on the complexity of algorithms makes it appear very unlikely that a method exists which takes time proportional to n or n^2 or n^3 or some higher power of n, instead of 2^n. For it has been shown that this would imply the existence of much better algorithms than are known at present for dozens of problems in mathematics, logic and computer science, for example the travelling salesman problem. It would also open the possibility of broaching the security of some recent cryptographic coding methods which depend on the apparent fact that it must take an astronomically long time to factorise large numbers.

However even if it turns out to be the case that there is no method which is better than exponential (i.e. of order 2^n) for all values of the number n of component propositions this does not necessarily mean that it is impossible to deal with most of the cases that arise in practice. One of the commonest types of optimisation problem, particularly in economic forecasting, is linear programming. The standard method for solving such problems, the simplex method, is known to take exponential time in the worst cases. But in practice — and thousands of such problems are solved every day — it works surprisingly well. A recent theoretical breakthrough by Khachian showed that there is a method of solution which in all cases takes only polynomial time in the number of constraints and variables and quite a low order polynomial at that, 120 mn^3 steps where m is the number of constraints and n the number of variables.

At first sight this appears to be a dramatic improvement on the simplex algorithm, which sometimes takes exponential time. However Dantzig (SIAM News, Vol. 13, No1, p 1, October 1980) has shown that a typical problem with 2,000 variables and 3,000 constraints would take 30 minutes by the simplex algorithm and 50 million years by a Khachian-type algorithm! What is important in practice is not the worst case behaviour for all inputs, but the average behaviour for the size of inputs likely to be encountered.

The second line of escape, and the most hopeful one, is that perhaps one never needs to deal with propositions with more than, say, a dozen components. This would certainly be true of the propositional logic directly arising outside mathematics. However propositional logic is very elementary; even for database queries, expert systems and robotics you need first order predicate logic, which deals with "all" and "some" and relations between individuals. And the most natural ways of dealing with that reduce quite simple formulae involving "all" and "some" into much more complicated formulae of propositional logic. Alan Robinson, who invented, some sixteen years ago, the method of "resolution" which is the basis of current mechanical proof procedures, describes elsewhere in this volume how well people have succeeded in getting round this difficulty. But I would like to round off this paper by explaining where first order logic fits into the picture. Statements involving the quantifiers, "all", "some" or, as mathematicians prefer to express it, "there exists", can be quite difficult to appraise. Consider, for example:

Abbreviations: $\forall x$ = for all x
$\exists x$ = there exists an x
$\rightarrow$ = implies

1. $(\exists x)(\forall y) F(x,y) \rightarrow (\forall y)(\exists x)F(x,y)$
2. $(\forall y)(\exists x)F(x,y) \rightarrow (\exists x)(\forall y)F(x,y)$
3. $[(\forall x)(\forall y)((R(x,y) \& R(x,z)) \rightarrow R(y,z) \& (\forall y)(\exists x)R(x,y)] \rightarrow (\forall x)(\forall y)(\forall z)[R(x,x) \& (R(x,y) \rightarrow R(y,x)) \& ((R(x,y) \& R(y,z)) \rightarrow R(x,z))]$
4. $(\exists x)(\forall y)(\forall z)\{[((F(y,z) \rightarrow (G(y) \rightarrow H(x))) \rightarrow F(x,x)) \& ((F(z,x) \rightarrow G(x)) \rightarrow H(z)) \& F(x,y)] \rightarrow F(z,z)\}$

We saw above that (1) is logically valid; whatever domain you take the individuals, x,y to range over and whatever relation between them you take F to be, (1) will be true. On the other hand (2) is not; assuming that it is the second commonest logical error of mathematical students (the commonest is thinking that $(p \rightarrow q) \rightarrow (q \rightarrow p)$). To see that (2) is not always true consider "The sun never sets on the British Empire". This used to be true in the sense "At every time there is a place in the British Empire where the sun is shining" but never in the sense "There is a place in the British Empire where at every time the sun is shining". (3) is recognisably mathematical in character; it is an easy exercise for a first year mathematics student. It is not immediately apparent whether (4) is logically valid or not.

Here there is no obvious analogue of the truth table method of just trying out all possibilities. There are now infinitely many possible domains of individuals, infinitely many possible different relations. Indeed, as I have already pointed out, it has been proved that there is no mechanical way of testing for logical validity. That is, you cannot write a program such that if you input an expression like (1), (2), (3) or (4) it will eventually halt and answer "valid" or "not valid".

But you can do the next best thing: you can write a program which, if the formula, like (1), (3) or (4) above, is logically valid it will say so, and actually produce a proof of it. Unfortunately, if like (2) it is not valid it may not halt at all, so you will never know whether it is not valid or whether the machine is just about to stop and say "valid". You can design the procedure so that for sufficiently simple classes of formulae, including (2) for example, it will always give an answer, but, by the general result I have just quoted, it will be impossible to do this for all formulae; there will always be cases where you will wait hopefully for ever and get no answer.

That it is possible to write such a proof-seeking algorithm follows from the work of Gödel and Herbrand in 1930. One of the first programs for actually doing this on an electronic computer was written by Hao Wang in 1958. His program proved the first 220 theorems of Russell and Whitehead's monumental Principia Mathematica in three minutes. These are all theorems of propositional logic, but his program could also handle quantifiers. An improved version due to Gilmore gave a proof of (4) above in less than a minute and a half. This is not to be despised; it took me half an hour to recognise that it is logically valid, and would have taken me another hour to write out a full proof. Alan Robinson in another paper in this volume tells how much more can be accomplished now with 20 years' experience of writing such programs and the much bigger and faster machines of today.

To sum up:
1. Complete mechanisation of mathematics or logic has been proved to be impossible.

2. You can write programs which look for proofs of logical statements and, if such a proof exists, i.e. if the statement is logically valid, will eventually find one. But if the statement is not logically valid the program may run for ever.

3. Such programs may be prohibited by computational explosion from proving hard theorems of mathematics but they are already capable of handling the logic needed for expert systems, databases, robotics and may be helpful in proving the correctness of programs.

Computers which were invented to speed up and take the routine drudgery out of numerical calculations are now beginning to do the same for logical reasoning.

2

Logical Reasoning in Machines

J. A. Robinson

Syracuse University

John Shepherdson's paper mentions Gödel's lesser-known result called his Completeness Theorem. Everybody has concentrated, because it was such a shock, on his Incompleteness discovery. But his Completeness work is essentially what people like me have been building on.

I first became involved about 20 years ago (1961) when somebody put into my hand a description of Gilmore's work which John Shepherdson mentions in the previous paper [1]. Like other logicians of that period Gilmore was well aware of Gödel's completeness discoveries and had been waiting impatiently for the computer to become a practical tool. He and several others — Hao Wang [2] among them — rushed off to those mid-50s computers and wrote down almost verbatim the methods Gödel and Herbrand and Skolem had laid out in the pre-computer age.

These algorithms that Gödel and Herbrand described were for the human computer, not an automatic machine but a person systematically following out a plan of working. It had always seemed to be a theoretical possibility that you might be able to make a machine do that too. Suddenly there were the machines, and Gilmore was first to the post with a running program to test out this idea.

It was good news and bad news. Good news that it could be done at all. Bad news in that only some of the examples that Gilmore tried actually were finished. I was shown this summary and was intrigued, not so much by the examples that were successful but by one conspicuous failure that Gilmore very honestly described — a logical formula not much more complicated than the ones in Shepherdson's paper. He had run it on the IBM 704 for 30 minutes using the Gödel-Herbrand algorithm. Then he simply abandoned the run because somebody was due on the machine. No information was at that time available on how much longer it might have taken to find the proof.

The paper that had been put into my hand was not by Gilmore. It was about Gilmore's work, by Martin Davis and Hilary Putnam [3]. They pointed out that if Gilmore had just thought a bit longer before rushing off to the machine he might have anticipated that such examples would turn up. They also corrected the actual programming, in such a way that the very same example that did not come out after 30 minutes of machine time, was done by hand by them in just a few minutes of work.

So suddenly, just by a little twiddle on the technique, by a better job of the programming of this same algorithm, there was this quite enormous improvement in the way it behaved. That was where I first came in. And I thought, My heavens, this is marvellous and what about trying to do more of that? I was thinking in a theoretical sort of programmer's way about this algorithm and trying to anticipate where it would be inefficient [4]. The upshot was that within a few years, with the help of some more obscure and, in fact, unknown, work that had been done by Herbrand at the same time as Gödel's Completeness discovery, it turned out to be possible to improve, rather dramatically, the performance of this very same algorithm. Some massaging of the ideas involved has resulted in gains of several orders of magnitude of efficiency.

We seem to be on a plateau now where we are not gaining very much more of that sort of advantage but, as I shall explain later, we are finding that the algorithm in the form that we now have it is surprisingly useful. We are beginning to discover all sorts of unexpected uses for it, one of which is as the inner engine of a new way of programming, a new kind of computation facility which appears to have many remarkable advantages.

Let me begin by reviewing where we stand. As John Shepherdson indicates, logic is a very old science. Aristotle got it well started, over two thousand years ago. Its subject matter is this idea of "following from" — the notion of logical consequence, that is the central idea of logic. As Shepherdson points out, this relationship depends only on the form of the assertions that you are dealing with, not on the content but only on the form. The syllogism form is exemplified by "All men are mortal. Socrates is a man. Conclusion: Socrates is mortal". This form of argument can be, and always is, stated with just letters in certain places in the pattern.

The reason you can use variables is that it doesn't matter what goes there. The significance of variables is that you can replace them by anything at all. The pattern revealed by the variables covers infinitely many cases all at once and it is a nice way of packaging a generality. In fact, in logic that is why variables are present. You wish to express generality by showing patterns which fit infinitely many cases, while all you really have is one thing. The one thing you have is a description of a form.

Logicians in one sense catalogue form. They study it, they look for ways of detecting formal configurations, formal properties in specific cases and ignoring all the rest — ignoring the content and getting at the relevant form. These forms, then, are capable of being represented symbolically as data structures — matrices, lists, and other kinds of data structures that you can completely represent inside computers or on paper. If you have the right ideas about representation then you can do things to the represented forms, quite concrete operations or manipulations and examinations, analysis, just like any other data. So because of the way that form can be handled concretely, there is really no mystery about logical reasoning, as seen by the computational logician. It is just a kind of data processing.

Because of the progress we have made since the advent of the computer, we now think that we can implement the logical data processing discoveries of that generation of Gödel and Herbrand, the 1930 generation. We can now run their algorithm quite respectably over a broad range of cases, and quite efficiently. Indeed, as I mentioned, we now are finding that the present state of implementation technique gives us access to a number of surprisingly useful applications. The goals of today's applied computational logicians are less ambitious and less arrogant than they were 30 years ago before we actually tried to do things. We are no longer saying we are going to replace the pure mathematician. I must admit that there was talk like that not all that long ago. We are now more modest.

Our work has led to some benefits for the mathematicians. In Illinois, for example, at the Argonne National Laboratory, there is a group of computational logicians who are providing software tools for the pure mathematician which are now being applied usefully to abstract combinatorial algebraic questions, group theory questions and the like, with some success. But that work is turning out to be quite messy, quite difficult. I would rather concentrate in this paper on the more mundane applications that some of us are now working on and try to give a feel for the general techniques in those cases.

A remark or two first. Computers do not have to imitate the way humans do things, although of course the great precedent for all this is that humans have been doing it for a long time. It turns out that one of the bottlenecks, one of the things that made Gilmore's program take so long on some of those examples, was that, without thinking, the algorithm had been put into the computer essentially in the form in which it was originally devised. That form was human-oriented. It was for people to think through and do, perhaps, on easy cases. So it had to be a human-oriented algorithm. That was the assumption everybody made. A quick way of saying what we have tried to do with the algorithm since then is to drop that assumption and do it the best way we could think of, whether or not that was the way that humans do it. That same point of course applies right across the board to all kinds of computing: do it the best way you can, whether or not it is simulating the way humans do it.

Another point: in order to find the machine's answers useful to you, you don't have to know how it arrived at them. That is not always true. But in this case it is. You can use the answer that a proof-finding machine gives you, if it does give you one, because it is a proof. And it is in the nature of a proof or an argument that its value is on its face. If it does not convince you totally of the correctness of its conclusion from its premises, it is not a proof.

That is what proofs are for. They are devices for acting on the human data processing system. The point of a proof is to convince humans about correctness. So computers, however complicated, create, construct,and print out these pieces of text, which are then used — and only then — to act as convincing arguments on the human user. Some people make this point by distinguishing between two contexts in terms of which you might discuss this matter. One is the context of discovery. One is the context of justification.

The context of discovery is that in which we are considering how the search for the proof is done, the kinds of intuitions involved in guessing right, and so on. That is a very mysterious business. To create an analogue of it inside the computer might be very messy and complicated and hard to understand even if we did it. The computer might even be guessing, in some implementations of a certain kind — invoking random number generators and so on. In the context of discovery, creativity in some general sense is at work. We all know that this is a very obscure process. However, the beauty of the theorem-proving problem is that you can ignore the messiness of the creativity part, because all you are really interested in is what it is that is discovered, the outcome. And that can be understood however it was discovered. We can all understand the proof, provided it is short and simple, of a theorem that withstood proof for centuries.

There are many examples of that. The creativity is in the context of discovery in which all the searching was done, all the ingenuity deployed. It is a very much easier problem indeed to understand that proof once we are given it. The picture (Figure 2.1) is reminiscent of one of Feigenbaum's diagrams (see Chapter 3). What we have in an expert system, or more generally a knowledge-based system, is, as he says, a collection of assertions gathered together in a knowledge base. This is the part of the system that contains one's facts, one's assumptions, one's definitions, one's heuristics, whatever is the content as opposed to the form of the application. We then have another part of the system, the inference engine, where the reasoning actually takes place. This reasoning takes the stylised form of questions coming in, and answers coming out, perhaps one or more answers for the same question. What happens in the inference engine takes into account simply the form of the particular problem, the theorem to be proved or the question to be answered, and whatever is relevant from over in the

LOGICAL REASONING MACHINES   23

```
Assertions                    Question
    │                            │
    ▼                            ▼
┌─────────┐                 ┌─────────┐
│Knowledge│ ──────────────▶ │Inference│
│  Base   │                 │ Engine  │
└─────────┘                 └─────────┘
                                 │
                                 ▼
                             Answer(s)
```

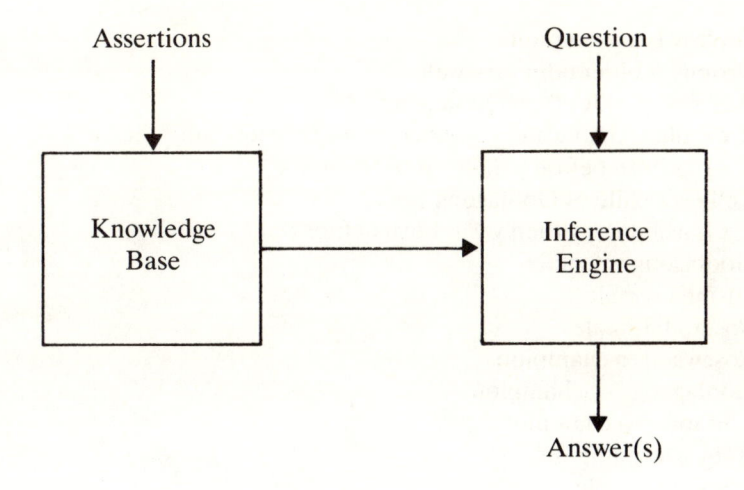

Figure 2.1 Structure of a knowledge-based system

knowledge base, again by virtue of its form and not its content. This inference engine does not care what you are talking about. It only cares whether what you say follows from what you have agreed to assume.

Feigenbaum properly concentrates on the inside of that box. He tells us about the general problem of getting the right pieces of knowledge about a particular subject-matter area. I shall ignore that problem. I shall just treat the knowledge base as a place where we go for the formally relevant pieces of knowledge that we need in order to go from the question to the answers.

Figure 2.2 gives an example of what might be found in the knowledge base. Here are 22 pieces of information that you can type in to a system of this kind. The information is about Wimbledon, statistics about some of the champions. The items marked with dots are a little bit different from the others. What we have here are two kinds of assertions. There are rules — those are the ones with dots. They are all of the form "*If,* something, something, something, *Then* conclusion". The others are data. They are specific assertions. The totality, all the data and all the rules together, make up the knowledge base.

Having put those into your knowledge base, you might want to ask questions. For example, you might want to ask that question: Which male champions are older than Kelly (Yvonne Goolagong's daughter)? Our system at Syracuse [6] would print out an answer as follows:
Connors Borg Rosewall Drobny.

That these persons are male and champions is explicitly given among the assertions, but that each of them is older than Kelly must be deduced. The

24   KNOWLEDGE-BASED REASONING SYSTEMS

1   Drobny is a champion
2   Drobny is older tahn Rosewall
3   Rosewall is older than Goolagong
4   If x is older than y and y is older than z then x is older than z
5   If x was born before y then x is older than y
6   Kelly is a child of Goolagong
7   If x is a child of y then y was born before x
8   Goolagong is female
9   Drobny is male
10 Rosewall is male
11 Rosewall is a champion
12 Goolagong is a champion
13 Connors is a champion
14 Borg is a champion
15 Connors is male
16 Borg is male
17 Borg was born before Connors
18 Connors was born before Kelly
19 Kelly is female
20 Evert is a champion
21 Evert is female
22 Evert was born before Connors

Figure 2.2 Example of a knowledge base. Its assertions are either rules (if . . . then . . .) or data

deductions involved can, if desired, be examined by the user. For example, one could request:
*Explain the fourth answer.
And the system would respond with the rationale shown as Figure 2.3.

Because our system implements a version of the Gödel-Herbrand algorithm for proving things, it purports to be ready to answer correctly — in full if you want to wait as long as it might take — any query that you can pose to it, provided only that the answer logically follows from the data. It will explore all of the conclusions of the form that you have asked about, that can be obtained from the information you have supplied. I said earlier that humans do not need to know how this is done, but only need to see the answer. If the answer is obviously right, that will do. On the other hand, if it is not obviously right, that, for example, Connors is older than Kelly, you cannot just see it at a glance. The whole point is that it takes a bit of argument. Such systems would weary us if, rather than just giving us the answer they always insisted on telling us why we should believe it. And so

* To show: Drobny is a male
   & Drobny is a champion
   & Drobny is older than Kelly.
* it is enough, by assertion 9,
* to show: Drobny is a champion
   & Drobny is older than Kelly.
* But then it is enough, by assertion 1,
* to show: Drobny is older than Kelly.
* But then it is enough, by assertion 4,
* to show: (there is a y:1 such that)
   & Drobny is older than y:1
   y:1 is older than Kelly.
* But then it is enough, by assertion 2,
* to show: Rosewall is older than Kelly.
* But then it is enough, by assertion 4,
* to show: (there is a y:2 such that)
   Rosewall is older than y:2
   y:2 is older than Kelly.
* But then it is enough, by assertion 3,
* to show: Goolagong was born before Kelly.
* But then it is enough, by assertion 5,
* to show: Goolagon was born before Kelly.
* But then it is enough, by assertion 7,
* to show: Kelly is a child of Goolagong.
* But then it is enough, by assertion 6,
   to show: nothing
* End of explanation.

Figure 2.3 The machine's justification for its line of reasoning (see text and Figure 2).

most systems of this kind have a facility for giving the reasons, but only when you ask for them.

For example, we could, as in Figure 2.2, ask why Drobny is listed in the answer. The machine (Figure 2.3) gives us its reasoning. It says: "Oh you want to know that Drobny is a male and a champion and older than Kelly, do you? All right. Well, referring to the knowledge base, to show that it would be enough, in view of what No 9 says (that he is a male) just to show you that he is a champion. We know he is a male — it is given. So as a first step, let us point that out." And then it says: "But in that case, if you only need to show those two things, then in view of what No 1 says, it is enough to cross off that Drobny is a champion and just show the final thing that Drobny is older than Kelly." That is the hard part of this problem. How do you do that? Well, the machine says that Assertion 4 allows you to reduce the problem. You say, If you could only show that there is a Y_1 such that Drobny is older than Y_1 and Y_1 is older than Kelly, you've got it. And your support for that is Proposition 4. So let's do that, says the explanation. In that case, regard Proposition 2 from your knowledge base. Take Y_1 to be Rosewall. You see, in finding this line of reasoning, you would have had to look around and try Rosewall and try other people. But it says, "Rosewall works, and here's why: If you make Rosewall the intermediary, Y_1, then you only need to show (since you know that Drobny is older than Rosewall) that Rosewall is older than Kelly. And that will do it." And so the cycle of explanation goes on, constantly revising the problem that you have left to prove, and chopping off bits that have been proved already. So now our problem is reduced to showing that Rosewall is older than Kelly. Again we try to find somebody who can be found to go between them (using the same rule, Assertion 4). Can we find another party? It turns out, yes. By Assertion 3, we can put Goolagong in between Rosewall and Kelly. And if we could only show that Goolagong is older than Kelly, we would have it.

Well we have got along very well by two applications of Assertion 4 so far. But it turns out that to keep this explanation going we have to appeal to a different rule now, the one encapsulated in Assertion 5. This says if we could show Goolagong was born before Kelly we would be able to show she was older. And finally if we could show that Kelly was a child of Goolagong, that would show (by Assertion 7, which is the other rule) that Goolagong was older and by Assertion 6 we have got it. This then completes the entire line of reasoning. We are left with nothing to show.

This explanation would be somewhat tedious, perhaps, if it were any longer. But it has a very easy, formatted, reasoning pattern which is linear, easily understood as constantly discharging one condition and perhaps, if necessary, trading it off for one or more other conditions, in a list of conditions. This list keeps getting modified and it seems to be a race in which you might find that the list of conditions you have left to discharge grows longer all the time. The length of the list does fluctuate, but eventually you have got them all out, and that is the way the reasoning works. There is really only one kind of inference step.

John Shepherdson mentions the propositional calculus that involved "And", "Or" and "Not" and "Implies" and in the predicate calculus we have the quantifiers as well — "For all" and "There exists". If you put all those things together and if you follow the analyses of some of the earlier, pre-computer logicians you find that they devised systems of inference which involve a very large number of inference rules. The problem of searching all the possible combinatorial patterns you can make up from this rich repertory is such that the complexity beats you. There are simply too many things to try.

You begin to gain on that problem if you strip down the number of moves that there are. Chess is hard because there are so many moves and noughts and crosses (tic-tac-toe) is not so hard because there are only a few moves. So the fewer moves you have, the easier it is to examine all possible lines of sequences of moves. So, here, we only have one kind of move that we make. It is technically called "resolution". It is a rule of inference that can be codified and described exactly. We know that resolution is adequate all by itself. It is the only rule you need in the predicate calculus. You can therefore confine your search engineering to the space in which the things that are to be looked at are all lines of resolution, steps of this one kind.

What is going on inside the inference engine that it can come up with this sort of thing? Let me propose a way of depicting these texts that may be easier to assimilate. Here (Figure 2.4) is a sort of chemistry notation for conditional assertions — *if/then* assertions. If we look at Assertion 4, there are two conditions, and a conclusion. *If* this and this, *then* that. Now I here just put the general pattern. We put the conclusion (the X is older than Z part) at the top in a little container; and put the two conditions that suffice to establish it according to this rule, depending literally from it. An unconditional assertion, like the datum that we had in the knowledge base, is just a conclusion that does not have any conditions on it.

Conditional assertions

if x is older than y
and y is older than z
then x is older than z

conclusion: [x is older than z]
            /   \   ‒ ‒ ‒ conditions
[x is older than y]   [y is older than z]

unconditional assertions

conclusion: [Borg is older than Connors]

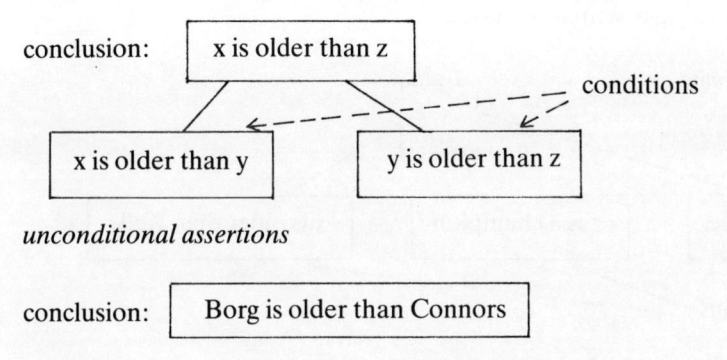

Figure 2.4 A representation for **if/then** assertions, as "atoms" (here shown as boxes).

28 KNOWLEDGE-BASED REASONING SYSTEMS

So there are these two shapes that we are going to encounter in the diagrams. We are going to explore the outright, unconditional shape; and the conditional one, with one or more (sometimes quite a lot) of things hanging off the bottom, representing the conditions to be established for a conclusion. Notice the variables, X, Y and Z. Those are where the power lies in these rules. Those are the things that you can replace by anything. Rules hold for all values of their variables, and in some applications "all" ranges over infinitely many things.

Inside the inference engine is a process of looking for opportune ways of substituting for the Xs, the Ys and the Zs in these rules. The rules come just with the variables. The job of the engine is to explore the possible ways of specialising these rules in each particular case. It is this that turns out to have been the bottleneck in the early versions, in the Gilmore-like versions of the Completeness algorithm. The old versions said: "The proofs that you can make with these rules will require you to find some clever way of replacing those variables by specific names. So make a list of all the ways of replacing those variables by specific names and start working down the list".

What Gödel and Herbrand proved was that somewhere in the list will be just the combinations you need. But if you were unlucky in the way you arranged that list, it might be a very long time indeed before you hit upon the right combination. And there were many places in the possible lines of reasoning where you had to appeal to rules. In each of those places it would be necessary to start searching down these (in general) infinite lists looking for the right combination. That was what killed those early programs.

What resolution does is cut out the need entirely for searching down these lists of ways of "instantiating" rules by concrete names. If you back off a little bit and think, it turns out that you can compute directly the ways of instantiating these variables which will work. So that accounts for the big improvement in efficiency that we got. We now calculate how to apply these rules instead of just search for ways.

answer template

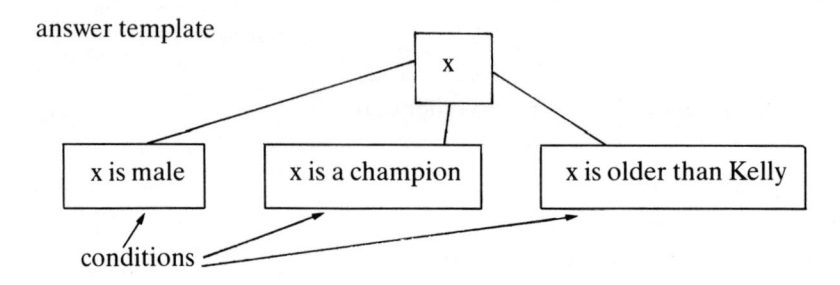

Figure 2.5 Answer template, given the question "what male champions are older than Kelly?" (see text).

I have introduced this "molecule notation" because I want a graphic way to show combinations of rules and data. We also want to do the same thing for questions (Figure 2.5). For example, "Which male champions are older than Kelly?" can be represented by the same sort of little diagram. But instead of a conclusion, we put what is called an "answer template" which is not a proposition at all. It is a sort of picture; in the simplest case, a single variable. This is verbalised as saying: "The question is, please find the ways of replacing the variable X in these conditions, for which there is a line of reasoning showing that those conditions are all true". As we saw earlier, there are four different lines of reasoning, corresponding to those four male tennis players, and this format, this diagrammatic way of saying what it is we want, is deliberately designed to be the same in appearance as these assertions that we have for answering such questions. We now have a sort of jigsaw puzzle to put assertions together in ways that satisfy certain conditions.

Let us say what reasoning patterns are in this notation. We saw that explanation coming out in a long straight line, and we have this phrase, "line of reasoning". It is a bit unfortunate, because reasoning in its most natural form is not linear: it is tree-like. At (A) in Figure 2.6 we have a question with three conditions. The black blobs are conditions, the top white blob is a question with which they are associated. The other white

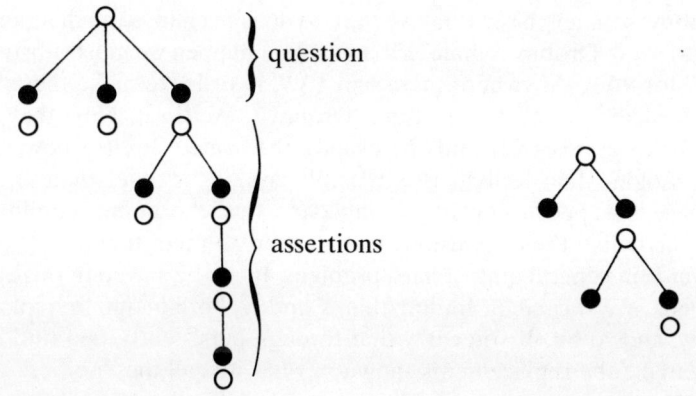

(A) Finished reasoning patterns are those with no conditions unmet.

(B) Unfinished reasoning pattern with two unmet conditions.

Figure 2.6 Reasoning patterns may or may not be finished and may or may not be correct. Correct reasoning patterns are those which have a unifier, hence provide an answer (see text). Examples of finished and unfinished reasoning patterns are given at A and B.

blobs are either data (unconditional assertions) or else conditional ones, i.e. a white blob with some associated conditions (black blobs). The left-hand diagram thus represents a finished piece of reasoning, in that there are no conditions that are unmet. They are all met by either an unconditional or a conditional assertion's conclusion. At (B) there is an unfinished line of reasoning because there are two conditions that are still unmet. It would need to have more stuck on the bottom of it in order to be finished.

What we are interested in is finding all of the reasoning patterns that can be clumped together from the knowledge base and the submitted question. We want to find all of the finished reasoning patterns with a given question at the top. They all start off with a question and assertions are arranged so as to build a finished structure. You start with a given question and actually what you're doing inside that engine is making all the different patterns that are finished. The engine must consider another condition which corresponds to the point I mentioned earlier. It must be sure that when a rule is put in all its variables are changed to concrete names of things, in such a way that every unmet condition is *exactly* met by the corresponding conclusion hanging underneath it. The earlier example is followed through as Figure 2.7.

At the top is the question again, and underneath the first two conditions we put the two pieces of data. Notice that what is inside box (a) and what is inside box (b) syntactically are different. One says "X is male", the other says "Drobny is male". Now what we have to do is to change the diagram so that box (a) says "Drobny is male". To make that happen we must substitute "Drobny" for "X". Anywhere there's an "X", in order to make these two boxes look alike, we must substitute "Drobny". We do it. Now that will result in making boxes (a) and (b) exactly the same. Box (c) now says, "Drobny is older than Kelly". Box (d) still says, X_1 is older than Z_1. So again, we go on specialising the variables so that the unmet conditions become *exactly* like the conclusions that purport to meet them.

Now that is in general quite a hard problem. It can be solved in this case, as it happens. We started off finding that X and X_1 both had to be replaced by Drobny, and so on. If you carry that through persistently, you find that when you make the replacements shown in what we call the "unifier" (the unifier is the set of equations showing what to put for the variables) a nice thing happens. When you actually impose these replacements on the diagram, all of the corresponding pairs where a condition is matched with the conclusion that meets it, become exactly alike, *exactly* alike syntactically.

The inference engine has a perfectly easy-to-understand task. It has got to fit together all these tinker toy things first, it has got to get finished reasoning patterns. Then it must discover whether a unifier exists for each pattern. It tries to find one, and if it does, it saves the result. In fact what it does is see

```
                          ┌───┐
                          │ x │
                          └───┘
        ┌──────────────┬──────┴──────┬──────────────────┐
(a) │ x is male │   │ x is a champion │   (c) │ x is older than Kelly │

(b) │ Drobny is male │   │ Drobny is a champion │   (d) │ $x_1$ is older than z │
```

x_1 is older than y_1

y_1 is older than z_1

Drobny is older than Rosewall

x_2 is older than z_2

x_2 is older than y_2

y_2 is older than z_2

Rosewall is older than Goolagong

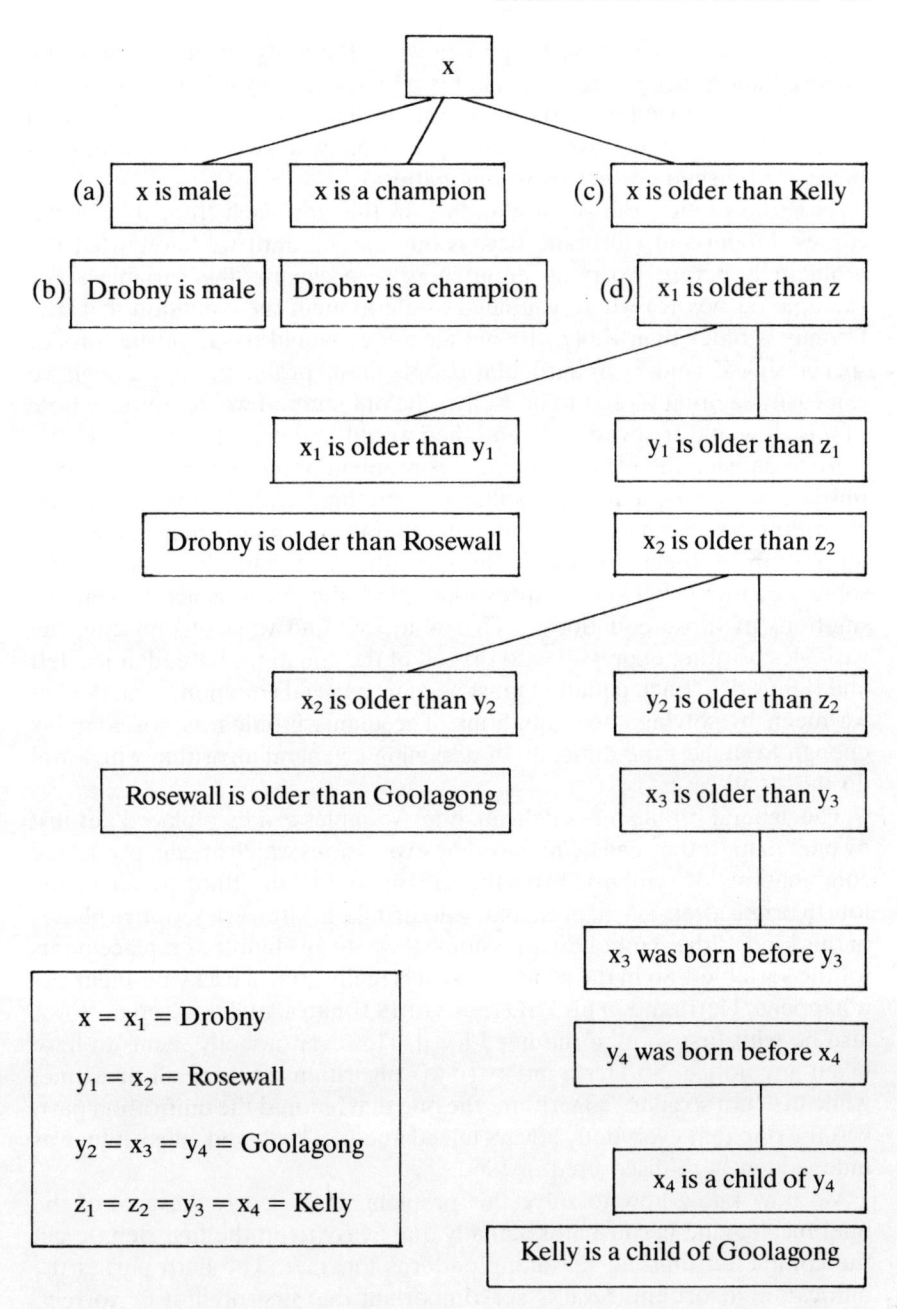

x_3 is older than y_3

x_3 was born before y_3

y_4 was born before x_4

$x = x_1 =$ Drobny

$y_1 = x_2 =$ Rosewall

$y_2 = x_3 = y_4 =$ Goolagong

$z_1 = z_2 = y_3 = x_4 =$ Kelly

x_4 is a child of y_4

Kelly is a child of Goolagong

Figure 2.7 Example of a reasoning pattern which is both finished and correct. The box on the left shows the unifier, i.e. its "certificate of correctness".

what happens to this answer template when the unifying substitutions are imposed and it prints that out. That is an answer. Any other combination that it can put together in the same way which is both finished and has a unifier, that's also an answer. There are as many answers to a question as there are finished correct reasoning patterns.

As I said earlier, the only difference in this approach from that of the earliest Gödel and Herbrand days is our waiting until we know what the problem is before worrying about how to specialise the variables. For example, at box (c) where you need a rule to meet the condition that says Drobny is older than Kelly; the old technique would try all of the ways of specialising Z_1 and Y_1 to particular people in the problem, even though we can easily see that Z_1 has to be Kelly. The old method would not take note of this. It would try everybody and then would find one of them was Kelly.

Systematising the idea of solving this problem of finding the unifier for a finished reasoning pattern results in something called "the unification algorithm". You can state the problem generally in a mathematical way. The unification problem, for which the algorithm is a solution, says: "Given some equations between expressions, find the most general symbolic solutions of those equations". That is to say, find ways of replacing the variables by other expressions so that all of the equations have identical left and right sides. Each equation must become a trivial equation. That is what we mean by solving such equations. The tennis problem is not complex enough to suggest the difficulty of designing a general algorithm which will do this in all cases.

The general problem is a delicate one. Variables can be replaced not just by bare names: they can be replaced by expressions which are deeply nested combinations of symbols, like "the square root of the third power of the fourth prime after. . ." In principle, you can take arbitrary descriptive phases of this kind as the symbolic expressions; they are all eligible as replacements for the variables. So in the general case it is really quite a tricky problem. As it happens, Herbrand in his PhD thesis of 1931 had actually solved it. It was also he who first spotted the need for it. However, nobody seems to have taken any notice. So Herbrand's "good" algorithm sat there all that time, while his "not so good" algorithm, the one that ignored the unification part, was the one that everybody always talked about. The "good" algorithm was independently re-discovered in 1960.

We now know how to solve this problem. It is clearly the guts of the inference engine because it is actually quite easy to do the first step, to get the completed finished reasoning patterns together. The hard part is the unification algorithm. So it is very important that first of all it be correct. Fortunately, it is. It not only solves the ones that are solvable but if there is no solution, the unfication algorithm very rapidly discovers that too, unlike the situations mentioned by John Shepherdson. In this case, the computer *can* decide correctly either way. And when the decision is positive it will construct for us (as it happens a unique) solution.

Not only is the unification algorithm correct, we also know how to implement it as a computer program so that it is extremely efficient. The unification algorithm started its existence as one of the most inefficient algorithms ever proposed. It was exponential in both space and time. Now we have progressed so far that, rather than being exponential, it is now linear. As it turns out, I recently met a computer scientist from Caltech, Professor Jim Kajiyah, who showed me a picture of a VSLI chip. It was a unification chip.

This efficiency of the heart of the inference engine, the unification module in there, shows up spectacularly in the University of Edinburgh's PROLOG compiler. This system, PROLOG, has been put together beautifully by a number of people in the UK and France over the last few years. PROLOG is basically one of those inference engine knowledge-base question-answer systems. The programmer user of PROLOG thinks that what he is doing is programming a machine that will then run on data. But the programming actually consists of asserting things into the knowledge base.

That is all your program is: assertions that you believe are true about your problem domain. You then formulate the question in such a way that it is an input to the program, and the act of getting the answers is the running of the program for that input.

There is a whole list of correspondences between what systems like this do and programmers' ways of thinking about it. The computational interpretation of the logical systems here is due originally to Robert Kowalski who is at Imperial College, London. He called the whole idea "Logic Programming" [10, 11]. Logic programming is just using one of these systems in the way that I have outlined. Kowalski thought of this in the early 70s. Quite quickly thereafter, in France, at the University of Marseilles, Alain Colmerauer and others implemented this idea. They called the resulting system PROLOG — Programming with Logic.

Their system was a good piece of software engineering. Soon David Warren of the University of Edinburgh, who is a genius of software creativity, thought it all out again, taking advantage of the pioneering implementation in Marseilles to produce another PROLOG Interpreter, this time for the DEC-10 computer. But he went one step further: he just pretended PROLOG was ALGOL or FORTRAN and he wrote a *compiler* too. It was a surprise that this could be done at all. Instead of regarding rules as pieces of reference text for an Interpreter which keeps looking and seeing what the rules say and then doing the appropriate changes, Warren's system regards these rules now as little programs and changes them into pieces of machine language which it runs when it wants to see what the rule would cause to happen in the search.

Compilers translate a high level description of a process into a low level, but very much faster, description of the same process, which can be run more directly on the computer. Those who knows what compilers do can appreciate Warren's achievement. As a result, the Edinburgh PROLOG system is now in very wide use. Wherever there are DEC-10s, on which it runs, one can invoke David Warren's system and develop very complicated AI programs. In fact, Warren's compiler was written in PROLOG and is itself a very complicated piece of software.

The image that these theorem-proving algorithms had 20 years ago was that Yes, they might be able to prove things but they'd better not be very big — two or three steps, or something that would take say, no more than half an hour to construct. The image now is that thousands upon thousands of assumptions can be in the knowledge base. Big programs can be in there. Even so, it will not take any longer than any other high-level language, such as LISP or ALGOL to get a problem out. Warren has published accounts comparing some problems, done in PROLOG and in LISP [12]. He finds that PROLOG is a bit faster, even, in some cases than other languages. So you can have this perfectly direct application of a logical "theorem-proving" facility without sacrificing the efficiency advantages of the older forms of language. In fact, you have gained enormously, in that PROLOG is very nearly a programming language that *anybody* can program in because all of the usual anxieties of programming have been taken away — sequencing events, worrying about small errors, and so on.

David Warren is fond of saying that there are no errors to make in PROLOG. The only mistakes you can make are (1) to omit some relevant piece of knowledge from the knowledge base and (2) to include some information which ought not to be there. These will lead to (1) failures to find some of the answers that you intended should be there and (2) getting some unintended answers. Such errors are not "system crashes": it is very natural that some questions have no answers from a given knowledge base. All you are doing is asking the system, "Does this follow from that?". And if it does, the answer is always "yes".

Now as John Shepherdson points out, if "This does *not* follow from that," you may or may not be told that the answer is "no". We are still subject to that limitation. There is no way around those zones of unattainability. They are the hard reality within which we have to do this work. They are like the thermodynamic realities for builders of steam engines.

We can build steam engines (or we used to be able to build them) and they ran very well, despite the fact that there are theoretical limitations on how well it can be done. The odd thing is that the steam engines were built *before* those limitations were properly understood, or even known. Now the gain is that we know, in some cases, that we have constructed almost the best possible steam engine, and that to do any better would be to start to crash into those limitations on what is possible.

We can treat the same "impossibility" constraints John Shepherdson tells us about in the same spirit. There they are. They are part of what the good Lord intended and we just work within them. In some cases, they are helpful because they tell us that we are working near to the limits of theoretical possibility. In that case, it is good evidence for not trying to get any better. So that unattainability result, although negative in form, is helpful.

References

1. Gilmore, P.C. (1960). A proof method for quantification theory. *IBM J. Res. Develop.* 4, 28-35.

2. Wang, H. J. (1960). Towards mechanical mathematics, *IBM J. Res. Develop.*, 4, 28-35.

3. Davis, M. and Putnam, H. (1960). A proof computing procedure for quantification theory. *J.A.C.M.*, 7, 201-215.

4. Robinson, J.A. (1963). Theorem-proving on the computer. *J.A.C.M.*, 10(2), 163-174.

5. Robinson, J.A. (1979). *Logic, Form and Function.* Edinburgh: Edinburgh University Press

6. Robinson J. A. and Sibert E.E. (1982). LOGLISP: an alternative to PROLOG. In *Machine Intelligence 10* (eds Hayes, J.E., Michie, D and Pao, Y-H), pp. 399-419. Chichester: Horwood and New York: Halsted Press.

7. Colmerauer, A., Kanoui, H., Pasero, R. and Roussel, P. (1973). Une systeme de communication homme-machine en Francais. *Rapport Groupe d'Intelligence Artificielle, Universite d'Aix Marseille,* Luminy.

8. Roussel, P. (1975). PROLOG: Manuel d'Utilisation. *Rapport Groupe d'Intelligence Artificielle, Universite d'Aix Marseille,* Luminy.

9. Warren, D.H.D. (1979). PROLOG on the DECsystem 10. In *Expert Systems in the Microelectronic Age* (ed D. Michie), pp. 112-121. Edinburgh: Edinburgh University Press.

10. Kowalski, R.A. (1974). Predicate logic as a programming language. *Proc. IFIP-74*, pp. 556-574. Amsterdam: North Holland.

11. Kowalski, R.A. (1979). *Logic for Problem-Solving*. Amsterdam: North Holland and New York: Elsevier.

12. Warren, D. H. D., Pereira, L., and Pereira, F., (1977). PROLOG — the language and its implementation compared with LISP. *Proc. SIGART/ SIGPLAN Symposium on AI and Programming Languages* (Rochester, NY). *SIGPLAN Notices*, 12 and *SIGART Newsletter*, 64, 109-115.

3

Knowledge Engineering: The Applied Side

E. A. Feigenbaum

Stanford University

Introduction: Symbolic Computation and Inference

This paper will discuss the applied artificial intelligence work that is sometimes called "knowledge engineering". The work is based on computer programs which do symbolic manipulations and symbolic inference, not calculation. The programs I will discuss do essentially no numerical calculation. They discover qualitative lines-of-reasoning leading to solutions to problems stated symbolically.

Knowledge

Since in this paper I often use the term "knowledge", let me say what I mean by it. The knowledge of an area of expertise, a field of practice, is generally of two types: (a) the *facts* of the domains. This is the widely shared knowledge that is written in textbooks and journals. (b) Equally important to the practice of a field is the *heuristic* knowledge. This is the knowledge which constitutes the rules of expertise, the rules of good practice, the judgmental rules of the field, the rules of plausible reasoning. These rules collectively constitute what the mathematician George Polya has called the "art of good guessing". In contrast to the facts of a field its rules of good guessing are rarely written down. This knowledge is transmitted in internships, PhD programmes, apprenticeships. The programs I will describe require, for expert performance on problems, heuristic knowledge to be combined with the facts of the discipline.

Expert Systems

The act of obtaining, formalising and putting to work these kinds of rules is what we call "expertise modelling". In the modelling of expertise, we construct programs called "expert systems". The goal of an expert system project is to write a program that achieves a high level of performance on problems that are difficult enough to require significant human expertise for their solution. A strategy of other areas of AI research is to choose a highly simplified problem sometimes called a "toy problem" and exploit the toy problem in depth. In contrast, the problems chosen by knowledge engineers require the expertise of an MD, or a PhD, or other very highly trained specialist in a field, to solve.

An expert system of this type consists of only two things: a knowledge base, and an inference procedure. The knowledge base contains the facts and heuristics; the inference procedure consists of the processes that work over the knowledge base to infer solutions to problems, to do analyses, to form hypotheses, etc. In principle, the knowledge base is separable from the inference procedure.

The Scientific Issues

What are the central scientific issues of the Artificial Intelligence field from which this more applied research draws its inspiration? I'd like to categorise these under three headings.

First is the problem of *knowledge representation*. How shall the knowledge of the field be represented as data structures in the memory of the computer, so that they can be conveniently accessed for problem-solving?

Second is the problem of *knowledge utilisation*. How can this knowledge be used in problem-solving? Essentially, this is the question of the design of the inference engine. What designs for the inference engine are available?

Third, and more important, is the question of *knowledge acquisition*. How is it possible to acquire the knowledge so important for problem-solving automatically or at least semi-automatically, in a way in which the computer facilitates the transfer of expertise from humans (from practitioners or from their texts or their data) to the symbolic data structures that constitute the knowledge representation in the machine? Knowledge acquisition is a long-standing problem of Artificial Intelligence. For a long time it was cloaked under the word "learning". Now we are able to be more precise about the problem of machine learning; and with this increased precision has come a new term, "knowledge acquisition research".

This is the most important of the central problems of Artificial Intelligence research. The reason is simple: to enhance the performance of AI programs, knowledge is power. The power does not reside in the inference procedure. The power resides in the specific knowledge of the problem domain. The most powerful systems will be those which contain the most knowledge.

This knowledge is currently acquired in a very painstaking way, reminiscent of cottage industries, in which individual computer scientists work with individual experts painstakingly to explicate heuristics. If applied Artificial Intelligence is to be important in the decades to come, we must have more automatic means for replacing the currently tedious, time-consuming and expensive procedures. The problem of knowledge acquisition is the critical bottleneck problem in Artificial Intelligence.

A Brief Tutorial Using the MYCIN Program

As the basis of the exposition of underlying ideas, I will use a well-known program called MYCIN (see Shortliffe, 1976). MYCIN is a program for medical diagnosis and therapy. It produces diagnoses of infectious diseases, particularly blood infections and meningitis infections; and advises the physician on antibiotic therapies for treating those infectious diseases. MYCIN conducts a consultation with its user, a physician. This physician is to be distinguished from another kind of doctor who works with MYCIN, the expert. The expert is the person who introduces rules into the MYCIN knowledge base. The user exploits these rules in a dialogue, an interactive consultation which finally terminates in a diagnosis and therapy. The consultation is conducted in a stylised form of English; the doctor never knows about the LISP program underneath. In the consultation the doctor is asked only for patient history and laboratory test results (exogenous data the computer could not possibly infer).

A program like MYCIN is using qualitative reasoning to discover a line-of-reasoning, leading to a result (in this case a diagnosis). We can expect that it should be able to explain that line-of-reasoning to the user. In fact, I believe it is necessary that expert consultative systems do so; otherwise, the systems will not be credible to their professional users.

Knowledge in MYCIN

Figure 3.1 shows a piece of knowledge in MYCIN. MYCIN contains about five hundred rules, about half of them for blood infections, half for meningitis infections. Each such "production rule" consists of an "if" part and a "then" part (sometimes called "situation" and "action" parts, respectively). The "if" part defines a set of conditions of relevancy such that if each of these conditions is true, then the conclusion follows. Any logical combination of the "if" side conditions can be used. The rule is shown in approximately the way the expert would enter it, and exactly the way the doctor would see the rule if it were displayed. This piece of knowledge will be evoked from the knowledge base if the conditions are true, and will be build into the line-of-reasoning.

If:
1) The infection which requires therapy is meningitis, and
2) The type of the infection is fungal, and
3) Organisms were not seen on the stain of the culture, and
4) The patient is not a compromised host, and
5) The patient has been to an area that is endemic for coccidiomycoses, and
6) The race of the patient is one of: black asian indian, and
7) The cryptococcal antigen in the csf was not positive
Then: There is suggestive evidence that cryptococcus is not one of the organisms which might be causing the infection.

FIGURE 3.1: A piece of knowledge in Mycin

Inexact Inference

In MYCIN, there is a way for the expert to state to what extent, on a scale from 0.0 to 1.0, he believes that the preconditions imply the conclusion. 1.0 is certainty; 0.9 is "very strong evidence"; 0.6 is "suggestive evidence" and so on. These indices are combined in MYCIN with a very simple and easily explained function, yielding an index called a "cumulative certainty factor", an index of "strength of belief" in the line-of-reasoning.

MYCIN Diagnosis and Therapy

Figure 3.2 shows a typical MYCIN diagnosis. Then MYCIN proceeds to conduct a shorter consultation with the physician about such things as the patient's known sensitivities to various kinds of antibiotics and the resistance shown by certain organisms to various kinds of antibiotics. MYCIN then produces a therapy recommendation such as shown in Figure 3.3.

INFECTION-1 is MENINGITIS
+ <ITEM-1> E. COLI [from clinical evidence only]
+ <ITEM-2> PSEUDOMONAS-AERUGINOSA [from clinical evidence only]
+ <ITEM-3> KLEBSIELLA-PNEUMONIAE [from clinical evidence only]
+ <ITEM-4> DIPLOCOCCUS-PNEUMONIAE [from clinical evidence only]

FIGURE 3.2: An example of a MYCIN diagnosis

My preferred therapy recommendation is as follows:
In order to cover for Items <1 2 3 4>:
Give the following in combination:
1) AMPICILLIN
Dose: 3.5g (28.0/ml) q4h IV [calculated on basis of 50/mg/kg]
2) GENTAMICIN
Dose: 119 mg (3.0 ml, 80/ng/2ml ampoule) q8 IV [calculated on basis of 1.7 mg/kg]
plus consider giving 5 mg q24h Intrathecal
Comments: Monitor serum concentrations
Since high concentrations of penicillins can inactivate aminoglycosides, do not mix these two antibiotics in the same IV bottle.

FIGURE 3.3: An example of a MYCIN antibiotic therapy recommendation

MYCIN's Line-of-Reasoning

MYCIN's line-of-reasoning is a chain of rules that concludes the (perhaps uncertain) presence of an infecting organism from laboratory test data and patient history. The line-of-reasoning is discovered by backward chaining. The search starts with the various possible organisms as "goals to be achieved" and terminates with the data.

The explanation facility can exhibit selected portions of the chain as requested by the user. It can answer a variety of queries during or after the consultation dialogue, such as: "Why (are you asking me for this information)?" or "How (was some particular conclusion reached)?" One interesting form of query is shown in figure 3.4. To answer it, MYCIN must keep track of not only acceptable lines-of-reasoning, but also the invalid lines explored, along with reasons for unacceptability.

USER: WHY DIDN'T YOU GIVE TETRACYCLINE FOR E. COLI IN REC-1
MYCIN: TETRACYCLINE was discounted for ITEM-1
(RECOMMENDATION-1) because there is evidence that this E. coli is not sensitive to it.

FIGURE 3.4: An example of MYCIN's explanation facility

MYCIN's Inference Procedure

We can remove the knowledge base of MYCIN and substitute a set of rules from another domain. That is equivalent to saying that the knowledge base and the inference procedure are separate things in an expert system. Removing from MYCIN its infectious disease diagnosis rules yields an inference "engine" which we call EMYCIN (for Essential Mycin or Empty Mycin or Engine Mycin, see van Melle (1979)).

Building a New System with the EMYCIN Tool: PUFF

Combining with EMYCIN a set of rules for pulmonary function diagnosis produced a diagnostic program called PUFF (Osborn et al. 1979). In this diagnostic situation, a patient is breathing in and out of an instrument called a spirometer, producing measurement of flow of air in expiration and inhalation, versus lung volume. Data reduction is done by a PDP-11, and data interpretation is done by PUFF. The PUFF report is reviewed by an expert physician, is signed if accurate, put into the patient record and sent to the referring physician. Currently, about 85 per cent of PUFF outputs are signed without modification.

PUFF consists of about 100 production rules of the MYCIN-like type. It produces reports like that shown in Figure 3.5.

INTERPRETATION: Elevated lung volumes indicate overinflation. In addition, the rv/tlc ratio is increased, suggesting a mild degree of air trapping. Forced vital capacity is normal but the fevl/fvc ratio is reduced, suggesting airway obstruction of a mild degree. Reduced mid-expiratory flow indicates mild airway obstruction. Obstruction is indicated by curvature in the flow-volume loop of a small degree. Following bronchodilation, the expired flow shows slight improvement. This is confirmed by the lack of change in airway resistance. The low diffusing capacity indicates a loss of alveolar capillary surface, which is moderate.

CONCLUSIONS: The low diffusing capacity, in combination with obstruction and a high total lung capacity would be consistent with a diagnosis of emphysema. The patient's airway obstruction may be caused by smoking. Discontinuation of smoking should help relieve the symptoms.

PULMONARY FUNCTION DIAGNOSIS:
1. MILD OBSTRUCTIVE AIRWAYS DISEASE. EMPHYSEMATOUS TYPE

FIGURE 3.5: An example of the output of PUFF

Another Application of the EMYCIN Tool

A group designing airplane wings for the U.S. Air Force uses a software package, called the MARC package, developed by the MARC Analysis

Research Corporation, for finite element analysis. The package is excellent but complex. Its use requires considerable expertise. The design group wanted a MYCIN-like expert system to consult with designers on the use of the MARC package. EMYCIN was used to create the expert system SACON (for Structural Analysis Consultant, Bennett and Engelmore 1979). An engineer brings to SACON his design specifications for the structure. SACON produces for him an analysis plan, which he can then translate into subroutine calls for the MARC software (Figures 3.6 and 3.7.).

---

if:
1) The material composing the substructure is one of metal,
2) The analysis error (in percent) that is tolerable is between 5 and 30,
3) The nondimensional stress of the substructure is greater than .9 and
4) The number of cycles the loading is to be applied is between 1000 and 10000,
Then: It is definite that fatigue is one of the stress behaviour phenomena in the substructure.

FIGURE 3.6: A piece of knowledge (production rule) in the SACON system

---

The following analysis classes are relevant to the analysis of your structure:

General-inelastic

The following are specific analysis recommendations you should follow when performing the structure analysis:

Activate incremental stress — incremental strain analysis.
Model nonlinear stress-strain relation of the material.
Solution will be based on a mix of gradient and Newton methods
User programs to scan peak stress at each step and evaluate fatigue integrity should be used.
User programs to scan stresses, smooth and compare with allowable stresses (with appropriate safety factors) should be used.
User programs to scan deflections, calculate relative values, and compare with code limits, should be called upon.
Cumulative strain damage should be calculated.

FIGURE 3.7: A SACON output (analysis plan)

Concluding Remarks on MYCIN-like Systems

Before leaving the topic of MYCIN-like systems, let me remark on two trends. The first is a trend in knowledge engineering to put in software packages what we know about building expert systems. EMYCIN represents one of the first of these packages. There are other packages, built for different types of inference procedure. The AGE system assists in the building of inference procedures of a type called "blackboard models", first developed at Carnegie-Mellon University in the HEARSAY-2 speech understanding project. Another package assists with knowledge representation. Called the UNITS package (Stefik, 1979) it is similar to the packages KRL and KL-ONE.

Second, let me mention a unique package that facilitates teaching of knowledge in knowledge bases built for expert systems. This package called GUIDON (Clancey, 1979) is capable of teaching whatever EMYCIN can reason about. Thus, GUIDON can currently teach infectious disease diagnosis and therapy; pulmonary function disease diagnosis; and the use of the MARC structural analysis package. GUIDON consists of a set of rules for another kind of expertise, the expertise of good teachers. If you blend the rules of good teaching with the rules of good practice in a field, then you can teach well the rules of good practice in that field. This is important because such rules are almost never taught explicitly. They are usually taught informally, by apprenticeship, as mentioned earlier.

Hypothesis and Theory Formation: DENDRAL and Meta-DENDRAL

The most widely used of the expert systems of knowledge engineering is the DENDRAL system (Buchanan and Feigenbaum, 1978). Initially, DENDRAL analysed mass spectral data, and inferred a complete structural hypothesis (topology only) for the molecule. DENDRAL was subsequently generalised to produce a set of structural candidates from whatever constraints happened to be available in the problem, not only the mass spectral constraints, but constraints from nuclear magnetic resonance, from other spectral data like IR or UV, or any other information that the chemist happens to know about the problem. Given a set of constraints from various kinds of available data DENDRAL will produce a set of candidate structures that are the best explanations of the data.

DENDRAL's Knowledge and Method

DENDRAL's knowledge sources are shown in Figure 3.8.

DENDRAL uses a three-stage problem-solving process. The first stage is one in which constraints on solution are inferred from spectral data. Given those constraints, plus all other constraints the chemist has noted, the program generates all structures satisfying the problem-specific and the general chemical constraints. Finally it tests the candidates to choose and rank the best. This method is called a "plan-generate-and-test" strategy.

Graph Theoretic	Connectivity, Symmetry
Chemical	Atoms, Valences, Stability
Spectroscopic	Mass Spectrometric Fragmentation Rules; Nuclear Magnetic Resonance Rules
Contextual	Origin of Sample, Chemical Properties, Method of Isolation
Judgmental	Goodness-of-Fit Between Predicted and Observed Data

FIGURE 3.8: DENDRAL's sources of knowledge

DENDRAL's Applications

DENDRAL has been used in thousands of chemical structure analyses. It has users in universities and industries throughout the US, Europe and Australia. Some operate over the international TYMNET to Stanford; others use DENDRAL on their own machines. DENDRAL has been "exported" to the USA National Institutes of Health. It has been re-coded for a PDP-10 in Edinburgh, Scotland (see Carhart 1977). It is running at Lederle Laboratories in Pearl River, New York and at other chemical and drug companies. Developed in LISP, it was rewritten in BCPL for efficiency. It has also been used to teach structure elucidation in the 1st-year graduate course in organic chemistry at Stanford, and also to check the correctness of published structures.

Knowledge Acquisition

The knowledge acquisition bottleneck is a critical problem. How is it that chemists arrive at their rules of mass spectrometry? They derive these rules or theories by induction from laboratory experience. The Meta-DENDRAL program was an attempt to model the processes of theory formation.

The "meta" level, or knowledge acquisition level, of DENDRAL accepts as input a set of known structure-spectrum pairs. Thousands of these have been stored in the computer. The output of Meta-DENDRAL is a set of general fragmentation rules of the form used by DENDRAL, viz. some particular subgraph of a chemical molecule gives rise to some particular fragmentation. (*IF* this subgraph occurs, *THEN* this fragmentation process will occur.)

Meta-DENDRAL's method is also a plan-generate-and-test method. The planning process is called interpretation and summarisation, interpreting each spectral data point as a fragmentation, collecting evidence for similar processes and bond environments. The generation process generates a space of plausible rules (not plausible structures as with DENDRAL, but plausible rules of mass spectrometry) constrained by the evidence and by some user-supplied context. The test phase tests the plausible rules, using all the evidence, positive and negative, and generalises or specialises the rules to improve support from the evidence, seeking a better fit between rules and evidence.

In a major knowledge acquisition experiment, Meta-DENDRAL inferred the rules of fragmentation for a family of complex steroidal molecules whose mass spectral theory was of interest to our chemist collaborators. A total of 33 rules (covering 3 subfamilies) was formed, all chemically plausible and of high quality (measured in terms of the amount of input data accounted for by each).

How good is Meta-DENDRAL? To what extent have we succeeded in forming by machine a piece of reasonable scientific theory, i.e. a set of fragmentation rules for mass spectrometry? We chose the classical scientific route for answering that question. We wrote out the results of the experiment described above and sent the paper to a respected scientific journal, as a scientific contribution. The contribution was refereed and published in the journal, the standard qualification for a piece of new knowledge entering the science (see Buchanan *et al*, 1976).

Knowledge Acquisition and Discovery

Another attempt at modelling knowledge acquisition and discovery was the development of the AM Program (Lenat, 1976). AM's task is the discovery of mathematical concepts, not necessarily new to mankind, but interestingly complex for a program to have discovered.

AM begins with a set of elementary ideas in finite set theory: the idea of a set, a multi-set, set equality, etc. The program contains heuristic knowledge relevant to generating new mathematical concepts, the kinds of heuristics that an expert mathematician would have. It also has heuristics for discarding the bad ideas generated and picking out the interesting new mathematical conjectures. These are the so-called heuristics of interestingness. Thus the knowledge base contains heuristics of combination ("generate") and heuristics of interestingness ("test").

The program searches a space of possible conjectures that can be generated from the elementary ideas, chooses the most interesting, and pursues that line-of-reasoning. As usual, the program is capable of explaining its line-of-reasoning. The user can interact with the program to give familiar labels to newly-generated concepts, such as: call that concept "add"; call that "prime". The program uses the label subsequently, so that the explanation trace is understandable to the human.

With its heuristics, the program searched the space discovering concepts like: list equality (a specialisation of general set equality); cardinality, therefore number; add, subtract, multiply, divide; factoring and the concept of a prime; and the fundamental theorem of arithmetic (the unique factorisation of numbers into primes). AM also made some conjectures in number theory which, though put forward many years ago, had not been explored.

The program eventually began exploring a bigger space than it could cope with, for reasons that are related to the earlier discussion of power and knowledge. As AM plunged deeper into number theory, its general mathematical heuristics became less powerful at controlling search. It needed more specific heuristics about number theory. These were not given initially because of the possible criticism that the program was initially biased toward discovering number theory. The program lost power as it needed the specialised knowledge that it did not have. A new project, called EURISKO, is exploring how a program can discover new heuristics, as it invents new kinds of things (e.g. as it discovers ideas in number theory, how can it invent heuristics about number theory?).

Two Major Principles of Knowledge Engineering

These have already been mentioned earlier and will be summarised here.

The first is that the problem-solving power exhibited by an intelligent agent's performance is primarily the consequence of its knowledge base, and only secondarily a consequence of the inference method employed. Expert systems must be knowledge-rich even if they are methods-poor. This is an important result and one that has only recently become well understood in AI. For a long time AI focused its attention almost exclusively on the development of clever inference methods. But the power of its systems does not reside in the inference method; almost any inference method will do. The power resides in the knowledge.

Second, experience has shown that this knowledge is largely *heuristic* knowledge: judgmental, experiental, uncertain. This knowledge is generally "private" to an expert, not because the expert is unwilling to share publicly what he knows, but because he is often unable to. This knowledge can be extracted by a careful, painstaking analysis by a second party (a knowledge engineer) operating in the context of a large number of highly specific performance problems. The expertise being modelled is multi-faceted; an expert brings to bear many and varied sources of knowledge in performance.

The Promise of Knowledge Engineering

There is currently considerable interest in the scientific, engineering and industrial use of knowledge engineering techniques. The promise, recognised but barely realised to date, is threefold.

Cost Reductions

There is a possible enormous cost savings in computation and instrumentation by using these methods. Here I would like to make the case concretely not abstractly. In signal processing applications, involving large amounts of data with poor signal/noise ratios, it is possible to reduce computation costs by several orders of magnitude by the use of knowledge-based reasoning rather than brute-force statistical methods.

One of the expert systems whose construction I supervised (Nii and Feigenhaum, 1977) involved the interpretation of massive amounts of signal data with very poor signal/noise ratios. The object of the program was to produce a continuously updated "situation understanding" of the objects producing the signals, their positions in space, and their velocities. Using standard signal-processing techniques of cross-correlation and auto-correlation, the computational requirements far exceeded the bounds of all computation available for the problem. In the statistical technique, no use was made of a wealth of knowledge available to interpret the signal data, for example: "textbook" information of the objects as signal-generating sources; "good guesses" available to the human controllers about the "most likely" moves of the objects over considerable periods of time; previously discerned patterns of movement; the laws of physics dictating what the objects could possibly do; what neighbouring observing sites had observed; and so on. This was the true symbolic "semantics" and context of the problem. The ongoing model of the situation could be inferred almost completely from this symbolic knowledge, with only occasional reference to the massive amount of signal data for hypothesis verification and for noticing changes. The expert system built using AI methods of symbolic inference was able to accomplish the task using an estimated two orders of magnitude less computation than the statistical methods required. There is an important lesson here. It makes little sense to use enormous amounts of expensive computation to tease a little signal out of much noise, when most of the understanding can be readily inferred from the symbolic knowledge surrounding the situation.

There is an additional cost saving possible. Sensor bandwidth and sensitivity is expensive. From a symbolic model it is possible, with prevision, to generate a set of signal expectations whose emergence in the data would make a difference to the verification of the ongoing model. Sensor parameters can then be "tuned" to the expected signals and signal directions; not every signal in every direction need be searched for.

Consider the DENDRAL program described earlier. Because the DENDRAL program knew so much about chemistry in general and mass spectrometry in particular, it could solve structure problems using low-resolution data that chemists could solve at that time only by using high-resolution instruments. Low-resolution instrumentation plus knowledge-based reasoning equalled the performance of high-resolution instruments. A low-resolution instrument costs only about $5,000 while a high-resolution instrument costs about $100,000. Therefore, $5,000 plus "smarts" can equal a $100,000 instrument.

The Inevitability Argument

There is a certain inevitability to knowledge engineering and its applications. The cost of computers will fall drastically during the coming two decades. As it does, many more of the practitioners of the world's professions will be persuaded to turn to economical automatic information processing for assistance in managing the increasing complexity of their daily tasks. In most of computer science they will find help only for those of their problems that have a mathematical or statistical core, or are of a routine data-processing nature. But such problems will be rare, except in engineering and physical science. In medicine, biology, management, indeed in most of the world's work, the daily tasks are those requiring symbolic reasoning with detailed professional knowledge. The computers that will act as "intelligent assistants" for those professionals must be endowed with such reasoning capabilities and knowledge.

The Most Important Gain: New Knowledge

The methodology that I have been describing allows a field to "get its hands on" the real knowledge of the field. The real knowledge of the field is not in the textbooks. The textbooks lack the experiential, judgmental, heuristic knowledge of the excellent practitioners of the field. When experts argue, the bases on which they argue are largely unspoken. The methodology we use gives a way of bringing heuristic knowledge to the surface and making it concrete, so that it can be discussed and consensus can be achieved. If consensus is not achieved, at least the alternatives to the consensus are available for examination. In the end it may be irrelevant that a computer program is available to be an "intelligent assistant". The gain to human knowledge by making explicit the heuristic rules of a discipline will perhaps be the most important contribution of the knowledge-based systems approach.

Problems of Knowledge Engineering

Though knowledge engineering has made great advances in the last ten years, and is witnessing the pressure toward industrial application, it faces persistent problems.

The Lack of Adequate and Appropriate Hardware

Artificial Intelligence is largely experimental, not theoretical, computer science. It builds and tests systems. Its laboratory is the computer, and it is suffering from lack of adequate laboratory facilities.

Currently applied AI is machine-limited. That was not the case for the first 15 years of AI. The capabilities of computers to process symbols exceeded our ability to conceive interesting ways to process them. In the last few years the field definitely has been limited by the size and power of its computers. For example, the DENDRAL program is now solving much larger and more difficult problems than we ever conceived that it would solve. System designers are always gentle to their systems: they know the computational boundaries of what is feasible; but users do not. The users have real problems that can easily exceed the computational capabilities of the systems that we provide for them. Problems in the physical sciences can command any number of large computers, while an AI project is worth only a small fraction of a DEC PDP-10. The scale must be changed.

AI researchers are now discovering how to construct specialised symbol manipulation machines. These computers have not yet been built by industry because industry does not yet perceive a widespread market. In the past we have adapted the classical computing machines for symbol manipulation. The list processing systems, particularly LISP, in which most AI work has been done, have been pasted on top of the instruction code of conventional computers. That is a mistake. We need specialised symbol processing devices.

The silver lining of the cloud is the emergence of two kinds of facilities. The first is the large memory machine. The era of the 18 bit address of the PDP-10 is ending. We are still using PDP-10s, but we envision machines with address spaces up to 32 bits. Of course the cost of memory is dropping dramatically. It is now possible to buy 2 million words of 36 bit memory for less than $200,000. Secondly, we see developments like the one at MIT, of a LISP machine (MIT, 1979), a piece of hardware and micro-code that runs a version of the LISP language. This provides highly efficient list processing in a personal computer environment. At the moment it is still too expensive to afford as a "personal" machine, but the cost should drop by about a factor of two every few years for the next decade.

Lack of Cumulation of AI Methods and Techniques

The second problem is the lack of cumulation of AI methods and techniques. Currently, in the AI field there is too much reinvention of concepts and methods that are well explored.

How does one cumulate knowledge in a science? One way is to publish papers and hope that other people read them and use the ideas. A more traditional way in computer science is to cumulate ideas in software packages, e.g. the cumulation of computational methods of statistics in the large statistical packages. The creation of software packages such as EMYCIN, AGE (Nii and Aiello, 1979), ROSIE (at the Rand Corporation), and the various knowledge representation systems, is a hopeful sign that we will solve the problem of cumulation.

Shortage of Trained Knowledge Engineers

One of the problems of knowledge engineering is the shortage of trained knowledge engineers. There is a strong and growing demand for such specialists. The universities are producing very few of them, but are themselves consuming almost the entire product.

There is significant industrial demand. The Xerox Palo Alto Research Center has hired a number of artificial intelligence researchers to investigate the office automation systems of the future — electronic offices. It is envisioned that programs will help process the "paper" that will flow electronically through the system, as well as perform other office functions such as calendar management, intelligent sorting of electronic mail, and intelligent access to files.

One company servicing the oil industry, Schlumberger, is beginning work on applying knowledge engineering methods to handle the following problem: the number of interpretations that have to be done for signals (coming from physical instrumentation of oil wells) is growing much larger, and it is expensive and difficult to train new interpretation specialists. Schlumberger is interested in replication of expertise. They want to discover what the expertise consists of and then copy it for use at their outlying sites.

Texas Instruments has established an AI group to explore educational uses of AI, and also some aspects of computer-aided design. IBM has a group in Palo Alto, California, studying the use of AI in system design, and in diagnosis of computer system failures.

A number of military applications of AI is being developed now. Hence the defence contact firms are also in the market for knowledge engineers.

Are there any silver linings to this cloud of shortage of people? I think there are. One is the recognition that the AI community must create for itself the equivalent of the aerospace industry to apply its skills and methods to real-world problems. Each new application cannot be done, in the future, by the few skilled technologists at the university laboratories. AI must have an industry that is capable of performing the process and producing usable devices.

The Problem of Knowledge Acquisition

Another problem of applied AI is a critical scientific problem — the problem of knowledge acquisition. Since the power of expert systems is in their knowledge bases, successful applied AI requires that knowledge move from the heads of experts into programs. The process is too slow. Therefore we seek more automatic methods for transferring and transforming knowledge into its computer representation.

We now have knowledge-acquisition systems that are interactive, involving semi-automatic ways of steering the expert to the right piece of knowledge to introduce into the system. We have also done experiments in automatic knowledge acquisition, extracting knowledge directly from "nature", i.e. from data, from evidence (e.g. the Meta-DENDRAL program described earlier).

Thus, there are silver linings with regard to knowledge acquisition, but the problem is an extremely difficult and important bottleneck problem in this field.

The Problem of Obtaining and Sustaining Funding

There is great difficulty in obtaining and sustaining sufficient funding for this kind of research. Why?

Like other empirical sciences, AI is much more expensive than its theoretic counterparts. AI projects do not fit the traditional academic model of professors and students. AI projects generally require full-time, post-doctoral professionals and programmers. Computer scientists and experts in the discipline are needed.

Knowledge engineering projects tend to be viewed as high-risk projects and off the mainstream of the target discipline. Hence, when these projects are reviewed, peer review is hard to obtain at all. In an era of budget stringency, these peer reviews do not provide the necessary judgments of high priority to fund such projects. When a project is given a peer review by a group consisting of some computer scientists and some specialists in the domain of expertise, the specialists in the domain will assign high priority to the laboratory work of their own discipline and not to some off-mainstream, high-risk adventure. The same is true of the administrative judgments made by funding agencies concerning programme relevance and priority. To put it another way, the knowledge engineering community is not yet well-established.

Historically the average knowledge engineering project has taken a long time to reach fruition. PUFF and SACON are exceptions, but generally quick results are rare. Therefore the hit-and-run approach for funding is inappropriate at this stage of the development of knowledge engineering. However, there are signs of improvement. The U.S. National Library of Medicine is funding five-year research programmes on knowledge representation. The US Defense Department support is solidifying. And Japan's Ministry of International Trade and Industry is considering large long-term support.

Adequate, long-term funding is important from the point of view of capturing the interest of experts in a domain. Intensive collaboration of experts is a key problem. These relationships between computer scientists and collaborators are very fragile. If the longevity of the grants is not sufficient, then the collaborations will dissolve, as has happened many times to applied AI projects.

The Development Gap

Finally, there is the so-called "development gap". There is lack of an orderly bureaucratic process in the research funding agencies for handling programs after they have achieved their first success as a research project.

Promising knowledge engineering projects, on whose success in application the future credibility of the field depends, have fallen, or will certainly fall, into the so-called "development gap". Industries, also, should be educated so that they perceive a commercial self-interest in filling the gap.

Acknowledgments

It is fitting, in conclusion, and perhaps instructive to the reader, to acknowledge the major sources of research funds for the work of my groups, the Heuristic Programming Project and SUMEX Project at Stanford University. The primary research funding has come from two agencies over the years: The Defense Advanced Research Projects Agency (DARPA); and the Biotechnology Resources Program of the US National Institute of Health (NIH). Project support for particular programs has been granted by the US National Science Foundation. Relatively recently we have received support from the US National Library of Medicine; from the Office of Naval Research; from Schlumberger-Doll Research; and from the IBM Corporation.

The work described in this article has been programmed on the facilities of the SUMEX-AIM Computer Resource at Stanford. SUMEX-AIM is a national computer resource for research on the application of artificial intelligence to biology and medicine. The national users (the AIM community) access the computer over the national computer networks TYMNET and ARPANET. The facility consists of Digital Equipment Corporation computers, a dual PDP-10 (KI) with 0.5 megawords, and a 2060 with 0.5 megawords. The research language used is INTERLISP. We are now expanding to significant use of a DEC 2060 with 1.0 megawords and a DEC VAX 11/780 with very large main memory.

References

Bennet, J.S. and Engelmore, R.S. (1979) SACON: a knowledge-based consultant for structural analysis, *Proc. 6th Int. Jnt. Conf. on Artif. Intell.* (Tokyo), pp. 47-49. Stanford, CA: Department of Computer Science, Stanford University.

Bobrow, D.G. and Winograd, T. (1977). An overview of KRL-0, a knowledge representation language, *Cog. Sci.* 1, 1.

Buchanan, B.G. and Feigenbaum, E.A. (1978). DENDRAL and Meta-DENDRAL: their applications dimensions, *Artif. Intell.*, 11.

Buchanan, B.G., and Smith, D.H., White, W. C., Gritter, R., Feigenbaum, E.A., Lederberg, J., Djerassi C. (1976). Applications of artificial intelligence for chemical inference. XXII Automatic rule formation in mass spectrometry by means of the Meta-DENDRAL program. *J. Amer. Chem. Soc.*, 98, 6168-6178.

Carhart, R.E. (1977). Reprogramming DENDRAL. *AISB Quarterly,* 28, 20-22.

Clancey, W.J. (1979). Transfer of rule-based expertise through a tutorial dialogue. PhD Thesis, Stanford University.

Clancey, W.J. (1979). Dialogue management for rule-based tutorials. *Proc. 6th Int. Jnt., Conf. on Artif. Intell.* (Toyko), pp. 155-161. Stanford, CA: Stanford University.

Lenat, D.B. (1976). An artificial intelligence approach to discovery in mathematics. PhD Thesis, Stanford University.

Lenat, D.B. (1983). The role of heuristics in learning by discovery: three case histories. In *Machine Learning: an artificial intelligence approach* (eds R.S. Michalski, J.G. Carbonell and T.M. Mitchell), pp. 243-306. Palo Alto, CA: Tioga.

LISP Machine Manual (1979). Cambridge, MA: Artificial Intelligence Laboratory, MIT.

Mostow, D.J. and Hayes-Roth, F. (1978). A system for speech understanding. In *Pattern-Directed Inference Systems* (eds D.A. Waterman and F. Hayes-Roth), New York: Academic Press.

Nii, H.P. and Aiello, N. (1979). AGE: a knowledge-based program for building knowledge-based programs, *Proc. 6th Int. Jnt. Conf. on Artif. Intell.* (Tokyo), pp 645-655. Stanford, CA: Department of Computer Science, Stanford University.

Nii, H.P. and Feigenbaum, E.A. (1978). Rule-based understanding of signals. In *Pattern-Directed Inference Systems* (eds D.A. Waterman and F, Hayes-Roth), pp 483-501. New York: Academic Press.

Osborn, J., Fagan, L., Fallat, R., McClung, D. and Mitchell, R. (1979). Measuring the data from respiratory measurements. *Medical Instrumentation*, 13 (6).

Shortliffe, E. (1976). *Computer-Based Medical Consultations: MYCIN.* New York: American Elsevier.

Stefik, M. (1979). An examination of a frame-structured representation system, *Proc. 6th Int. Jnt. Conf. on Artif. Intell.* (Toyko), pp. 845-852. Stanford, CA: Department of Computer Science, Stanford University.

Van Melle, W. (1979). A domain-independent production rule system for consultation programs, *Proc. 6th Int. Jnt. Conf. on Artif. Intell.* (Toyko), pp. 923-925. Stanford, CA: Department of Computer Science, Stanford University.

4

A Prototype Knowledge Refinery

D. Michie
University of Edinburgh

Introduction

The question has been raised whether there are too few ideas to justify public expenditure on research facilities. In Britain the "hit rate" of ideas, in the sense of laboratory success transformed into commercially viable activity, is very low, as we all know. But it is not low because of shortage or poverty of the ideas themselves. Observed exploitation does not remotely reflect the potential exploitability of British laboratory work. All established information scientists, especially if they are active in software technology, could make a short list of recently discovered principles or phenomena, which could ultimately generate new industries. But they do nothing about it. First, to do so is not their trade. Second they are convinced that to follow new ideas through into a profitable new craft or a new industry, even a new product, is more often than not politically impossible. As an illustration I shall take one of these cases out of my own experience. Others could produce equally pertinent examples, but this has certain exaggerated features such as its low cost and its large effect on society. Bill Read has volunteered to put forward afterwards ideas for funding and technical management, not for this idea specifically but as a general plan.

The case I put before us is: Why do we not, since the phenomena are well known, build a "knowledge refinery" as the basis of a new industry, comparable in some ways to the industry of petroleum refining, only more important in the long run? The produce to be refined is codified human knowledge. This is the material in textbooks and technical papers which, rather like crude oil, is still in an unsatisfactory state. Improvement can be brought about by a machine-based technique known as *knowledge refining*. The idea is simple but no-one foresaw it.

Let us first consider some general questions:
Have there been genuine observations of this purportedly new and exploitable

phenomenon? Three years ago there was none. But there are many now.
Is the necessary software there? It is.
Is there plenty of room for product-improvement? Certainly.
Is there availability of suitably trained labour? Any good software company has people who in a short time could adapt themselves to this type of work.
What are the capital and running costs? Relative to other industries, negligible.
Is there potential social impact? Greater, in the long term, than oil refining itself.
Could it constitute a United Kingdom specialism? Britain is a particularly appropriate country to do this.

Knowledge Refinement

The chance observation which first brought it to my attention was made in our Edinburgh laboratory in the following manner. Ivan Bratko, a Yugoslav computer scientist and chess master, was then on a visit to Edinburgh. He chose for study an elementary piece of chess knowledge, namely: How to mate with king and rook against king from any legal starting position. Although an elementary mate, it is not easy to program, taking (unless artificial intelligence methods are used) approximately two or three months of a graduate student's time. Furthermore the resulting program is never completely correct in its play.

Using one of our local advice languages, Bratko was able to complete the programming in two weeks. Subsequently he proved, both exhaustively by computation and also by symbolic proof, that the program was complete and correct. He then translated the program rules back into English. This produced six rules only. They were complete and correct, unlike grandmaster codifications which turn out to contain errors when subjected to the pulveriser approach of exhaustive computation (see Bratko, 1978).

The improvement in the knowledge representation when back-translated from an advice program was unexpected. However, when the possibility was drawn to the attention of workers in other laboratories they confirmed that they too were able to see indications of the same phenomenon. For example, MYCIN, developed in Feigenbaum's laboratory, was the first expert system of the modern type (Shortliffe, 1976). Although its knowledge is not broad enough to make the program of significant utility to clinicians it is nonetheless an observed fact that particularly before examinations the program is heavily used by medical students. They find this a better source of knowledge than the text-books routinely available to them. Notes are given below on other cases where back-translation from an advice program has produced an improved text for the human learner.

Internal medicine

Dr Jack Myers at Pittsburgh Medical School is the equivalent of a grand master in internal medicine. In his later years he had planned a series of volumes as a monument to his life-time achievement in codifying knowledge about internal medicine. But he was drawn by Harry Pople, a computer scientist, into a project to put what he knows into expert system form (Pople, 1977). The significant development from the knowledge-refinery point of view is that medical collaborators with the project make continuing use of photocopies of parts of the Myers-Pople knowledge base in their subsequent clinical careers.

Oil platform diagnosis

Another example of the same phenomenon comes from Edinburgh work on oil platform fault diagnosis. Even though our study was a feasibility study and does not pretend to be a field system, production engineers have asked us for copies of our inference net (in which the machine's knowledge is coded) for instructional purposes.

Organic chemical synthesis

In organic chemical synthesis at the University of California, Santa Cruz, organic chemists use printouts from the Wippke knowledge base (from Wippke's program SECS, Wippke, 1977) in those areas of synthetic chemistry where it has expertise. They regard it as superior to conventional sources.

More striking cases occur where the system is assisted by inbuilt learning capabilities. Inductive learning programs enable the expert to convey through *examples* some of the diagnostic descriptive concepts on which his skill depends. He relies on the system "getting the hang of it" from examples. This is the method which he is accustomed to use for communicating with a student or a colleague, instead of having to spell everything out. The following examples come into this category.

Soybean pathology

Until recently, the best classification of soybean diseases, which are of economic importance in the state of Illinois, was that by the plant pathologist, Dr Jacobsen, who collaborated in a study directed by R. S. Michalski in the University of Illinois (see Michalski and Chilausky 1980). The refinement phenomenon was assisted in this case from machine generalisation over examples by Michalski's program AQ11. Thus in this case the machine was part-author of the resulting classification system, which gave 99% correct allocation of diseased plants as against about 83% for the old Jacobsen system. Jacobsen then took it in hand to try and improve his system, using the machine to test and recycle and debug his theory. With great difficulty he refined his own system so that it achieved a 93% success rate. Unable to improve it further, he then decided to accept the machine-generated taxonomy. He uses it now as a basis of his professional work.

Mass spectroscopy

Another valid example where the product is handed back to the original source as a greatly improved codification comes from mass spectroscopy, the domain of the DENDRAL project at Stanford and of the Meta-DENDRAL module which is the inductive learning part (see Buchanan and Feigenbaum, 1978 and Chapter 3 of this book). A somewhat obscure family of organic chemicals called the mono- and poly-keto-androstanes formerly lacked any spectroscopic theory. In the *Journal of the American Chemical Association* (1967, see Buchanan *et al*) there is a paper with six authors describing spectroscopic rules for interpreting mass spectra in the case of the keto-androstanes: but the substantive contribution to the construction of the theory was Meta-DENDAL's.

The question arises: does a different program have to be written for each of these application areas? The knowledge put in by the expert must of course be domain-specific, but we have at least one example of generality.

Lymphatic cancers

In the differential diagnosis of lymphatic cancers Ivan Bratko successfully used a learning algorithm derived from Ross Quinlan's ID3 which was in turn based on Earl Hunt's CLS (see Hunt, Marin and Stone, 1966). The Edinburgh version of ID3 was developed using the domain of chess. Strategies for chess end-games were conveyed by examples, in the way that the chess master teaches a human pupil. The resulting correct and complete theory of King and Pawn against King is itself of interest to chess masters.

When Bratko returned to Yugoslavia, he used exactly the same program in a collaborative study with a clinical colleague at Ljubljana. The clinical expert had attempted to develop a definitive classification for the lymphatic cancers for diagnostic purposes. With this program, ID3, Bratko and the clinician were able to construct quite quickly a classification substantially better than the preceding codification which the clinicians had hand-crafted.

But with the aid of a medical student to help him extract the facts from the case histories, he was able to use the rules of machine origin to perform as though he were a medical expert (see Bratko and Mulec, 1980).

Necessary ingredients for knowledge-refining

What are the necessary ingredients to make knowledge refining work?
1. Knowledge-engineering software: i.e. "advice languages", "inference engines" (that part of an expert system able to make inferences from data supplied and to retrace and display its lines of reasoning) and "induction modules" (that part of an expert system able to generate rules from examples).
2. A good development environment. UNIX and INTERSLIP are two examples of particularly good software environments for this type of work.
3. One or more experts. Even with knowledge generation automated to the limit of current technique an expert is still needed to choose the repertoire of primitive measurements or attributes to evaluate as relevant to the given problem domain.
4. One or more knowledge engineers, namely computer scientists with some experience in this particular craft. But you must be prepared for progress to be slow. An average rate of progress is three or four finally accepted new rules added to the knowledge-base for each man-week's work.

That can be seen as a lot or a little. Compared with traditional software engineering, the rate is rather good, since you may have a commercially useful system when you only have two or three hundred rules in memory.

Alternatively it can be seen as ridiculously slow because each rule would only take a few minutes to convey to a human apprentice. We incline to the second view. Like other knowledge engineering laboratories, we are impatient to integrate inductive learning facilities with this type of software so that the expert can program his knowledge into the system by examples.

As performance systems, expert systems now have commercial promise. In one or two cases they are making money. There is a system of over 2,000 rules, called R1, used at Digital Equipment Corporation for configuring computing systems to customers' needs (see McDermott, 1982). It already out-performs their best technical salesman. But attention is not being directed here to that application of expert systems. I am talking about a potential new craft, perhaps an industry, in which the focus is not on the product that expert systems were originally designed to deliver, namely interactive advice in conversation with a client, but on the unexpected by-product, the finished knowledge-base itself. Expert system languages can be used to get knowledge into the machine, to test it, to debug it, to fill gaps, to extend and modify it in practice, until finally the knowledge can be put back into the human world as an unrecognisably superior product. Thus, the possibility now exists of superseding (as the automobile has superseded the horse) a handicraft which has been going on for several thousands of years, namely, the writing of manuals and texts on how to do things.

Clearly there could be an enormous effect on social life if this were ever put on a factory basis. It would then become possible to turn out unrecognisably improved codifications of human knowledge and know-how *in bulk.*

What sort of applications exist? Legal and financial codifications have certainly reached the point where some knowledge refining is becoming a matter of urgency. For instance, at the Department of Health and Social Security, the human codifications are so large that nobody who asks the question, "Am I entitled to benefit?" gets it answered from the book. An experienced social security officer makes a good guess. Similar circumstances surround the training and maintenance manuals for complex equipment. Whitehall and other large bureaucratic establishments are drowning in a surplus of unusable procedural guides and starving for lack of usable ones.

Suppose machine-refined material could be turned out in bulk, 100 times more complete, correct, comprehensible and compact than anything produced without this computer-based technique, would there be customers? Large organisations, particularly the Open University, which are in the business of retailing knowledge by older methods would be high on the list. The Open University's export business alone brings in millions a year.

It would not be feasible for me or my colleagues to seize on this or other similar development and try to push it along the path to applicability. However, Bill Read who by reason of his profession knows a very great deal about business, about exploitation, and about investment in technology, has agreed to give us his comments on these problems.

Commentary and Panel Discussion

The following is a summary of points made in Mr Bill Read's commentary.

Mr Read. I have nothing specific to say about the knowledge refinery idea. But on the general question of how a development idea can be financed and a business created as a result, if I were the Government I would raise and administer development money as follows:
1. Cause 2½% of all the major pension funds to be placed into a unit trust. Then augment from public funds the interest yielded.

2. Allow private investors to subscribe to the same fund, subject to a limit, encouraged by a tax break, i.e. part or all of the interest to be tax-exempt.
3. About £500 million per year could be generated this way. About 10 per cent of this could be earmarked for development ideas such as Donald Michie's.
4. Give the management of the development fund to an investment corporation with bright, enlightened people in the boardroom.
5. Save overheads by piggy-backing each new venture during its formative phase on the central resources and facilities of the corporation. In effect the new company would operate as a division, until it had proved its capacity to be free-standing.

Sir Ieuan Maddock. Concerning Donald Michie's Knowledge Refinery, I am not surprised it turns out this way. It is an old truism that you do things better by having to think them through into a computer system. So much knowledge is disorganised, indeed so much knowledge is bad. It is not surprising that by a systematic approach one can de-pollute the information and make it more efficient. I think there is something in that: I hope that it progresses.

When we come to Bill Read's ideas, I am very interested in what he is saying. I will now sing the praises of an existing organisation with which I am associated which starts off with £25 million in the kitty. There is plenty more to come if ideas can be found that are really opportunity limited rather than project limited. This organisation, Prutec, does much of what Bill Read was saying in the sense of taking long-shot risks and without asking for high guarantees and things of that kind. It is in the gambling business but the likelihood of some successes has got to be good enough to pay for what will undoubtedly be numerous losses.

I think that Donald Michie is saying : "What about the idea of a government safety net?" There are plenty of venture houses looking for technological opportunities. In criticising the banks and the finance houses we have got to remember that in the past they did put up a lot of money into technology. They consistently got their fingers burned. A lot of money went into the Nuclear Consortium — and the thing was a failure. A lot of money went into early computers now in the burial grounds. Above all, a lot of money went into the aircraft industry. And don't forget a lot of people lost a leg and an arm in a company — a noble company known as Rolls-Royce.

So there is a bad record. If you are running an investment house, you have to assess the offer of an opportunity. Imagine Bill Read trying to sell the idea of a knowledge refinery to one of the great City companies as opposed to an option on another oil well or bingo hall. In looking for a project one would have to give some kind of a test ultimately of "Is this viable and credible?"

That I think is going to be the big problem — testing out these ideas to see what are reasonable-sounding gambles. It cuts both ways.

There are promising things which turn out to be very poor in the event, like some of the ones I've mentioned. But there was a case of a first-generation Scandinavian working in America. He came up with a ludicrous-seeming idea and hawked it around for a very long time. Ultimately he found a company which was in the extreme gambling life-or-death phase and they took a chance on it. They asked for a market survey. The first market survey said, "Forget it, there's nothing in it". Years later, the product had been improved by very intensive development (not so much research, development) and they had another market survey that said, "You might make about a quarter of a million to half a million dollars a year out of it". And the product was Xerox and had been offered to Kodak, 3M and IBM, I believe, and turned down in all cases. I think ICI in Britain turned it down, too.

The other problem is that somewhere fairly early along you have to get a milch cow. You have to get some project which comes through reasonably well, reliably providing a good supply of funds so then you can afford to run the risks of these other projects.

I strongly believe in the basic principle Bill Read is enunciating: that the hope of reducing unemployment comes from the birth of lots of new companies rather than by any tinkering around with the long-established companies which can be very slow in generating jobs. But we do have to remember that creating a new company does not automatically mean reducing unemployment. The very newness of the company can be knocking out another company elsewhere. The classic example is the growth of the aircraft industry which demolished the old ocean liner industry. And the growth of television put down the old cinema industry. One has to watch this displacement.

Professor Michie. It would be wrong not to hear from Parliamentary Government on this subject, particularly since I know Ian Lloyd has given a good deal of thought to these issues.

Mr Lloyd. I remain in no doubt that the flow of first-class thinking which has ultimately an industrial application is still as strong as ever in Britain. But it is subterranean and seems in many senses to go out of the country.

Everyone in this room will remember a case, when a young RAF officer by the name of Whittle invented a thing called the gas turbine, and could get no support whatsoever. He then happened to meet a former colleague of mine in the House of Commons by the name of Rolf Dudley Williams. And Rolf Dudley Williams almost overnight wrote out a cheque for something like £15,000 to £20,000 — pre-war pounds — out of his own personal account. And that was the start of the real gas turbine industry, certainly in the UK.

Today, there are very few individuals in the UK who are capable of writing out a cheque of the modern-day equivalent of £15,000 to £20,000 which is probably of the order of £250,000. Now the philosophical question which is presented to us is: Whether you need that kind of individual to be able to take a very quick, short and effective decision when he sees something he likes and wishes to back; or whether you have to go down Bill Read's path and create, as it were, a fairly big national institution which, in my experience, however well-designed, however well thought out, by its very size, and conspicuous position in society, becomes to some extent inflexible, codified and bureaucratic.

So I have a certain scepticism about Bill Read's solution. Also I think I know something of the enormous political difficulties which would be created by the proposal to use pension funds. There are some who would argue that it is excellent and there are some who would argue that it simply can't be done.

But never mind that. Let me come to my specific example. About two years, ago I happened to be in Silicon Valley doing something else and I went to see this organisation called Cetus. I was extraordinarily impressed — purely as a layman because I have no technical judgement in these fields whatever — but I think I can recognise a first class laboratory when I see one. And I think I can recognise the enthusiasm of the individuals working in such a context when I meet them and talk to them.

I went round to Cetus and had a fascinating hour with the man who started it. This is a man called Dr Pete Farley. He qualified as an MD. After that, when he decided that he had an idea with immense industrial implications, he went to a business school and spent a couple of years training there. A most unusual type of qualification.

He then launched Cetus. He did so by appealing to the venture capital organisations in California and raised the necessary minimum of money. At the stage where the scientific work in the laboratory which he had created, coupled with that which he had brought from the university, illustrated very clearly that there was an enormous industrial potential, he said, "Well this company is not going to be a large-scale manufacturing company. We are going to be a research and development company. We are going to continue to create the best research and development in the world in the field of bio-technology and we are going to sell it. And that is going to be the commercial operation of this organisation." Very interesting concept.

He then did another interesting thing and relevant to the problems we are addressing here. He said, "Even though I may be an experienced biotechnologist, my own capacity in this field is doubtless going to come under considerable strain and I am not going to be able to cover the whole range of problems".

So he created a board of directors, which in itself was most impressive because of the general background of those concerned. And then he did another thing, very relevant to this field. He created a science advisory board, on which I believe there are two or three Nobel prizewinners. With this, he went forward to the point where the company went public and raised the largest amount of risk capital ever raised on a first issue in the United States. I think the sum was something like $135 million.

The next point is this: That the moment they discerned the industrial applications of this area they began to develop associations with major American industrial companies across quite a broad scale. In each case, as he put it to me: "We see a billion-dollar industry arising out of this bit of science, another billion-dollar industry arising out of that bit of science". And there were, I think, four or five major projects where he was absolutely convinced that a billion-dollar industry can be created. At this stage, what he does is to take the team or the group of people in Cetus working in this area and say: "We will create a sub-organisation with you and with the major industrial partner, who will put in the industrial capital to create the major industrial facility. But you, the team, four or five people working in this area will have, say, 20, 25, 30% of the equity." So the gearing is enormous. And as a result these people inevitably have an enormous incentive to succeed.

Now I well understand the different kinds of opinion in the United Kingdom which regard this thinking with great suspicion. That may have other and very considerable merits which no-one would dismiss. It is a difference in style of life, completely. But we are wanting the same results. Of that there is no question. And so far it seems to me we have not yet devised effective mechanisms for producing this kind of result. I would have thought this was one of the most successful mechanisms which one can create.

But it needs a different attitude on the part of the scientist in university. It needs, I think, different mechanisms on the part of the capital supply industry. And in this context, some of the most interesting things I have come across recently, not only in the United States, are financial institutions where there is a very impressive scientific capability within that institution.

I can give you one example. There is a firm of stockbrokers in San Francisco all five of whose partners have PhDs in some area or another of science or technology. Literally across the road is another one where although the main partners are essentially financial and economic people, they have a very strong science advisory team of four or five people recruited from the best technological universities in the States.

And so the thing operates in a sort of circuit. The successful young man comes out of university, and starts with some large organisation: but from early on he has at the back of his mind the idea of starting his own company.

Statistically, probably three out of five do this, and two fail. The other three, by the age of 35, have created a company with a turnover of, shall we say, $25 or $30 million. At that stage, quite frequently, I understand, they sell the company and go back into the academic field.

This creates a great challenge to our own academic community, by asking people to do things which in a sense are academically not quite respectable. We have got to ask ourselves the question: can we make it respectable and have some British way of institutionalising it?

Professor Michie. I would like to add an afternote to what Ian Lloyd has said and remind people that there are many different kinds of scientists, all of whom are capable of working in a dedicated and useful way. Some of them are more motivated by money; others are more motivated by enablement. The motivating effect of enablement is often forgotten. If somebody were to set up in our field an R and D company and it got around, not that there were tremendous pay rates, but that there was no red tape and enormous facilitation, university scientists would forget about respectability. They would be lining up to join such an organisation.

Comment from the floor. I think we ought to be doing that. People here are talking about their wonderful ideas which industry should be building into businesses. But no-one else will do it for you. You've got to do it. This is what Bill Read was saying. The people whose idea it is have got to get into the company.

Professor Michie. Let me put this to the scientific members. What do you think of the proposition that if your innovatory work begins to go well you should be willing to change over, to become a businessman? I'd like to hear both Michael Duff and Bob McGhee speak to that question.

Dr Duff. I don't think I've got any capability at all for business. And to acquire the knowledge, I would presumably have to go through a very long education process.

Dr McGhee. In industry I could not do exactly what I want to do. In a university I can.

Lord Balfour. I think it would be absolutely wrong in these two cases to ask for any change. You are doing the jobs you should be doing, and making a supreme success of it. My quick question would be. If Bill Read thinks he could get 500 million from Government why hasn't it happened? Sir Ieuan Maddock could tell us many more tales than I could about the lessons of past Government involvement. When Harold Wilson came in in 1964 with a white hot technological revolution, all this was going to happen. Why didn't it? It is a very long story. It is extremely difficult for Government or for anybody else to expose money and make profitable innovation happen.

There are things which, with respect, I think Bill Read overlooked. You can set up a framework for finding money, for paying people, for supervising the entrepreneur. All these things have been done over and over again. There is an organisation called Cosira which is very much less ambitious for helping small businesses and providing all these technical and managerial assistants. But the key is finding the entrepreneur who is prepared to go through the hell and high water of employing people and getting a project off the ground. An industry that is to be successful must be an organic development.

Professor Michie. I do not think academic scientists are in the least averse to working with entrepreneurs. Aversion is not the point. What *is* the point is that you may be a very good song composer and quite good on the piano and then people say to you: "Now go out into the real world, and sing it, too". You may be better off if you collaborate with somebody who actually can sing. Scientists should be asked to collaborate with entrepreneurs, not to become entrepreneurs.

Mr Read. I think that what I've had in the back of my mind was something much larger than the various things that have been tried. I'll also go back to Ian Lloyd's point concerning the American management style where they do try and give incentives. At least you have the carrot as well as the stick, to try and do things on a much larger scale. Whereas if you go round a lot of these other companies that have been put together to try and do this in a smaller way, I think you will find that the incentives were not very good. The managing directors or chairmen were not earning very much money at all.

References

Bratko, I. (1978). Proving correctness of strategies in the AL1 assertional language. *Information Processing Letters*, **7**, 223-230.
Bratko, I. and Mulec, P. (1980). An experiment in automatic learning of diagnostic rules. *Informatica*, **4**, 18-25.
Buchanan, B. G. and Feigenbaum, E.A. (1978). DENDRAL and Meta-DENDRAL: their applications dimensions. *Artific. Intell.*, **11**.

Buchanan, B. G., Smith, D.H., White, W.C., Gritter, R., Feigenbaum, E.A., Lederberg, J. and Djerassi, C. (1976). Applications of Artificial Intelligence for chemical inference, XXII, Automatic rule-formation in mass spectrometry by means of the Meta-DENDRAL program. *J. Amer. Chem. Soc.*, **98**, 6168-6178.

Hunt, E.B., Marin, J. and Stone, P. (1966). *Experiments in Induction.* New York: Academic Press.

McDermott, J. (1982). XSEL: a computer sales-person's assistant. *Machine Intelligence 10* (eds Hayes, J. E., Michie, D. and Pao, Y-H.), pp. 325-37. Chichester: Horwood, and New York: Halsted Press.

Michalski, R.S. and Chilausky, R.L. (1980). Knowledge acquisition by encoding expert rules versus computer induction from examples: a case study involving soybean pathology. *Int. J. for Man-Machine Studies*, **12**(1), 63-87.

Michie, D. (1980). Expert systems. *Computer Journal*, **23**(4), 397-376.

Paterson, A. and Niblett, T.B. (1982). ACLS Manual. Edinburgh, UK, and Champaign, USA: Intelligent Terminals Ltd.

Pople, H. E., Myers, J. D. and Miller, R.A. (1977). DIALOG: a model of diagnostic logic for internal medicine. *Proc. 5th Inter. Joint Conf. on Artif. Int., IJCAI-77*, Pittsburgh: Computer Science Department, Carnegie-Mellon University. (This program was subsequently re-named INTERNIST. It is now called CADUCEUS.)

Quinlan, J. R. (1979). Discovering rules by induction from large collections of examples. *Expert Systems in the Microelectronic Age* (ed D. Michie), pp. 168-201. Edinburgh: Edinburgh University Press.

Quinlan, J. R. (1982). Semi-autonomous acquisition of pattern-based knowledge. *Machine Intelligence 10* (eds Hayes, J.E., Michie, D. and Pao, Y-H), pp. 159-172. Chichester: Horwood and New York: Halsted Press. Also appears in *Introductory Readings in Expert Systems* (ed. Michie, D.), pp. 192-207. London, Paris and New York: Gordon and Breach.

Shortliffe, E. H. (1976). *Computer-Based Medical Consultation: MYCIN.* New York: Elsevier.

Wipke, W. T. (1977). Computer-assisted 3-dimensional synthetic analysis. *Computer Representation and Manipulation of Chemical Information* (eds Wipke, W.T., Heller, S.R. and Hyde, E.), pp. 147-174. London and New York: Wiley Interscience.

PART II

Engineering Tomorrow's World

5

Seeing Machines

M. J. B. Duff

University College, London

Introduction

Extending automation to the recognition of patterns would not at first seem to be particularly difficult. It would be a valuable aid to inspection in manufacturing processes and would speed up analysis of star maps, for example. It might be applied wherever the structure of data, rather than the individual items, carries the significant information. But serial computing to do this may be prohibitively lengthy and unwieldy, so speedier and more economical techniques are being evolved to do a great deal of the necessary processing in parallel, in much the same way that the human visual system operates. Logic cells for use in special arrays are being developed for the task.

It could be argued that one of the chief aims of technological innovation is to emulate, and eventually to improve upon, man's natural capabilities. For many years the most sensitive detector of light was the retina of the eye, while microphones could not equal the high, broad-band sensitivity of the ear. But now the reverse is largely true and it is possible to construct devices which out-perform man. For example, man-made devices can certainly detect light and sound with greater sensitivity. It is obvious, too, that man cannot compete when it comes to mechanical performance, such as travelling at high speed or handling heavy weights. The impressive calculating speeds of electronic computers make it possible to complete, in a few seconds, computations which would have taken many man years in the days of slide rules and hand-operated mechanical calculating machines.

But in spite of the entertaining, though sometimes frightening, predictions from the science fiction writers, there is one field which is still the almost undisputed territory of man himself: intelligent behaviour. It has been suggested that our position is unassailable, through definition of the word "intelligent", for some would not accept behaviour as being intelligent if a machine could generate it without human assistance. Others have put forward the alternative view that many computers and their programs are already exhibiting what might be called primitive intelligence, involving the solution of problems, prediction and ability to learn. Clearly, their intelligence, if that is what it is, stems from their man-made architecture and man-written programs, and from being exposed only to carefully regulated data. But could not this also be said of Homo sapiens in his normal growth and education?

Recognising Images

One kind of intelligent behaviour which has long seemed as though it would lend itself to automation is pattern recognition. It is not clearly defined but is usually taken to include activities such as recognising spoken and written words or, more generally, interpreting visual and aural "images" in such a way that we identify their components. A pattern-recognition program might be asked, for example, to pick out rivers in an aerial photograph, or to classify a fingerprint to speed up identification. Programs now being written will attempt to make sense of spoken sentences with a view to controlling machinery by verbal commands. The ability to recognise patterns is necessary in a great many situations, so pattern recognition is a convenient description for those operations in data processing where it is the structure of the data that carries the significant information.

In this article, I will keep to visual pattern recognition but will extend the word "visual" to include all "images" that could be transformed into pictures carrying the same information. For example, ultra-violet images might be regarded as visual even though the human eye cannot detect them. The essential qualification is that the patterns can be represented meaningfully as pictures.

Tessellation

Assuming a limit to how far we can resolve the picture, it is possible to transform a visual pattern into a regular array of numbers, each representing the average optical brightness in a small element of the picture. This process of breaking up a picture into a regular mosaic of small "cells" is called tessellation. Sometimes numbers are assigned to each cell to define the local image intensity, or grey tone, fairly precisely; more usually, however, a "threshold" level of grey is arbitrarily chosen and all elements darker than the threshold are treated as being black, all lighter ones as white. When this thresholding process has turned the grey tone image into a black and white one, each cell is labelled either 0 or 1 according to whether the element is

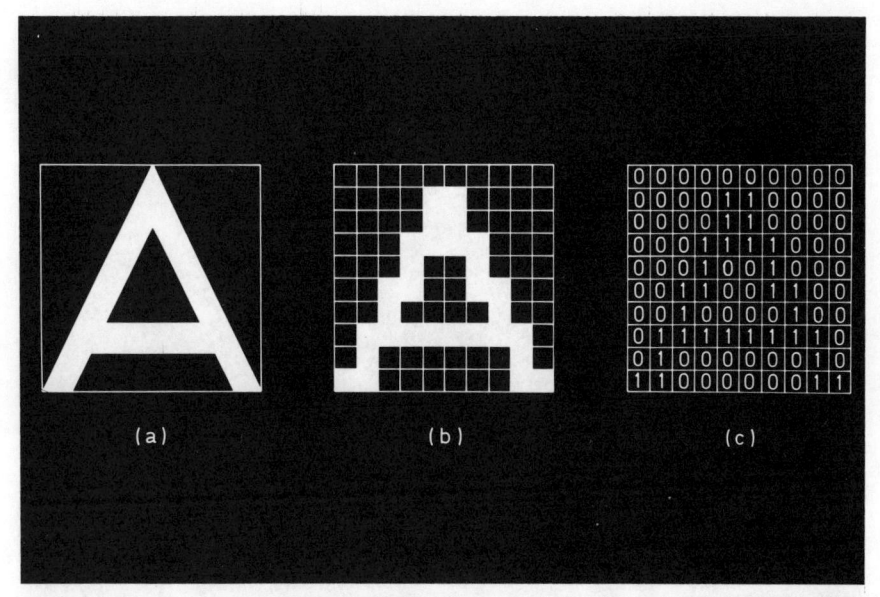

Figure 1. In this tessellation of the letter "A", the character is first broken up into a number of small cells (b) and each cell is given a binary coding 0 or 1, as in (c).

black or white. Figure 5.1 shows the result of a typical tessellation operation, in this instance on a letter A.

At this stage, the task of pattern recognition can begin. What operations should be performed on the array of numbers representing the picture to identify it unambiguously as an A? It is not my purpose here to discuss the many ways of calculating answers to problems, devised in the development of optical character readers, nor to consider in detail the principles employed in any pattern-recognition system, except as far as this is necessary for an understanding of the use of cellular logic arrays for the task. Within this limitation, however, let us examine the sort of processes which might be useful in recognising the letter A.

The first point to note is that the letter will usually not be as well formed as in Figure 5.1. For example, Figure 5.2 shows what the number "3" can look like when produced on a typewriter and greatly magnified. A typical sequence of operations is as follows. First, it is probably necessary to carry out some cleaning-up operation, perhaps following this by a thinning process designed to reduce the figure to a set of smooth lines of uniform width. This preliminary activity is called pre-processing.

The next processes are intended to explore the structure of the figure, discovering line ends and junctions and looking for closed loops such as the

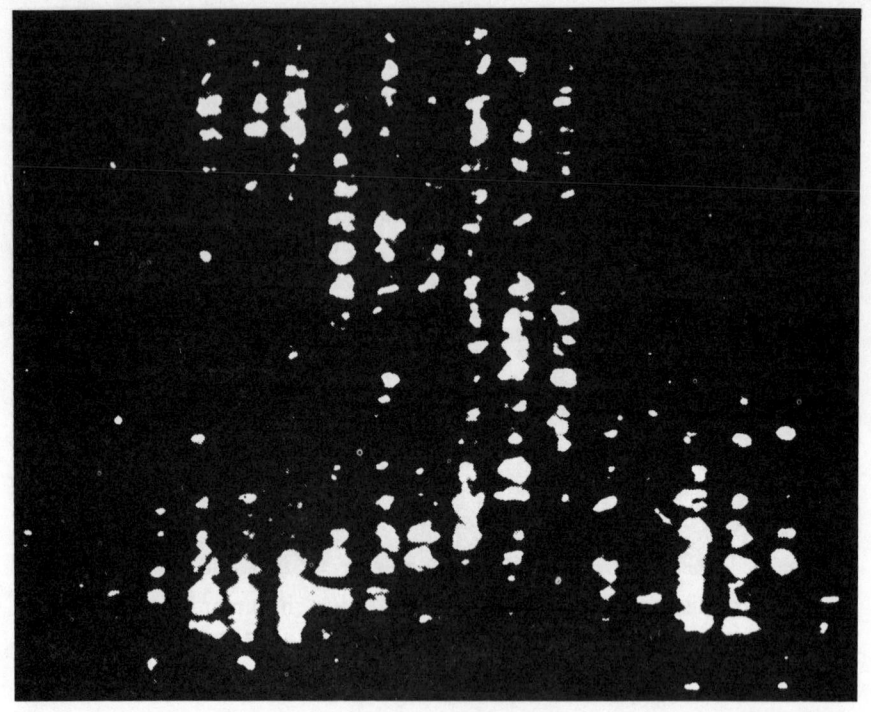

Figure 2. A photograph of a typewritten number 3, greatly magnified.

upper part of the A. This stage is called feature extraction. The features can then be listed and compared with stored lists from reference letters or figures. Ideally, the pre-processing and feature extraction stages of the operation should produce feature lists which are similar, no matter how the print quality varies and regardless of the size and orientation of the sample. The more refined programs should also allow for small distortions of the shape of the character and should accept a reasonable range of type styles.

Many pattern-recognition programs follow this broad scheme. At the heart of the problem of achieving effective pattern recognition is the need to select "good" features, that is, features which are consistently present in the data and which reliably characterise it. It is probably true to say that most pattern recognition systems which fail do so because it has not been found possible to define and extract a set of good features for the data they have to handle.

Even if difficulties such as these are successfully overcome, a further problem can, and often does, arise. Although a picture may have quite poor resolution it nevertheless may be made up of a large number of cells, whereas a high-resolution picture, such as a television frame, tessellates into an extremely large number of cells (nearly 400,000 for a 625-line picture) if information is not to be thrown away. If a conventional serial computer is to make calculations on every cell in the picture, the process is bound to be lengthy. Furthermore, structure in a picture can be revealed only if the contents of each cell are examined in relation to the contents of immediately adjacent cells, so it is clear that the number of individual calculations needed for the whole picture could become so large as to be prohibitive. In fact, the computing system is not the right one for the job.

Consider a simple example; suppose a picture contains only lines of single-cell thickness, represented by an array of '1' cells (the white background) on which there are chains of '0' cells (making up the black lines.) The problem is to identify the ends of lines and produce a new picture in which only these appear as black dots (0 cells) on a white background (1 cells) cells). Each cell has eight immediate neighbours, so a line end can be defined by a 0 cell with only one other 0 cell among these neighbours. A conventional computing system would scan the data cell by cell and, whenever it detected a 0 cell, would check each of the eight neighbours to see if one of them, and one only, is also a 0 cell.

This simple example highlights the factor which is common to many pattern-recognition and picture-processing operations; there is no logical reason why every cell should not be processed simultaneously. It is merely the structure of the computer, operating in a serial progression, which prevents the work on all the cells being carried out in parallel, with the enormous savings in processing time this would mean. Indeed, a lot of operations in picture processing would be better done in parallel. It is significant that the human visual system is believed to be organised in a parallel way, particularly in the earlier stages of nerve circuits which are used for the first processing steps.

Cellular logic arrays are now being used to put into effect the idea of a two-dimensional computer, organised in a parallel way for processing this sort of data, which itself has a two-dimensional structure. The basic unit of the array is the logic cell, which combines a selection of logic "gates" with a certain amount of storage. (A gate is an electronic circuit which passes a signal through only when it is told to do so by another, independent, signal.) The term "cell" is used in two senses here, to mean both a small picture element and a unit of the array of processors. Each cell is connected to all or some of its close neighbours; typical schemes for interconnecting arrays are shown in Figure 5.3.

Processing Power

Let us assume that the number assigned to each picture cell (1 or 0) can be

(a) 6-CONNECTED HEXAGON

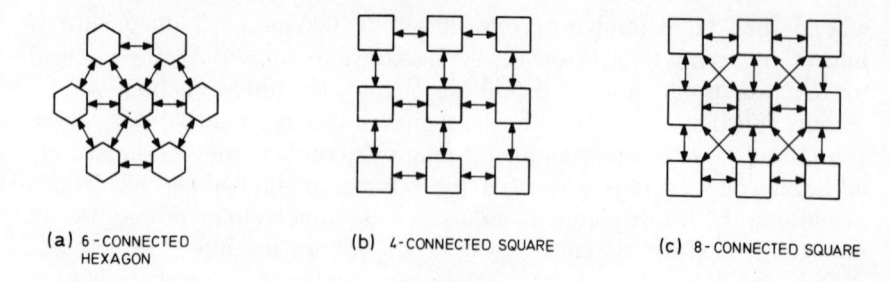

(b) 4-CONNECTED SQUARE

(c) 8-CONNECTED SQUARE

Figure 3. Typical schemes for inter-connecting processors in an array: in (a) the central processor or cell has six connections to a hexagon of neighboring cells arranged within a square, and in (c) there are eight direct connections, to all the neighboring cells.

entered into the corresponding processor cell. We now have to decide how much processing power each cell must have for the array to be able to handle the very many different operations involved in processing a picture. If the processing power is allowed to be unnecessarily high, by using a microprocessor to form each cell for example, the cost of the array would be prohibitive for most applications; if the processing power is kept very low, it might still be possible to perform the necessary operations by successive applications of the array to the data, but the performance in terms of speed, and therefore time, might well cast doubt on the wisdom of using an array processor at all, rather than a conventional serial machine. Obviously an acceptable compromise between these two extremes needs to be found, and the main purpose of the cellular logic array research programme at University College, London, has been to find the best possible compromise. In this work, done with support from the UK Science and Engineering Research Council, we have constructed and operated several trial arrays. One in particular, known as CLIP 4 (CLIP stands for "cellular logic image processor") is a large-scale integrated circuit array using a semiconductor chip specially designed for its application and comprising eight processors. A prototype image processor using these chips has been in operation since early 1980. It is expected that a commercial version of CLIP 4 will be put into production and marketed during 1983. It is used to process a picture of 96 x 96 cells, making up the central portion of a television frame.

Boolean Processor

The basic features of the CLIP 4 cell are shown schematically in Figure 5.4. Consider, for the sake of simplicity, that the image making up the input has been "thresholded" so that the image element entering the cell is either a 0

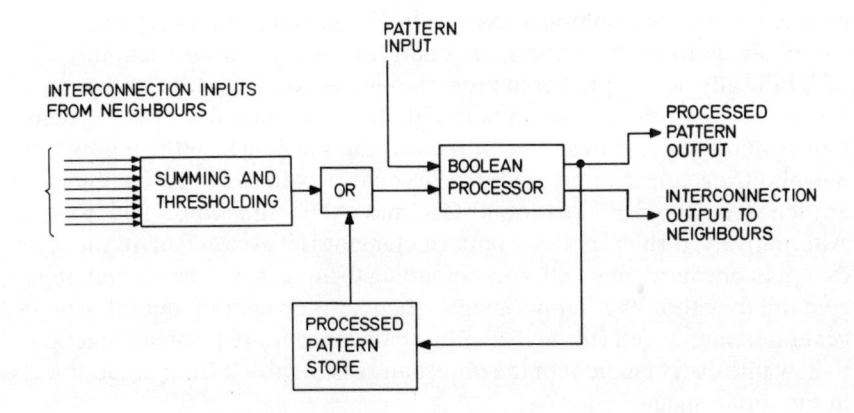

Figure 4. Schematic logic system of the CLIP-4 cell, described in the text.

or a 1: that is, the elements are in binary form. At the core of the cell there is a Boolean processor, which accepts two binary inputs and transforms them to give two independent binary outputs. Clearly, the two inputs can present any of four possible combinations of elements, 00, 01, 10 and 11. For each of these there are four possible output combinations, depending on the particular function the processor performs. This gives a total number of 16 possible output states. It is easy to show that the number of possible transformations from input to output is equal to the number of output states raised to the power of the number of input states (4^4 or 256). The transform function is selected by appropriately setting eight control lines entering the processor. (Eight lines are needed: 256 is 2^8.)

One of the two outputs is regarded as a new pattern element and is loaded into a store. The other fans out to each of the neighbouring cells, and it is these signals that, after gating, and OR-ing go to form one of the binary inputs to the Boolean processors in the cells. Each signal is compared in an OR gate with a pattern element from the cell's store. (When one or both the inputs to an OR gate are 1, it passes an element 1, but when both inputs to it are 0, it gives an output element 0.)

Instructions

It must be emphasised that the control lines which determine the function the processor performs run in parallel to every cell in the array; similarly, the interconnection input gate selection is applied to cells in parallel. The instructions which select pattern elements from the stores for feeding to the OR gate, to contribute to the input image element (except for the initial picture input), are common to every cell. Through this, every cell in an array can be made to perform the same operation at a given instruction.

A radically new approach to programming is necessary for a computer of this nature, and there is room here only to point out a few of the system's more interesting features. One of these is the way in which the inputs from neighbouring cells can be inhibited, to enable patterns to be combined in any chosen Boolean operation (OR and AND functions, and so on). Alternatively, if the processed pattern element is 0 everywhere in the array except in one particular cell, corresponding to any cell of a significant object contained within the input image, then a propagation output can be generated in that cell (through choice of an appropriate Boolean function), to flow into every element of the object and distinguish it from other objects in the input image.

The Boolean processor can then complete its task by producing an output image containing just those objects which are in the propagation path. This whole operation is effected by not more than four machine instructions to the array: two load instructions, a SET instruction to define the cell's function, and a process-initiate-and-store-result instruction. In CLIP 4 the operation takes 10 microseconds plus one microsecond for every cell step in the propagation path.

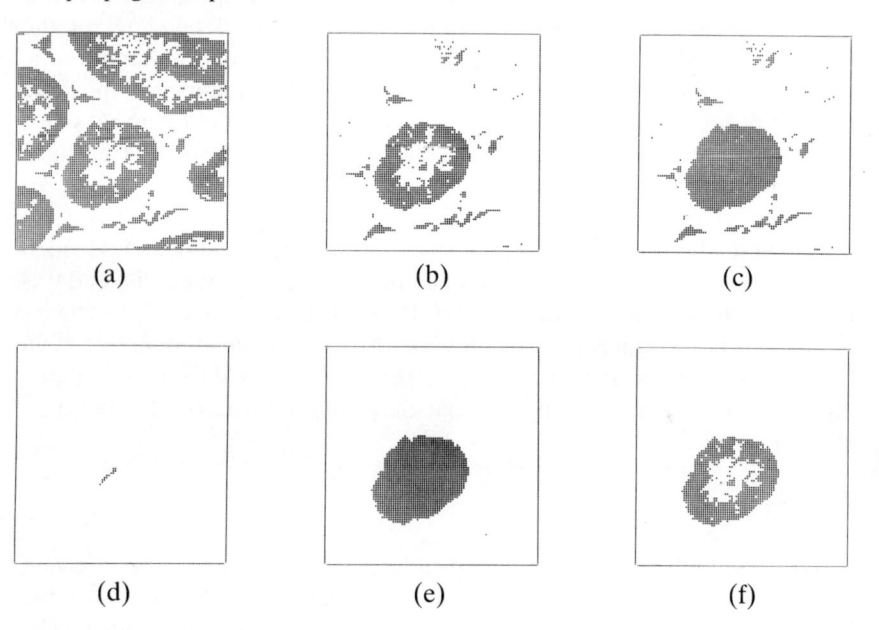

Figure 5. Steps in extracting detail of a biological cell from a microscope section (see text).

Sequences of instructions such as I have described go to make up picture processing programs. Figure 5.5 shows steps in a program designed to extract detail of a biological cell from a microscope section (a). The steps are: (b) Remove edge-connected objects. (c) Fill all closed black loops. (d) Shrink until a further shrink would empty the picture. (e) Extract the largest object in the picture obtained from step (c). (f) Use this picture to "mask out" the wanted cell from the original input. All steps except (d), which involves a loop of instructions, are achieved by a single pair of instructions.

The cellular logic array processor is a powerful computing tool for pattern recognition; what we need now are equally powerful algorithms, ways of tackling problems, to take advantage of the computing systems which are becoming available.

6

Walking Machines

R. McGhee

Ohio State University

For almost 30 years I have been trying to understand the problem of co-ordination of motion in articulated mechanisms. By an articulated mechanism I mean something that has a lot of hinges.

The first engineering work I did in this area related to the automatic control of aircraft and guided missiles. Let us consider an airplane since most of us are more familiar with those. When it is flying along, it has three sets of hinges. One set has to do with the up and down motion of the airplane. This set is called the elevators. Another set has to do with turning to the right or the left. This control surface is called the rudder. And finally, in order to make a proper turn so that the passengers do not experience discomfort, the pilot must be able to bank his airplane. This involves a set of hinges which is associated with surfaces called ailerons.

There are therefore three degrees of freedom associated with the motion of an airplane in steady flight. Of course there are many other degrees of freedom associated with problems like landing and take-off and change of speed, etc. But we can say that in a certain sense the complexity of the pilot's task is very much related to the fact that he has these three degrees of freedom to control in a co-ordinated way. I claim that this co-ordination goes on at three distinct levels.

First of all, there is the logical level. When I speak of the logical level, I am talking about a kind of information processing which leads to discrete decisions which can be explained using natural language. In fact, these decisions always involve language, conversations between the pilot and co-pilot, conversations between a pilot and the ground control, messages such as: "Begin your descent"; "clear for take-off", etc. The co-pilot and engineer may give confirming signals to the pilot that the landing gear is up. So we can say that at the logical level one is concerned with discrete events.

There is, however, another level of control which requires rather specialised training. And that I choose to call the geometrical level because it deals with continuous motion. If you happen to be involved in a field called human factors, you might be very much concerned with how the pilot manages his tasks. This is extremely important and a great deal of effort and funds are expended in designing the cockpit of an airplane so that it is convenient for the pilot and makes a good match to his muscular system. The description of actions that take place at the geometrical level involves curves. We cannot describe it precisely with natural language, but have to use some sort of geometrical or kinematic language. We can make it mathematical, but the most straightforward way is to present the curves of how the pilot's joints move as he controls the airplane. And of course these motions are not independent; they are co-ordinated, depending upon each other so as to achieve the necessary action. It is not fully understood how human beings accomplish this kind of co-ordination.

Finally, even deeper into the nervous system, or robot, or aircraft, is the dynamic level. In order to achieve motion, it is necessary to apply forces. And in order to understand the relationship between forces and motion it is necessary to have the concept of acceleration which really means understanding calculus, going back to the time of Newton and the laws of mechanics.

Now, from an information science or biological point of view, one can observe that there are two kinds of processes going on, or two kinds of relationships between these levels. First of all, there is a downward task-decomposition at work. The pilot begins, perhaps, by thinking "I have got to go to work today". He then makes a plan of how to get to work and as he gets to the airplane this plan becomes more detailed and so on. When he is actually flying the airplane, after he has trained, his joint motions are co-ordinated at a subconscious level. And at a still deeper, inaccessible, level is the problem of providing the necessary electrical impulses to the muscles governing the motion of the pilot's limbs. There are some 800 or so individual muscles in the human body and it is finally at this level that the motion is accomplished.

After 15 years of working on guided missiles and aircraft, I became interested in human motion, especially as related to providing better aids to the handicapped. When you work on weapons long enough, you start wondering about the people who are on the receiving end. I observed that artificial limbs and braces were very primitive and had not changed very much, and that electronics did not seem to be making much of a contribution. So somewhat naively, I thought that it might be possible to use the automatic co-ordination techniques used in guided missiles and aircraft to build a powered artificial limb in which some of the motions would be automatically co-ordinated.

It did not take long to find out that that problem was too hard. With more than 200 "hinges" in the human skeleton controlled by more than 800 actuators, there are too many degrees of freedom. So rather quickly, I and my colleagues at the University of Southern California regressed to a simpler problem: the problem of co-ordinating robot motion. The term "robot" was not accepted, so we said we were working on walking machines. We still say that to distinguish the machines we work on from robots in general.

The reason that it is attractive to work on robots is that at the present time they have many fewer degrees of freedom, ranging from about 4 up to 18. You are probably most familiar with industrial robots, but I want to make it clear that I am not talking about industrial robots.

The industrial robot is a machine which is immobile, except when it it brought to its workstation by a forklift truck. It does a repetitive job in a highly structured environment in a factory. That is the reason that it is effective. Today industrial robots are replacing human beings in the dirtiest, most repetitive, most inhuman kinds of job. However, there are needs for robots in other circumstances which require mobility. A very important one is in the nuclear power industry. Recently, in Paris, I saw in operation a prototype of a pipe inspection robot for the Super Phoenix Breeder Reactor. It is necessary to check the integrity of welds in this reactor from time to time in a very high temperature and high radiation environment. The surface of the reactor is at 200 degrees Centigrade, the level of radiation is quite high. And so M. Jean Vertut of the French Atomic Energy Commission has built a very clever device which uses a combination of wheels and legs to move about through the confined spaces of the reactor and inspect the integrity of welds. There is no other way to do that job without shutting down the reactor. The intention is to do this online, during reactor operation.

Another possibility where robot systems might function more effectively than human beings is in space. NASA is talking more and more about constructing large systems in space, large antennas, perhaps solar-powered generating systems, and so on. These structures cannot be constructed on earth because they are too flimsy. If they were not too flimsy they would be too heavy. I am told it costs $50,000 an hour for a man to work on a tether in space. It certainly would make sense to have a mobile robot capable of moving about on a large structure and performing simple assembly operations.

The area I am personally working on most intensively at the present time is in the area of terrain adaptive vehicles. What we are looking for here is, roughly speaking, an artificial horse. We would like something that could cross very rough terrain, without shaking up the rider and without requiring an excessive expenditure of energy.

We are able to consider this range of possibilities in a realistic way only because of microelectronics. I was frustrated for the first 15 years of my research into artificial limbs and robotics by unavailability of sufficient computational power at an acceptable cost. The machines shown in the Figures with computer co-ordinated motion (see later) are all tethered to a computer via a cable. None of them yet has self-contained computers. We expect that within three years this will be possible because of the availability of the appropriate chips.

The question may be asked: "Why walking robots? Why use legs rather than wheels?" After all, the wheel is usually taken as the very symbol of an advanced society and it is often said that the North American Indians, for example, got stuck at a certain level of development because they failed to invent the wheel. That may not be right. It may be they got stuck there because they failed to invent the mechanical leg. Because, after all, they didn't have highways and wheels are not much good without highways. If you look at the development of wheeled transportation in Europe and Asia, it went right along with the development of highway technology.

The most likely possibility for significant support in the near future for the development of walking machines lies in the area of military logistic support. If you look in the hills around you, you will realise that we don't have vehicles that can traverse this terrain. On the other hand, animals live there. They are able to do so because the nature of the interaction of a wheel with terrain is quite different from that of a leg. This is very straightforward. If you put a wheel on soft or rocky soil, the first thing it does is sink into the soil and in so doing it creates a hole which it must continuously climb out of. A leg, on the other hand, a biological leg until now, experiences a contrary effect. If you try to climb a hill or walk through soft soil, the motion of your leg pushes the soil backward, not forward, and it creates a depression which helps you. And that is the fundamental reason that legs are better than wheels in rough terrain. This phenomenon accounts for the fact that roughly 50% of the land surface of the Earth is not accessible to any wheeled or tracked vehicle. Many of these areas are, of course, accessible by helicopter but helicopters are very expensive machines. They only function in good weather and they have a lot of other limitations.

Another reason for using legs rather wheels is to carry out economically worthwhile activities in fragile or difficult terrain, such as tundra regions, for example. It has been noted that when herds of hundreds of thousands of caribou, which are very large animals, move through an area they damage the terrain. However, that damage heals over within approximately a year. On the other hand, if a caterpillar tractor makes one pass through the same area, it may take up to 100 years for the scar to heal and it may not heal at all. It may induce erosion which will create gulleys up to 20 or 30 feet deep.

Again the reason for this is to be found in soil mechanics. Animals create discrete footprints which are small in area. Caterpillar tractors first of all interact more vigorously with the soil in overcoming the before-stated problem and secondly, and more importantly, they produce a continuous track which induces erosion.

I have already referred to space assembly. Not only do wheels require roads to function efficiently, they also require gravity. A wheel is a device which must be biased, it must be drawn down to the surfaces to travel over. The physical force available for this purpose on earth is gravity. Gravity does not exist in space. So you cannot have automobiles in space.

Finally, the example I referred to earlier, of hazardous environments, goes beyond nuclear reactors. It also includes fire-fighting, underground mining and many other possibilities, places we would like to put machines, not men. But the machines are not there for lack of mobility. The fireman goes into the burning building, not because his intelligence is needed there but because his legs are the only things we have at the moment that will pull a hose. He could stay outside and work with television if he only had something to drag the hose into the building.

The Figures which follow include several of the categories mentioned above. Figure 6.1 is based on a drawing which is about 15 years old and represents capabilities still not achieved. Up until about 1943 the United States Army used pack animals to transport supplies through difficult terrain. And a US Army mule, which was an especially heavy breed of animal, was able to carry 400 lb for 15 miles or 250 lb for 30 miles in one day through very rough terrain. Now mules have some serious problems. First of all, they are stubborn, so it is difficult to get them to do what you want. Secondly, the fuel they run on is not very dense. Hay is harder to carry around than gasoline. Thirdly, 250 lb is not always enough, especially for a modern army. If you want to put a radar system on the top of a mountain, for example, it may be very difficult to break it down into 250 lb modules and the mule may throw a critical piece off his back. So the U.S. Army launched a project through the Defense Advanced Research Projects Agency (DARPA) in the second half of the 1960s to try to realise the kind of vehicle shown in the Figure. They did not get what they wanted but they did get some scientifically significant results.

I referred earlier to robots in space. Figure 6.2 shows a drawing which appeared on the cover of a magazine called *Robotics Age* which was provided by Dr Ewald Herer of NASA. It shows a space shuttle at work building a large structure in space — it might be an antenna, it might be a solar power generation system — and you see that the idea is to keep the man inside the shuttle where he is not so expensive and not exposed to the dangers of working outside the shuttle. We see a number of robotic devices

Figure 6.1: Planned ambulating quadruped transporter. An artist's conception of a more biddable substitute for the US army mule (taken out of service in the 1940's).

Figure 6.2. Artist's conception of possible uses for mobile robots, including legged machines, for use in space (reproduction by courtesy of Jet Propulsion Laboratory, NASA).

functioning in this picture. First of all the shuttle itself has an arm. That is a reality soon to be tested. In this concept, the arm passes panels out to the spidery object which has a set of legs which allows it to crawl around this structure, receive panels, and assemble them into larger structures. It also has a reaction engine which is burned as little as possible but in this concept when the panels have been assembled into larger sub-assemblies the reaction engine is used to move them around. Lower down we see some in motion. One of the robots is moving a large panel, handing it over to a space crane which does a further assembly. That is also just an idea. But Figure 6.3 shows something that is a reality. This is a Swiss-manufactured machine called the Menzi Muck (possibly the name sounds better in Swiss). It has five legs, or maybe four legs and one arm, and like insects it exhibits limb specialisation. You might think of it as a kind of mechanical praying mantis which happens to be interested in excavation. The rear portion of the machine is a very powerful arm capable of excavation or of cutting trees with a special tool. The back two legs are for mobility, so they have wheels associated with them. There is no power in those wheels, the power comes from the scoop. And in the middle, there is a pair of legs whose function is stabilisation.

Figure 6.3. A Swiss-manufactured walker, known as the Menzi Muck. There are two legs with wheels, for mobility, and a centrally-placed pair of legs for stabilisation. The fifth "limb" is a very powerful arm which can be used for excavation or for cutting trees with a special tool (photograph courtesy of North Central Forest Experiment Station, USDA Forest Service).

Figure 6.4 shows the General Electric Quadruped Vehicle which was constructed during the beginning of 1964, completed and first tested about 1967. The machine uses the human being for both the logical and co-ordination levels of control. He is given a power assist and does not have to provide more than 1% of the full force associated with limb motions. Thus, when the man moves his legs or his hands the machine amplifies that motion and applies 100 times more force than the man is applying. So the man is not receiving very much assistance here except for power amplification. He must himself co-ordinate 12 joints, three in each leg, two at the hip and one at the knee. Despite this very heavy load on the operator (twice as many degrees of freedom as a helicopter), a few men were able to achieve a remarkable degree of dexterity in operating this machine. The principal difficulty was that the work was exhausting. Even the best operator, who happened to be the designer of the machine, was only able to operate it for about 10 minutes a day: then he was exhausted. When I became aware of this machine, I thought that we ought to be able to convince the people concerned that they needed an auto-pilot. So I decided with one of my students, who is now a professor, Dr Andrew Frank, to build the machine shown as Figure 6.5 which was subsequently christened The Phony Pony. It had only one purpose — to show that joint motions could be co-ordinated electronically. We had no microprocessors at that time so we built our own special-purpose computer. It had just 16 flip-flops in it and it still took a rack of equipment. But it proved the point. We showed that motion could be co-ordinated electronically, and did not necessarily require biological intelligence.

I showed a short film about these ideas at a meeting in Yugoslavia in 1969. It attracted more attention from researchers in the Soviet Union than in the United States. They went back home and began to work themselves on the problem of motion co-ordination, and by 1972 had solved a major scientific problem. The scientific problem which was solved was: How should one co-ordinate the motion of the limbs of a walking machine in order to maximise its stability? The solution is what is called a wave gait. It involves a wave of motion from the rear of the machine to the front of the machine, with the placing of legs on the righthand side and the lefthand side half a cycle out of phase. Through a very intensive, long-term computer study, the Soviets proved that this was the optimal way to use the legs of a six-legged machine. The extra pair of legs had been added because it has been found that for machine co-ordination of motion, trying to produce an artificial quadruped was too ambitious. The balancing problem is too difficult. Thus the Soviet walking machine has an extra pair of legs in the middle to simplify the stabilisation problem.*

---

* This work is described in Machine Intelligence 9 (eds Jean Hayes, L.I. Mikulich and D. Michie) published by E. Horwood in 1979

Figure 6.4. The General Electric Quardruped Vehicle, developed during the 1960's. The machine uses a human being, with power assist, for both the logical and co-ordination levels of control.

92 ENGINEERING TOMORROW'S WORLD

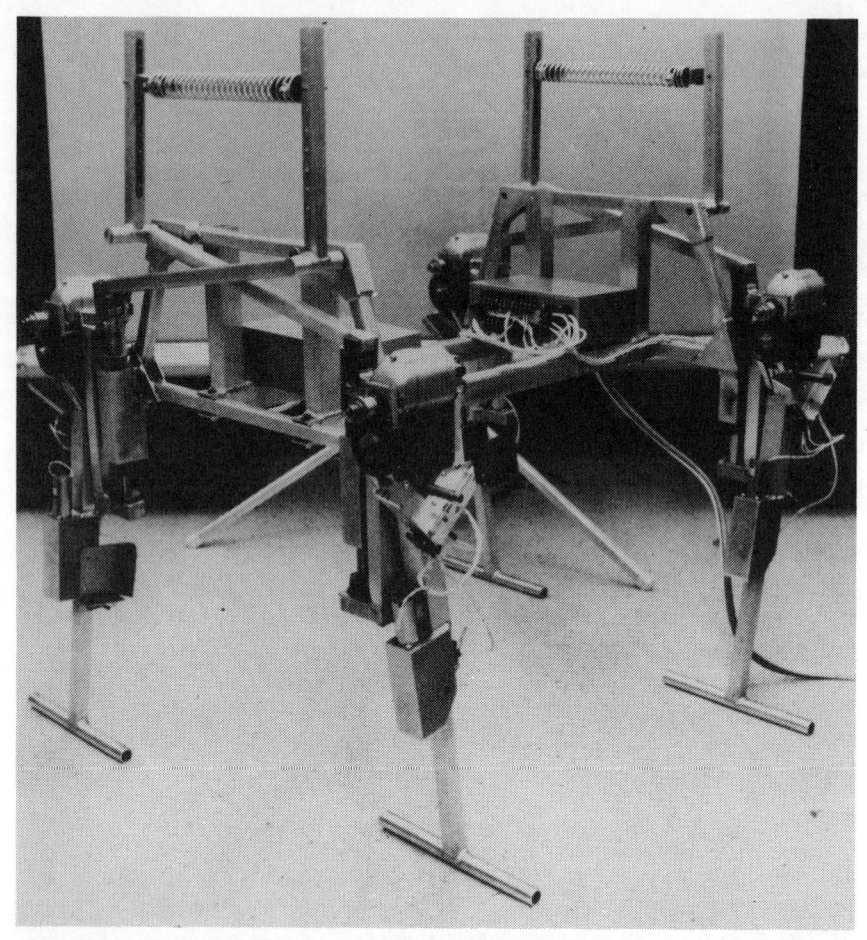

Figure 6.5. The Phony Phony, developed to demonstrate that joint movements could be co-ordinated electronically.

This produces 18 degrees of freedom, three in each leg (that is the minimal number needed to place each leg arbitrarily). With so many degrees of freedom (18 compared to the six or seven in an industrial robot) a very rich kind of behaviour is possible. There is not a unique trajectory associated with the body motion over a given terrain but one can decide what to control. You can decide, for example, that it's important to keep the body level. And that can be done. You can decide that, unlike a wheeled or tracked vehicle, it is not necessary to bounce over every stone but do what a human being or a horse does, either stepping over it or on it. And in this way, rather large obstacles can be overcome.

I saw a film of this work in 1972 and was very impressed. It is quite important to realise that what was shown was not an artist's conception, but an allegedly real-time film in which a computer was making all of the decisions concerning motion. However, I came to the conclusion that this kind of idealised motion was not what was really wanted. At least it is not what animals do. Animals adjust their body so that it is more or less parallel to the local terrain slope. This is to avoid two kinds of problem: it is unpleasant for an animal to scrape its belly and so it likes to keep it off the ground; on the other hand, if it gets its body too high, it runs out of leg length and that is equally embarrassing. So it seems more sensible to follow the biological solution in most circumstances and not try to keep the body level but rather roughly parallel to the terrain.

By 1976 the Soviets had made another advance, having become aware of the importance of some kind of remote sensing. To be effective, a robot (Soviet work has been concentrated on true robots, machines without human operators on board) needs some kind of primitive vision. It needs to discover obstacles before it runs into them.

So they did an excellent simulation study in 1976 in which the action of a triangulation range-finder is assumed. This is not imaging vision. It is felt in the Soviet Union, and I agree, that at this point in time the kind of imaging vision systems that Michael Duff discussed in Chapter 5 are too difficult and too advanced for control of locomotion. But we can have something that amounts to radar: a device that scans a terrain and provides a relief map, using the mechanism of triangulation. The scanners are on top of the vehicle, the receivers are in the body and if you compute the line of intersection of the image with the source, you then know where the terrain is. This is still to date the most advanced demonstration I am aware of, of a walking robot finding its way through difficult terrain.

Also in 1976 construction was under way both at my institution in Ohio State and at several points in the Soviet Union, to realise in hardware the kind of behaviour demonstrated by simulation studies. Our machine (Figure 6.6) first walked early in 1977, and to the best of my knowledge, the first Soviet machine walked about four months later. Since 1977 we have been studying the problem of higher level control: How can a man and a computing machine co-operate effectively to regulate and co-ordinate the motions of the joints of the robot?

We recently made a film to demonstrate two kinds of communication between the human operator and the robot. The first kind of communication is symbolic, using a greatly simplified language. The language consists simply of isolated commands of which there are about a dozen. One is "Try out your legs and see if they are working OK". Thus if any portions of the system are not functioning we discover this before trying to walk. Originally

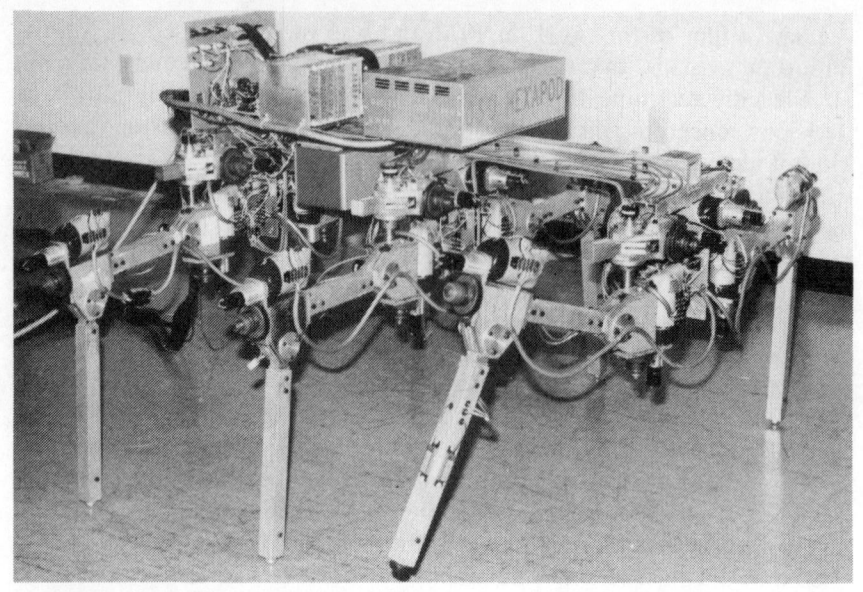

Figure 6.6. The OSU Hexapod, which first "walked" in 1977. The right front leg is equipped with sensors.

we used to lift the Hexapod off its stool to walk. That took four people because it is very heavy. We finally figured out, "Why don't we just tell it to stand up?" All the operator has to do now is hit the U key on its console and the machine stands up. Before walking it has to take its mark, positioning its limbs properly for the initiation of walking. For the second type of communication with the robot we need something like a pilot's controls. This particular scheme involves a three-axis joystick. Twisting the joystick causes the robot to twist its body — determines its rotational rate, in fact. Fore/aft deflection determines fore/aft velocity, right/left deflection determines right/left velocity and of course co-ordinated motion is possible. So now the operator only thinks about what he wants the body of the machine to do and the computer worries about what the legs should do.

When the robot walks, the motion is quite slow. This is because of another defect in this machine that we have discovered, through experience. I referred earlier to the stubbornness of a mule. A mule won't harm itself. In fact, it is more intelligent than a horse. You can force a horse to harm itself by asking it to do things that exceed its muscular capacity. A mule won't do it.

This machine is even more agreeable than a horse. It will do whatever you tell it to do — such as ripping its front legs off. We think it important that a real walking machine, a practical walking machine, must be given an artificial sense of pain so that it will refuse to do things that will damage the machine or harm the operator. Currently, machine capabilities include co-ordinated motion, forward motion, turning, and some motion to the side. It is capable of side-passing, i.e., it can keep its body in a constant orientation and move strictly laterally. To back up, one simply pulls the control level to the rear and if it is twisted at the same time then the vehicle begins to turn.

The computer is not on board, though there is a considerable amount of on-board digital electronics. The box which says OSU Hexapod (Figure 6.6) on it contains a communication system which transmits to the control computer via cable three pieces of information for each leg: namely, the position of each of the three joints, the velocity of each of the three joints, and (at present for one leg) the force of reaction with the ground, so the computer knows what forces the robot is encountering as it goes over the terrain. This feature, which permits terrain adaptation and efficient use of energy, is being added to the other legs of the machine. Before long, we expect to be able to put railroad ties (sleepers) around the floor of the room and repeat this experiment with the machine passing over the railroad ties and making the adjustments automatically.

For this it has to have a vertical sense, which it now has, with a vertical gyroscope and two pendulum sensors. When the experiment is over we again ask it to stand up.

The above is a short account of recent work in Ohio State University. We are in contact not only with researchers in the Soviet Union but also in Japan, where some very advanced work is going on. In particular, my own early ideas about logical or finite state control have been picked up by Japanese researchers, Professor Hirose, in particular, and advanced to a considerably higher level to produce a quadruped machine with several interesting features. First of all, the legs were designed by a mechanical engineer (I am an electrical engineer.) A mechanical engineer has sense enough to get the actuators off the limbs where they simply produce unnecessary weight and consequent energy inefficiency. He put the motors in the body and moves the joints through tendons, much like the human body. Another feature of the machine is that it has a tactile sense which allows it to discover the presence of obstacles and adjust to them. A defect of the machine is that it is too autonomous. There is no human communication. When it is sent out on a path it finds its own way and you cannot call it back. Another defect is that having only four legs it has an inferior degree of stability. It is not able to move its legs and its body at the same time which illustrates again the necessity for more than four legs.

The first commercially viable machine that I would be willing to call a walking machine is the Menzi Muck mentioned earlier (Figure 6.3). It is very clever and apparently cost-effective, selling for $80,000 to $100,000. In one case it has been adapted to timber harvesting. The hydraulic shear on the arm is able to cut a tree of up to 12 inches at one snip. And the operator can pile the trees up for later collection and processing.

The OSU Hexapod walking machine (Figure 6.6) is something analogous, perhaps, to a walking stick insect which is not very advanced. If you look at more advanced insects, there is limb specialisation. The grasshopper is an example. Its back legs are used for jumping, its front legs are used for holding food and its inner legs are for stabilisation. The same kind of specialisation is seen in the Menzi Muck because this is a machine for a specific function, not a research machine. The co-ordination is very primitive, however. I think that productivity could be improved if the operator had a microprocessor assisting him. He ought only to have to concern himself with what the end effector is doing and not pull levers constantly to move joints one by one. When he wants to move to a new site, the power comes from the arm. The rear legs — their motion is simplified by the use of wheels — and the inner legs are used for support and stabilisation.

That is where we are today. Within three years we hope to have developed a new man-carrying machine derived from the OSU Hexapod vehicle. It will probably have an internal combustion engine like a Toyota with about 80 horsepower. The machine is likely to weigh 3,000 or 4,000 pounds and will certainly at the beginning have six legs. We would like to be able to get rid of the middle pair of legs but do not think we can deal with the stabilisation problem adequately without them.

The actuation mechanism is likely to be hydraulic, although that is a serious problem. The efficiency of conventional hydraulic actuators is unacceptable. We expect the operator will have aircraft-type controls and will be concerned with controlling speed and direction. On-board computers, at least one microprocessor per leg, at least one central co-ordination computer, and probably a completely independent fault detection and fault correction computer will be included to provide safety for the men and the machine. The whole thing will, we hope, travel at something like 5-8 miles per hour. The speed may not be impressive, but we hope its mobility will be.

Remaining Problems

I believe that we understand the co-ordination problem quite thoroughly. On the other hand we do not know exactly how decision-making should be apportioned between the man and machine. That is, we do not understand the logical level as thoroughly as we understand the geometric or kinetic levels.

But there is another problem which is really serious. There is a curve derived from work done 30 years ago by Gabrielli and von Karman and shows that for all known modes of transportation there is a kind of an asymptote along that line which relates top speed to specific power. The vertical axis shows the size of the engine per ton required in a vehicle, beginning with 0.1 horsepower per ton and going up to 2000 horsepower per ton. As the speed goes up, of course the power requirement goes up. And it is interesting to note that (to no-one's surprise) horses are very efficient. A horse can move a ton with a little less than one horsepower or a little more than a horsepower, depending upon how fast he is moving. He is much more efficient than a human being. If you want to get around efficiently, apparently it is better to use four legs than two. Human beings require roughly three or four times more energy than horses. They are not able to go as fast and are not able to travel as efficiently. We are still very much better than tracked vehicles for off-road locomotion. Tracked vehicles require roughly 10 to 20 times more horsepower per ton than a horse. A tank requires several hundred horsepower and weighs tens of tons. Walking machines are still further up. Despite their adaptability, the energy costs are unacceptable. So a major challenge to us, and half of our programme at my university, involves moving the walking machines' curve downward on the graph. The mechanical engineers think they know how to do it.

Questions and discussion

Q. I have a question about human control on your projected futuristic vehicle. You seem to have placed so much emphasis on having a person there. Why doesn't the operator just sit in front of a CRT, on which is simulated the state of affairs, with an electronic joystick and make electronic decisions about what this gadget should be doing?
A. Would you like to fly in an airplane when the pilot was doing that?
Q. The pilot does that all the time!
A. Not in landing and take-off. But you're right, he does it much of the time. I would say it depends very much on the task and for routine locomotion that would be sufficient. If one were crossing a ploughed field, it wouldn't matter exactly what route were taken. And certainly the vehicle ought to be able to accommodate the terrain irregularities in that case. But if it came to a problem like crossing a fence, for example, then I think human intervention is required.

We think that all of the human senses will be important, e.g. we think that the kinaesthetic senses of a human operator will prove to be valuable. There is an analogy to be found in the field of manipulators. There are two kinds of electronically controlled manipulators: one type is used in manufacturing, we call it the industrial robot; another type is used in the nuclear industry and it is called a remote manipulator. A human operator using a remote manipulator is able to deal with far more varied tasks and accomplish much more than an industrial robot can. If the task is highly structured or relatively highly structured, we think the man is probably not needed. But if one gets into completely unforeseen circumstances, we think it is best to have the man there in the vehicle, at this stage in development. Of course we want to automate his functions as highly as possible. But in our opinion, he is still needed there.

Q. You have shown that six legs are more stable than four. It all goes to show that the human system of standing up has a control system that is immensely more sophisticated than anything.

A. Indeed.

Q. Why don't you go back to your first idea of having a human driver in, with the electro-mechanics made so much more efficient that he is not exhausted? That must be the most efficient way of getting over really unknown territory.

A. In fact what we see is a hierarchy of control schemes. In relatively benign circumstances the operator should be able to put the machine on auto-pilot and put his feet up and do nothing. As the terrain becomes more and more difficult and the decisions become more and more complex, we expect that he will have to take control at a lower and lower level. So we are building a flexible system in which the operator has a selection of modes for operation. The lowest level would be one at which he is worrying about what happens to every joint. In fact, we don't think it's necessary to go to that level. We think that probably in very difficult terrain, say climbing boulders, the operator should directly control the front pair of legs. There is no reason that the second and third pair cannot follow and use the same footprints.

Q. Is your funding military?

A. Primarily but not exclusively. We have had support over the past 15 years from five agencies. They are the Air Force Office of Scientific Research, National Science Foundation, NASA, National Institute of Health and currently our largest supporter is the organisation which started this whole field of research, DARPA — Defence Advanced Research Projects Agency.

Q. The latest prediction was that we will abandon the highly spread, spider-like configurations.

A. Right. It has to do with the question of energy efficiency, or rather with the trade-off between energy efficiency and stability. The wider legs are more suitable for a machine that is plugged into the wall. For laboratory investigations, for studying problems relating to climbing, to various kinds of operator interaction, we want a machine which won't crash. That's the important thing in the laboratory. So we spread the legs wide. But for efficient locomotion, it turns out that if you look at what is needed at each joint it's better to tuck the legs under the body as all cursorial mammals do. You find no high-speed, very efficient mammals which do not tuck their legs under their bodies.

Q. Are you looking for high speed?

A. No. We are concerned with energy efficiency. Setting aside the case of climbing round a space craft where widely spread legs are probably desirable, we are concerned simply about making a machine that will function at all, at five miles per hour, and be entirely self-contained and give a reasonable mileage. We must achieve something like three to five miles per gallon or the machine will not be competitive with commercial vehicles. So speed is not the question. It's energy efficiency. It is a complicated question which has taken some time to understand it. But there are good engineering reasons why you do not find any mammals with legs like insects.

Q. I would like to ask a question about seabed exploration. There are all sorts of devices under development for digging trenches for pipeline laying and so forth. What are the modes of progression on the ocean bed and does your kind of technology come in here?

A. That depends very much on the nature of the floor of the ocean, which varies enormously. There are areas of the world in which the floor of the ocean is composed of very soft mud. The screw type of propulsion has been investigated and seems to be most appropriate to that kind of surface. There are other areas where large rocks and boulders are found on the surface and there isn't any satisfactory way of moving about over that kind of terrain. If one uses a floating vehicle, it is in danger of being dashed against the rocks by ocean currents. A walking machine might be appropriate in those circumstances.

Q. How far have you got with what you called the "artificial sense of pain"?

A. We have just realised that it is necessary and we have a graduate student and one faculty member working on that problem. It is not as difficult as it might seem. The pain computer must have access to everything that all the limbs are doing. Whereas a leg controller needs access only to its own leg, the machine which produces resistance to destructive motions must be able to know what all of the legs are doing. So this computer will be independently connected to all sensors and will also be aware of what the man is trying to do. It will then refuse to co-operate if this will be harmful to the man and the machine.

7

Computers in Medical Bio-Technology

W. F. Bodmer

Imperial Cancer Research Fund, London

Although I started at Cambridge as early as 1957 with computer modelling in population genetics, I owe much of my present interest and attitude to computing to my period in Stanford during the years 1961-70. I was, I think, the first person to use a computer in the Stanford Genetics Department, and my wife and colleague Julia Bodmer showed Joshua Lederberg how to use a punch card. Soon we were learning from him, and Lederberg went on to launch Ed Feigenbaum in founding and building the world's leading centre for the application of computer intelligence in medicine and bio-technology.

Bio-Medical Potential

Going beyond personal research interests, my viewpoint now relates to the needs of research organisations covering basic and clinical work in the bio-medical areas. Foremost, as I see it, is the need to overcome resistance to the use of computers. In setting up advanced computing facilities recently at the Imperial Cancer Research Fund, a major goal has been to get these facilities and their potential broadly appreciated. The very suddenness of some of the developments makes this far from easy.

Speed of Onset

The theme of this collection of papers is to look 10 years ahead. Ten years is not so long from some points of view, and particularly not in computing. In the 25 years since the first primitive applications of computers to genetics we have seen the rise of artificial intelligence, interactive access, on-line information retrieval. Perhaps the next 10 years will see what is now already done by few people done by many. I have in mind electronic mail, bulk information handling, electronic office functions, and medical diagnosis.

These are general developments which happen to be of great importance to the bio-medical worker, and one can now extend the list to include not only increasingly intelligent databases but also full-fledged knowledge-based management systems, as described earlier by Feigenbaum. One must add the increasing scope of computer-based statistical analysis, which can be turned to account by the epidemiologist, for example, to analyse diseases in ways previously impossible.

Contrasted with these are specific utilities such as the specialised databases and knowledge-bases themselves, diagnostic aids oriented to the GP, packages for analysis of DNA sequences, software for the control and interpretation of particular laboratory instruments, and so on.

Application to Instrumentation

Some applications to instrumentation are spectacular and rapidly accepted. Examples are image analysis of X-ray photos, the tomography scanner, and automatic planning of radiotherapy. In some of these we see sophisticated developments of image analysis in areas where there were no alternatives and the advantages were obvious. Other areas have proved more problematical, as the following example illustrates.

The importance of being able to identify, by computer, individual human chromosomes from photographs of microscopic preparations cannot be overstated. As you probably know, the genes that determine our inheritance are carried on elements called chromosomes (which simply means coloured bodies because that is how you see them, by using a stain). The human organism has 22 pairs, one member of each pair coming from either parent, plus X and Y which are the sex chromosomes. It is important in many cases to know what the chromosome constitution is because there are abnormalities that are connected with having an unusual chromosome, one that is a bit longer or a bit shorter, or with having an extra copy of one. Many of you may know that Down's syndrome results from possession of an extra copy of Chromosome Number 21. Each of these chromosomes is individually identified by its own visible properties. In order to do chromosome analysis, which is cumbersome on a large scale, essentially for epidemiological purposes, one would like to automate this process. A group in the UK and other groups elsewhere have attempted for a long time to automate the analysis of human chromosomes. But the complicated problem of pattern recognition was never really solved in spite of large expenditures. Now new approaches are being tried, for example the use of cell sorters to sort individual chromosomes. These have overtaken the initial approaches.

There is so often the difficulty of deciding when the effort is worth the reward. A current example is full automation of DNA sequencing. There are many examples in the instrumentation area which appear on the face of it to be straightforward, and yet are as complicated as they are important. Consider for example the analysis of the two-dimensional surface of a gel used to separate the proteins of a whole cell. There may be upwards of a thousand spots to be seen, irregularly distributed and irregular in shape and size. The technique is called 2D gel electrophoresis and is used to separate mixtures of proteins or other macromolecular substances into their constituent pure species. Computer-based image analysis has great potential here.

Impact in Hospitals

The arrival of some of these computer-based techniques in medical diagnosis has brought about a revolution. The whole approach to systematic analysis of images produced by X-rays or by radioactive materials that are taken by people and taken up by different organs has had major effects. In any large hospital nowadays with a medical physics or nuclear medicine department, computers and complicated equipment run by computers and taking data from computers are a *sine qua non*, and this is a phenomenon that has happened only within the last few years. It is going to have major ramifications that interact with new developments in biology.

I might just mention briefly one of them. The body reacts to foreign substances by producing antibodies. These antibodies can be made by animals in response to the injection of different types of cells. Recently, a technique for making so-called monoconal antibodies, very pure and potent reagents which can be made as if by micro-organisms in culture, has come into play. This is a revolution in many areas of medical applications, because it allows you to produce reagents that are more specific for different types of cells. It is going to change our approaches to the diagnosis, for example, of cancers, because it is going to define the cell types in a way they have not been defined before. If you take these reagents, these antibodies, put a radioactive tag on them and give them to a patient, they will go to the places where there may be unexpected cancer cells, the so-called metastases: this sort of work is now being done. Emission tomography, a camera which takes pictures of the radiation, will play a major role in identifying the location of these unusual cells and will provide a "non-invasive" approach to diagnosis. This is going to be extremely important and will depend in a major way on computer applications for the detection of these radiating signals and their proper analysis.

Proteins and their Shapes

Another application of fundamental interest goes back to some of the earliest days of computing. When I used Edsac II at Cambridge I used to stand in the queue with physicists and physical chemists who were analysing electron density maps produced by X-ray diffraction, a technique for looking at protein molecules. These techniques were pioneered in Cambridge for working out the three-dimensional structure of a protein. A protein is a string of amino acids, basic building blocks, of which there are 20 different sorts. And that string, although you can lay it out in a line, in real life takes up very complicated folded structures which give the protein its shape. It is its shape that determines what it can do, and what things can interact with it. These techniques of X-ray diffraction can produce a map in terms of the density of electrons of all these different structures. But without computers it would never have been possible to work out the structure of proteins.

Developments in this area continue. It is not enough to know of the single protein molecule what its shape is. We need to know how its structures are disposed when that protein molecule is embedded within different parts of the cell. We need to know something about higher order structures and that is an enormously complicated problem, much more difficult than some of the basic linear problems of genetics to which I shall come later. Already there are very imaginative image analysis programs that will store all the data on an electron density map, give you the picture of a protein from any direction, rotate it, take bits of it out, match them up with other bits. Just as those familiar with the theory of continental drift can see how South America matches up with Africa, so students of protein structure can use computer image-handling to do the same thing with different protein molecules, or with protein molecules and the things they interact with, to see how the shapes are inter-related and what this tells about their functions. For instance, if you want to know how a drug interacts with another molecule, you may use this approach to help predict what sorts of drugs to make and how they might work.

General Applications

Electronic Mail

Since we had our computer facility set up in the ICRF we have learnt what electronic mail is. It seems a simple thing but, it may have quite fundamental implications for improved communication between people. They don't necessarily have to be far apart. My wife, Julia, and I work together in the same building about 10 feet away from each other but we find we often communicate by electronic mail on the computer. There are all sorts of ways in which you can inter-relate and bring together a group of people in a research institute with electronic mail, a kind of internal Prestel: for example, listings of forthcoming seminars, library accessions, new methods available, new reagents available, new techniques and so on. And if you have an organisation with remote sites, as we do, information exchange is even more important.

Word Processing

It has been said that there was a difficulty in getting office automation ideas accepted. My experience is exactly the opposite. As soon as it is available, everybody wants to use it, including the secretaries. The problem is not lack of interest or willingness, but simply the time it takes to train enough people to use the equipment available.

It is commonplace to say that word processing facilities must be directly interlinked to your central computer, so that you can have immediate transfer of information on references, tabular material and all sorts of other things from store which the scientific worker needs when preparing a paper for publication. Of course, eventually there is no longer any need for the published paper: the computer will be your means of communication. Relevance is obvious not only to office applications but to the organisation of hospital and medical records and so on.

Primary Care

Office aids in the most general sense will be most important in the field of primary medical care. In the British system, that means the GP and the social worker.

A need mentioned earlier (see Chapter 4) arises from the fact that we have a most cumbersome system of social services in the UK. It is important for a social worker or GP to know what benefits are available and to know under what circumstances eligibility may be claimed by different people. An aid via the computer, whether it is a free-standing microcomputer or plugged into a larger system, would obviously be enormously useful. The barrier is not that we do not know what to do. The people in the field know exactly what to do. The barrier is to get the new techniques accepted.

Exploding Information

Another area is the need to cope with the explosion of information in science. There is, I think, a greater problem in the bio-medical sciences than the physical sciences. In the physical sciences the information is in relatively few journals, although they are very large ones. But in the bio-medical area it is spread over hundreds of journals. It is impossible tell where something useful might be found.

Thus, there is a great need for the use of computers for information retrieval and for making the information properly accessible in easy ways to the working scientist.

Machine Intelligence

It is time to turn to machine intelligence and to the potential of knowledge engineering. I would like to start with work in which my wife and I were involved at Stanford University. We worked on something now called the HLA System. The HLA System is a blood group-like system in white blood cells: it is detected as if it were a blood group, and the determinants of it are the differences that exist between people that are used when you match individuals for transplantation. If someone needs a kidney graft or a bone marrow transplant, then it is important to match them as far as possible for these HLA determinants, because that will help with the rejection problem. It has also come to be realised that this genetic system, which is a very complex one, is involved in the way the body responds to foreign things, the way it makes antibodies, the way it mounts what is called the "immune response". This, in turn, therefore, is associated with some of the major chronic diseases of the present time. There are genetic susceptibilities that are of major importance in rheumatoid arthritis, in juvenile-onset diabetes and so on. Today it is a major area of medical research. Every issue of *The Lancet* or the *British Medical Journal* has something involving the HLA System.

Why do I mention that in this context? It is probably not realised by the medical world that its development depended entirely on the application of computers. Nor is it realised by people in the computer field that relatively simple computer applications made that development possible. The reason that computers were important was that we had to interpret a lot of messy information, reagents that reacted with cells from different people; they did not react very well, they were not reproducible. We had to use clustering algorithms to define the types that were inherited and then, having defined those types with clustering algorithms, to construct logical rules that told us how, when we typed new individuals the assignments should be made. We were doing this in the mid-1960s, as ideas on machine intelligence were developing, and we did not realise that that was what we were doing in a very simple-minded sort of way.

Early Diagnosis

Something must be added about the applications of these logical approaches to dealing with knowledge in medical diagnosis. Ed Feigenbaum's group has pioneered these approaches. Let me say something about one particular area where from our point of view, involved in cancer research as we are, these applications seem particularly important. In Britain, the critical care, the point of first contact of the patient with his doctor, is the general practitioner. In the days when little could be done about different sorts of diseases, it might not matter if the GP gave the wrong diagnosis. Whatever the diagnosis was there was not much he could do about it. My father, who was a GP, used to say: "If you go to a doctor and you have got flu, it will go in seven days; if you don't, it will go in a week".

That is not true any more in many areas. And so the more important it becomes to get the correct diagnosis at an early stage — especially in a disease like cancer where early diagnosis is paramount and can make the critical difference. If one is involved, as I often am, in talking to the public, the public that helps us raise money, one frequently hears the complaint: "Why did my friend not get referred as soon as was possible, when it might have been possible to do something?"

The problem is not really the fault of the GP. He has a difficult job covering the whole range of different medical applications. Any one thing he may see relatively infrequently. I think it is essential to provide aids for the GP, to diffuse culturally to the GP the expert knowledge which he cannot expect to acquire. So it is important to develop the right approaches to aiding the GP in the primary medical care situation in diagnosis. Once again I think the problem is not so much that we do not know what to do. We can already use some of the existing sophisticated knowledge bases. The challenge is not to create them but to get the GP to use them in his ordinary practice. Probably the only way will be to get a few GPs to work with these systems themselves, evolving them in particular areas.

Perhaps a start could be made by helping GPs a little with their office problems, providing something mundane that is useful, and then getting them to take an interest and be involved in these other more sophisticated applications.

Analysis of DNA Sequences

Let me turn to one of my own major areas of interest, the analysis of DNA (de-oxy-ribo-nucleic acid) sequences. Essentially this amounts to the analysis of the genetic language. DNA is the essential material of which genes are made. It is by now a household word and most of you have heard of Watson and Crick and the double helix. The genetic language is made out of four different "letters" which are chemical substances, A, T, G and C. And the chromosome is really a very long double string of letters with a very simple rule, according to which letter is opposite which. So an A is opposite a T, a T opposite an A, a G opposite a C, a C opposite a G. DNA is just a long string of those letters, a very long string. The total human genome contains something like three times 10 to the ninth power, three American billions, of those letters, divided into 20 or so packages, the chromosomes. To make proteins which are the working substances of the cell, a template has to be formed from the DNA. This template is the RNA (ribonucleic acid) from which is read off the sequence of the 20 amino acids in the protein. So the RNA string is simply a copy of that DNA sequence. This copied sequence from the DNA is used as the template from which, three letters at a time, the corresponding amino acid is linked into the chain.

The logic is simple. There is a four-letter language in the DNA, a 20-letter language in the protein and a simple code that tells you which combination of three letters goes to which amino acid. A complicated machinery in the cell carries out the process of making protein from the information carried in that linear array of letters, that very long string. This DNA language is the blueprint from which everything is made. From it we can in principle derive all information about bodily functions, including the variations between individuals, normal and abnormal.

Let us return to these three times 10 to the ninth based pairs. A strange phenomenon in higher organisms is that, of this vital information, about half of it does not code for any protein component or have any other function. It is, in a sense, rubbish. Some of us have called it "selfish DNA". So the functional part of the DNA is about half of one and a half billion pairs. But that information is divided up into groups that reflect these protein products, the products that the cell uses to carry out its functions. For instance, haemoglobin, the stuff that makes red blood cells red, and carries oxygen around in the blood, is one of the major proteins and the first whose structure was studied. It actually occurs in slightly different forms. Different versions of it are used in the embryonic and foetal and adult lives and it is made of two components that are slightly different from each other. So it is not a single protein, but a family of proteins. We call these families of related things "clusters". So when considering the number of basic genetic functions, you should not think in terms of the numbers of these letters, nor even in terms of the numbers of proteins. You should think in terms of the number of families of these proteins or gene clusters. Various calculations based on new data suggest that a reasonable number for these clusters is of the order of 5,000. It is important to realise that although the total number of letters in the language is enormous, the number of functional clusters involved is a much more comprehensible magnitude. We may not be all that far from knowing something about most basic genetic functions, whether of haemoglobin or the proteins that go to make up the muscle cells or what tells the cell how to divide or about relationships between one cell and another.

We should begin to accumulate a knowledge base on genes, a sort of genetic data bank which tells us about genes, all the way from their DNA sequence to the protein product and through to the functions of those products.

Determinants of Individual Differences

Cancer is essentially a disease at the cellular level where the cell goes out of control because some of its genetic functions are misused or changed. You can ask in any particular cancer: "What genes have changed? What's going wrong? What are the functions involved?" You can ask that same question in a variety of other diseases. You can ask it with respect to normal functions, e.g. with differences in intellectual or athletic ability. What is it that makes these differences? Some of it is in the genes. These are areas, of course, of great controversy. But there is no denying the fact that genetic data tells us that there are contributions from our genetic differences to differences between people. And that in principle if we knew something about all these genetic functions in the end we should be able to say which one of them has changed in a way that contributes to particular differences, whether normal or abnormal, between individuals.

The only way to get to this point is by accumulating this information in a systematic manner in a knowledge base. This is interrelated with having the DNA sequence information. The more we learn about products and their functions in relation to the primary language, the more we shall be able to predict, when we have a new sequence, what it is likely to be doing, even though we may not actually know in detail what it is doing.

This analysis of normal differences between people, and also the differences that contribute to disease, is going to be one of the major contributions that molecular biology will make to society in the future. There is no doubt that computers will play a major role. The conventional approach, e.g. with an IQ test or other measure, height or weight or disease incidences, has many pitfalls, especially in the human situation. In the view of many of us the only way to avoid those pitfalls is to have a genetic approach which is unequivocal: to find a DNA sequence difference which is associated with the differences under study.

In human genetics until recently the ways of studying the sequence differences in the genetic material have been limited. We have not had enough genetic markers, i. e. heritable differences between individuals that are sufficiently well-defined. Without going into the details one can say that the approaches of genetic engineering are solving that problem. Now we can study differences between people in the most objective and clear-cut way, differences in their DNA sequence.

Remember that the chromosome is an entity which carries a DNA sequence. There are about 20 or so of them, so within each chromosome is about one-twentieth of the total set of nucleotide pairs. If you think of it in terms of gene clusters, that means a chromosome may have on average two or three hundred of these genetic clusters that are the primary functional entities. If we have a series of genetic markers, a series of reference points that we can identify on the chromosome that are inherited, we can use those to say: If there is a particular gene here that is influencing whether I get diabetes or heart disease or have perfect pitch we will find it because it will be associated in certain ways with these well-defined markers on either side. So we localise the lesion in the genetic material, where the genetic influence lies, even though we know nothing about its function. Now you can divide things up so that the segments within which you can localise an effect may be within about a tenth or so of the chromosome. The point about making this calculation is that if you knew the whole DNA sequence and had it all recorded, and you knew what those 25 or so functions were within the lesion where that genetic influence lies, you could begin, by the accumulation of knowledge, in your knowledge base, to say: Which of these different functions is likely to be the important one in the individual difference under study?

Through these approaches I think that we shall see in the future a much more complete understanding of the genetic basis for all sorts of individual differences. This will make a contribution even before we have any idea of how that particular function works, a much more complicated problem.

Brains, Machines and the Interface

Finally, one cannot discuss medicine and biology without making some reference to one of the major frontiers of research, to the understanding of how the brain works. I therefore find very interesting the development of the CLIP information processor as M. J. B. Duff has defined it (see Chapter 5). His is perhaps an approach that is analogous to the way the brain works and gets down to a level of efficiency that is in some ways comparable with the brain. The brain, as we have heard so many times, is by far the most efficient computer from some points of view, especially in recognition of patterns and in dealing with imperfect data by filling in gaps. I think the brain is essentially a heuristic machine and that is why knowledge engineering and related heuristic approaches are so important. Learning to understand mental processes will have major implications, particularly in dealing with mental disease. As a geneticist I have been involved in these areas because of ways of understanding genetic contributions to mental disease. There is no doubt, for example, that there is a major genetic component to schizophrenia, and a major genetic component to depressive states. These can be established in quite objective ways.

Conclusion

I have tried to give you a vignette of different possibilities in the bio-medical research area. Here, as elsewhere, it is important not to keep reinventing the wheel. The need commented on by Ed Feigenbaum about keeping up with the building blocks available for doing this sort of work is vital. These building blocks then have to be compatible between the different groups that use them, and as always, compatibility between computational methods is a key problem.

In conclusion, I think the greatest need for compatibility is between the human brain and the computer application. All the techniques that we have talked about will fail unless they are made acceptable to the people who use them. That is going to be the challenge of the next 10 years. If we believe that these applications are going to be of major value to our society then we must overcome the resistance of potential users by producing things that are really usable and hence valuable for man.

8

Technology and the Universities

D. B. Thomas

Rutherford and Appleton Laboratory

Introduction

A significant proportion of the most highly qualified manpower in science and engineering in the UK is employed by universities and polytechnics both in teaching and in research. It is pertinent to ask what can be done, particularly in a period when British industry is experiencing difficulty in competing internationally in technology, to marshal this manpower resource to the greater economic good. Clearly the principal role of this section of the academic community is to train the young engineers and scientists upon whom UK industry will largely depend for its future success. Such a contribution will however by its very nature produce results only in the longer term. In contrast some of the present research activities in universities and polytechnics, when taken collectively, are close enough to the immediate interests of industry to offer economic benefits to the nation on a considerable scale in the shorter term.

In a number of branches of science the natural development of the subject over the past few decades has created the need for expensive research facilities beyond the capability of any one academic institution to sustain. This in turn has led to national, and in some cases international, facilities being set up to support research teams from universities working in collaboration. The most striking example of this type of development is in high energy physics where the situation has been transformed over the last thirty years from one in which an individual university could itself contemplate building and operating a state-of-the-art particle accelerator to one in which the highest energy accelerators can now only be afforded by the richest countries, or by groups of smaller countries working together.

This trend towards centralised facilities in science has been mirrored in more recent times in some branches of engineering. In the last half-decade, for example, the need for such central facilities to support academic research in computing, microelectronics and information technology has become apparent in most advanced countries.

This paper outlines the response of the Science and Engineering Research Council towards satisfying these requirements in the UK. It describes the central engineering facilities which have already been set up, the overall objective being to organise in specific areas of technology co-ordinated programmes involving academic researchers with common technical interests and goals. This approach towards increased co-ordination frequently itself creates the need for central facilities to support the research, and later creates the need to link the results of the work into British industry. An important point to note is that the very existence of a coherent academic community with a common research programme in a particular area of technology makes for a single interface with industry. This in itself eases the problem of technology transfer.

On the industrial front, collaboration in research between individual high technology companies in the UK has recently become more evident. Such a move could further simplify technology transfer in cases where a single collaborative academic activity has to interact with a single collaborative industrial one. Several examples will be quoted later in which a further merger of interests has taken place resulting in the evolution of common projects involving engineering teams from industry, government laboratories and academic circles working in a fully integrated fashion on a day-to-day basis.

This volume has as its sub-title, "The Unprecedented Opportunity". It thus calls for an assessment of future progress by extrapolation of present rates and trends. The technical programmes described later have all been launched within the last ten years. The speed with which this has been accomplished can be used as a yardstick against which to measure future projects and this is done in the final section of the paper.

The Last Ten Years — the Difficulty in Getting Started

A major reorganisation in 1956 of Government support of science in the UK led amongst other things to the establishment of the Science Research Council (SRC). The role assigned to SRC was principally to support academic research by providing grants to universities, by operating national research facilities, and by paying the subscriptions to international organisations such as CERN and ESA to provide access for UK researchers to more major research tools.

The support of engineering research was included in the original remit of SRC. It did not however figure largely at first, the initial emphasis being rather on the continuing support of "big science", nuclear physics, radio astronomy and space research. The former two subjects had begun to be highly organised immediately after the Second World War, building on the experience of team work which had earlier produced atomic weapons and radar. The continuing worldwide progress in civil and military applications in these fields in the post-War years, followed by the launching in 1957 of the first earth-orbiting satellite which opened the way to space science, provided the backcloth against which the support of "big science" flourished.

Rutherford Laboratory, the major laboratory of SRC with a staff of 1250, was in the late 1960s largely occupied with operating and mounting experiments on its own 7GEV proton synchrotron. It was also involved in preparing experiments to be run on the accelerators at CERN, these activities being undertaken in support of a community of about 400 UK university high-energy physicists.

At that time, no integrated UK engineering community comparable in size to any of the "big science" communities had assembled itself around any sub-discipline of engineering research, nor were there any central facilities operated by SRC laboratories in support of engineering. It was not until 1969 that SRC set up a separate Engineering Board with the objective of promoting and revitalising engineering research in universities and polytechnics. In its early years the Board concentrated on increasing the number of grants given in support of engineering. By 1973, in recognition of the coming need for central facilities for engineers, a dialogue had commenced between the Engineering Board and Rutherford Laboratory. This was shortly followed in 1975 by the decision of the Board to set up the Interactive Computing Facility (ICF) as an interlinked network of multi-user minicomputers which would be accessible from terminals installed in the majority of academic Engineering Departments. Rutherford Laboratory was commissioned to manage the installation and operating of the network. Today it serves a community of users in excess of 2000 in number. At about the same time the Engineering Board approved a number of minor projects involving collaboration between one or more universities and Rutherford Laboratory. These ranged from rheometers for polymer research, to a superconducting AC generator test rig, an experimental magnetic levitation transport system and a high pressure fluidised bed combustion rig. As none of these minor projects was in the field of information technology, they are outside the scope of this paper and will not be described further here.

In 1977 approval was given by the Engineering Board for the establishment of five new major centres specialising in various aspects of microelectronics. Silicon processing facilities were enhanced at Edinburgh and Southampton Universities, ion implantation research was intensified at Surrey University, a materials-preparation centre for advanced semi-conductor compounds was created at Sheffield University and an Electronic Beam

Lithography Facility (EBLF) set up at Rutherford Laboratory to provide a mask-making service. This range of facilities aimed to enable SRC to fabricate prototype integrated circuits in-house to designs by academic researchers. The facilities have been operational for several years and are now serving a community of more than 100 designers of integrated circuits and other special solid-state devices.

In 1979 decisions were taken by SRC leading to some international rationalisation of its research establishments. These resulted in Appleton Laboratory, which specialised in radio propagation studies and the support of space research, being merged with Rutherford Laboratory on the latter's site. By 1981 Rutherford Appleton Laboratory (RAL) with a total staff of 1600 was established at Chilton. One result of this move was to increase the technical base at Chilton from which projects in information technology could arise, combining the existing computing and microelectronics expertise with incoming expertise in radio propagation, satellite communications and other branches of telecommunications.

The first big national project in which RAL has a leading role involving the telecommunications aspects of information technology was launched under the name Project UNIVERSE early in 1981. A collaboration involving industry, government laboratories and universities was formed to establish local area networks of computers at seven sites in the UK and connected together via links to the existing Orbital Test Satellite. This research project is scheduled to become operational in the second quarter of 1982.

In recognition of its own increasing role in engineering, and of the importance of the subject to the national economy, SRC successfully petitioned the Privy Council to modify its name. In April 1981 it became the Science and Engineering Research Council (SERC).

From the above, it can be deduced that over the last decade there has been a considerable shift of resources into the support of UK academic engineering research. In 1970 virtually the whole budget of SRC was devoted to science with only minor support to engineering. By 1980 the Engineering Board commanded a budget of £4m per annum (20% of SERC's total budget) and about 300 out of the 2500 permanent staff of SERC were engaged in support of Engineering Board programmes. This shift of resources has taken place against the background of a growing realisation that the leading industrial competitors of the UK are organising their efforts in some fields of engineering, such as microelectronics, on a national basis, and that to defend its position the UK may have to do the same.

Although the growth of SERC resources devoted to engineering has been very significant in recent years, it is interesting to speculate why it was not even greater at a time when a great national debate was in progress on ways to improve the industrial performance of UK engineering. Some possible answers to this question are attempted below, particularly since they may give some clue as to likely future growth rates.

Scientific research and engineering research are in direct competition with one another within SERC for an essentially fixed level of funding. The Council makes financial allocations to its three Science Boards and to its Engineering Board, and in these allocations reflects national priorities. The underlying factors governing these allocations are too complex to be described in detail here but a few of the main influences can be mentioned.

Firstly, many pure science subjects are totally dependent on SERC for funds whereas for more technological subjects funding can be sought from other government agencies and from industry as well as from SERC. Secondly the criteria used in judging grant applications in engineering by SERC are more complicated than in science because of the differing nature of the subjects. Allowing for some over-simplification in presentation, the one criterion used to judge scientific proposals in SERC can be encapsulated in the question: "Is it good science?". In engineering a number of questions have to be asked. "Is it good engineering research, and not development." SERC does not support development work. "Will the results be of interest to industry?" If the answer is no, then it is unlikely the grant will be approved. If the answer is a very positive yes (i.e. there is great and immediate interest from industry), then the grant application could also be turned down with the advice that industrial funding is more appropriate. Although it would be wrong to overstate the difficulties in judging proposals in engineering compared with those in science, the added complexity of the procedure should be appreciated. Thirdly, university scientists recognised many years ago the need to form themselves into big teams to tackle "big science" projects involving expensive central facilities. Only now are university engineers beginning to recognise the need to work in this manner and to accept the resultant changes in personal work pattern and attitude which collaborating in these new ways entails.

Computing and Microelectronics

In this section the existing six SERC-supported central facilities established to provide technical assistance to academic engineers working in the fields of interactive computing and microelectronics are described. Reference is also made to a number of SERC-supported MSc Courses which have recently been stated specifically to train integrated circuit designers. Finally a collaborative project with industry to produce a new set of computer-aided design tools for use with gate arrays is mentioned. A quarterly newsletter called *Microfabrication* is circulated widely in the university community describing the latest developments.

Interactive Computing Facility

Launched in 1975/6, the Interactive Computing Facility (ICF) had as its hardware objective to establish a computer network linking engineering departments in universities and polytechnics in the UK and as its software objective to produce a number of standardised suites of applications programs in various branches of engineering and make them available over the network for general academic use.

By 1981, after a capital investment approaching 10m, ICF was serving a community of over 2000 engineers, mainly in universities. Twenty-nine minicomputers are linked into the network. A policy of standardising whenever possible on two specific types of machine, one from the UK (from GEC Computers) and one from the USA (from Prime Computers), was introduced. Interactive graphics terminals, also of standard types, are located in over 100 engineering departments and linked into the nearest computer on the network.

Telecommunications links between the 29 computers and between computers and terminals are in general private telephone lines leased from British Telecom. These allow data transfer rates of about 10 kilobits per second to be achieved between most points on the network. Some less intensively-used terminals are linked into the network by dialling-up via the public telephone network. The network can also be used to access SERC's mainframe computers, dual IBM 360/185 machines with an IBM 3032 front end.

The network is managed by a team at Rutherford Appleton Laboratory. This team has the responsibility of purchasing all new computers for the network and arranging for installation at the selected site. Bulk purchasing of graphics terminals and other equipment is carried out to provide a loan pool of equipment which can be called on by university workers with approved SERC research grants. Telecommunications for the network is also managed centrally by the RAL team including all negotiations and contracts with British Telecom. Maintenance agreements for items in the equipment pool are also handled centrally.

On the software side a number of Special Interest Groups, composed primarily of university research engineers, have been established to define standard suites of software. At the present time Special Interest Groups are active in the following fields:
— Artificial Intelligence;
— Circuit Design: Analogue and Digital;

— Computer-Aided Architectural Design;
— Control Engineering;
— Electromagnetics;
— Finite Elements: Structural Geotechnical and Fluid Mechanics;
— Graphics: Pre-Processors and Post-Processors.

The Groups operate by first surveying what software is already available in universities or commercially. They then procure what is appropriate and commission the writing of whatever additional software is needed to produce a comprehensive suite of programs covering the needs of that area. Documentation of the selected suite is considered of the utmost importance, the principal objective being to make a user-friendly system, particularly for postgraduate students who may have little initial familiarity with computing techniques.

To keep users in touch with software and hardware developments on ICF, a quarterly Newsletter is circulated both by electronic mail on the network itself and in normal printed form by post. One new development to be introduced in the near future is the Single User Mini or Personal Computer. Individual engineering researchers who use interactive computing extensively under SERC support will each be provided with one of the latest new powerful Single User Minis which will be networked into ICF.

Electron Beam Lithography Facility

Designers of special integrated circuits in the universities have access to computer-aided design circuits to be produced in the form of digital data. The principal program used for layout is GAELIC and a whole range of simulation programs including SPICE are also available.

Once a final design layout has been prepared in digital form and stored on disc, a set of mask-plates can be manufactured from this data. This is done in the Electronic Beam Lithography facility at RAL using a Cambridge Instruments EBMF-2 e-beam machine. Chromium-on-glass mask-plates are produced, the service offered as standard being a 2 micron minimum feature size service. Smaller feature size, down to 1 micron and lower are undertaken on an experimental basis. Experiments involving direct-writing on other substrate materials (such as lithium niobate for Surface Acoustic Wave devices) are being undertaken.

Over 500 mask-plates were produced in the Facility in the last year and the demand continues to increase. To meet this demand the EBMF-2 has been upgraded so that its writing speed, and therefore throughput, has been increased by a factor of close to 5.

The Facility also takes part in the development of an advanced 3-beam lithography machine with joint Department of Industry-SERC funding. The object is to produce an even faster machine, hopefully by a further factor of 10. The development is taking place in collaboration with Cambridge University which is manufacturing the electronic optics column and with Cambridge Instruments which may market the machine or some sub-systems of it. A programme of evaluation of advanced electron-sensitive resists is also in progress to match the increased writing speed (and therefore reduced exposure dosage) of the new machine.

Preliminary experiments in x-ray replication are also scheduled using the SERC's Synchrotron Radiation Source at Daresbury Laboratory.

Silicon Processing Facilities at Edinburgh and Southampton

Both Edinburgh and Southampton Universities have SERC-supported microelectronics facilities specialising in silicon processing. Both offer a standard NMOS process with 6 micron minimum feature and common design rules. Development is proceeding towards a similar 3 micron process that will allow 10,000 to 20,000 gates per chip. Both centres have commercial Lintott ion-implanters for introducing dopants into silicon.

Libraries of standard circuits, such as for example shift-registers, are being built up from designs that have been proved experimentally on the NMOS process offered. These standard circuits can be used in combination to produce complex systems.

At Edinburgh a gate array has been designed based on the NMOS process, particularly with use by students in mind. This gate array consists of 90 cells which can be configured as 2 input NAND and 2 input NOR gates. Silicon wafers incorporating this gate array design can be processed in quantity and then held in stock. The student designs his circuit by specifying only how a final layer of metal tracks shall interconnect the standard pre-processed gates. In fabrication terms, all that needs to be done to realise this circuit is to produce one mask-plate with the required pattern of interconnects on and use this to transfer the pattern on to pre-processed wafers. Not only is the design of systems using a gate array much simpler for the student than a fully customised design but also the processing required to lay down the pattern of aluminium interconnects is so much simpler than fabricating a customised design. These two factors mean that the turn-around in fabrication from the time the student completes his design to the time he receives prototype packages chips can be as short as a few weeks.

Southampton University has also designed a gate array for student use, in this case based on I^2L technology (Integrated Injection Logic). This array has 282 uncommitted gates which can be similarly interconnected by one metallisation layer to produce the required circuit. Again the objective has been to provide an easy-to-use vehicle for student projects. Development work is also in progress at Southampton on other bipolar technologies.

Advanced Semi-Conductor Materials Work at Sheffield

Research on devices based on compounds of elements from Groups III and V of the Periodic Table has been in progress at Sheffield for over a decade. Studies of binary, ternary and quaternary mixed crystals have been carried out with microwave applications and more recently optoelectronic applications in mind. Both liquid phase epitaxy reactors and Metal-Organic-Chemical-Vapour Deposition techniques are in use to grow layers of the required materials. As many as four layers of differing composition, each typically of a thickness of 1 micron, have to be grown on top of one another for some applications. Novel devices have been constructed using these techniques and mask-sets supplied by the Electron Beam Lithography Facility at RAL.

The Sheffield Facility is able to offer a range of well characterised epitaxial single crystal layers to suit university customer requirements in Gallium-Arsenide, Gallium-Aluminium-Arsenide, and Indium-Phosphide.

Ion Implantation Research Facility at Surrey

Ion implantation of dopant impurities into pure silicon to produce regions of semi-conducting material is one of the basic techniques used in integrated circuit fabrication. The importance of this technique is such that a research facility devoted to it has been set up at Surrey University with SERC support. Ion implantation and ion beam analysis can be undertaken using a 500keV implanter. A wide range of species of elements have been successfully implanted.

UK5000 — A Computer-Aided Design System for a Large Gate Array

Perhaps the key to making the design of special integrated circuits accessible to a wide spectrum of engineers and scientists is to automate the layout on silicon of the circuit. If this could be done the engineer or scientists would need only to generate a logic diagram describing his circuit. The computer-aided design software would take over at this point and automatically produce the magnetic tapes to control the mask-making machine.

A project which aims to do this is UK5000, a collaborative project involving four industrial companies, GEC, ICL, STL and TMC, plus British Telecom, RSRE (Malvern) and RAL. A gate array is to be designed in ISO-CMOS technology with 5000 usable gates — actually 6000 gates to allow for some inefficiency in usage. The structure will be designed for ease of interconnection via two layers of metal tracks by software auto-routing techniques. This software will be produced as part of the project as will other software for automatic test pattern generation. These latter programs will be applied to the completed gate array after the two layers of interconnections have been made, to check that the design performs correctly.

The project will involve a total of about 35 man-years of effort divided between the participating organisations. It is scheduled for completion in late 1982. Once available, the software will be mounted on SERC computers of the ICF to make it accessible to systems designers in the universities. This project is an example of the ever increasing sophistication of the software tools that are needed for design of today's complex integrated circuits. It also illustrates the importance of collaborative working between organisations as a means of keeping development costs to each within bounds.

MSc Courses in Integrated Circuit Design

The importance of securing an adequate national supply of trained integrated circuit designers led SERC to support three MSc courses from October 1980. The courses are at Edinburgh University, UMIST and one shared between Brunel and Southampton Universities. In the first year of the courses about 25 students were trained and in the year beginning in October 1981 the number had risen to 50.

The students on these courses normally come with first degrees in electrical engineering or computer science. They are taught to design integrated circuits using graphic terminals at their universities connected through to an ICL at RAL on which the design software packages are maintained. Once completed their designs go for mask-making at EBLF, followed by silicon processing at either the Edinburgh or Southampton Microfabrication Facilities. Prototype packaged microchips are returned to the students for testing. Similar support from the SERC Central Facilities is given to an MEng course at Durham University and an MSc course at Queens University Belfast.

The Present — Some Examples of "Systems" Projects

Two examples of the type of "systems engineering" projects which SERC would like to encourage universities to undertake are mentioned below. The first of these is CLIP4, an array-processor for robot vision systems, developed by Dr Michael Duff of University College London. It is described in Chapter 5 of this volume. The second is Project UNIVERSE, a project to research the interconnection of Local Area Networks of computers at remote sites via links to the OTS communications satellite.

CLIP4

SERC has supported University College London in the development of the CLIP series of array processors since 1973. In 1980, when the CLIP4 prototype first operated, it was decided by SERC that the concepts involved in the machine were both important and novel enough for a more fully engineered version of CLIP4 to be manufactured. The National Research Development Corporation, which carries the responsibility for exploiting SERC-supported inventions commercially, had unsuccessfully attempted over a number of years to interest UK industry in marketing CLIP4. Because of this RAL was called upon to produce the engineered version.

CLIP4 in its usual form of a 96 by 96 array processor has a small computer associated with each of its 96 by 96 array points or pixels. A special custom-designed microchip providing 8 of these elementary computers had been developed and fabricated in sufficient quantity (i.e. about 1200 chips) to permit the prototype machine to be built and tested. The rapid advances in microelectronics during this process meant that it was already proving appropriate to redesign the CLIP4 chip so that it could be produced at a cheaper price and to a higher technical specification. This was accomplished in 1981, the redesigned chips costing only one-quarter of the original price (£5 rather than £20 each) and being capable of performing at 5 times the speed (5 MHz rather than 1 MHz).

Two machines embodying this new chip are under construction at RAL, one for use at University College London and one for the Medical Research Council's unit at Edinburgh. Proposals for two further machines, one for the Scientific Instrument Research Association and one for RAL, are under consideration.

The objective behind this construction programme is to enable CLIP4 to be evaluated as a pattern recognition system in various fields of science, medicine and engineering. The machine should, for example, be capable of being used in conjunction with a medical microscope and TV camera for automatic scanning for cancer cells or chromosome abnormalities in smear samples. If applications such as these can be successfully demonstrated, greater commercial interest in CLIP4 may follow.

Project UNIVERSE

As described earlier, SERC operates networks of inter-linked computers scattered widely across university sites in the UK. Leased telephone lines are used to make the interconnections and this essentially limits the rate of digital data transfer at present to less than 10 kilobits per second. Experience has shown that there is a need for data transfer rates 10 or 100 times as great, if these can be accomplished. In the longer term, when the planned use of optical fibres for the public telephone network becomes a reality in 5 to 10 years' time, transfer rates in the megabit range will be readily possible.

The same pattern of need for higher speed communications between computers is also showing itself even more strongly on individual sites. Here the accepted solution is to provide a Local Area Network at each site into which all computers, word processors and other devices which need to communicate with one another at high data rates can be connected.

Project UNIVERSE is a research project to establish Local Area Networks at each of seven sites in the UK and connect them together by a Mbit/s link via the existing Orbital Test Satellite (OTS). The participants are GEC-Marconi Electronics Ltd, Logica Ltd, British Telecom, Cambridge University, Loughborough University of Technology, University College London and SERC-RAL with the Department of Industry providing considerable financial support. New earth terminals to access OTS will be set up at the GEC-Marconi site at Great Baddow, Essex and by SERC at the three University sites. Existing earth stations at the BT Research Laboratories, Martlesham Heath, Suffolk and at the RAL site at Chilton, Oxfordshire will also be used.

The seventh site, that of Logica Ltd in London, is within 1 km of University College and can thus make use of the earth station there via a high-speed terrestrial data link which has been provided by BT. There are likely to be in excess of 50 computers and associated devices connected into the overall network, each able to communicate at will with any one of the others. Various types of Local Area Network will be evaluated, including Ethernet, Token Rings and Cambridge Rings, with the last being the preferred choice. RAL is responsible for co-ordinating the project.

The research programme to be carried out will have as its principal objective the development of software protocols to control the data traffic on the network. There is a great deal of international activity towards the standardisation of such protocols. The research done under Project UNIVERSE should contribute significantly to the emerging standards.

The cost of this programme will be about £3.5m over three years commencing in mid-1981 and will be shared by the participants. The limited residual life-time of OTS means that any experiments beyond that period are likely to have be to be transferred to another geostationary satellite, perhaps ECS1 or ECS2.

The Next Ten Years — the Unprecedented Opportunity

The principal target in information technology to be pursued by SERC in the coming years will be to encourage the build-up of "Systems Engineering" in universities and polytechnics such as CLIP4 and Project UNIVERSE and in subjects such as
— novel computer architectures;
— computer networking concepts;
— telecommunications;
— intelligent robots;
— pattern recognition;
— office automation;
— data banks and data distribution;
— software engineering and standards;
— knowledge engineering and expert systems.

This is by no means an exhaustive list, for similar systems approaches will be applicable to most branches of human activity. SERC, with its first priority as ever in the training of postgraduate students, will continue to be conscious of the need to produce "systems engineers" of the highest quality skilled in these subjects, and in sufficient numbers.

There will also be a continuing need for SERC to provide the infrastructure to enable postgraduate students and university staff alike to embody their ideas for new systems in customised integrated circuits, both quickly and cheaply. The aim should be in a few years to make it as easy to design a special microchip as it now is to write a computer program. With the technology of integrated circuits advancing so rapidly (towards Very Large Scale Integrated Circuits with close on one million gates on a microchip), it will be necessary to continue to invest in updating the existing SERC facilities in computing and microelectronics. As the technology increases progressively in complexity over the coming decade, the time is likely to come when the cost of providing this infrastructure will exceed the resources available to SERC for deployment in this field. This will lead to increased co-operation with other governmental organisations and industrial companies in the establishment of national facilities serving all these organisations, or even perhaps within Europe, international facilities. A prerequisite for future success in information technology could well be the ability to establish and manage national and international programmes involving massive numbers of staff engaged in co-operative high technology ventures.

9

Robots of the Future

E C Joseph[*]

Sperry Univac, Minnesota

Throughout history there has been a cyclic process when one technology is substituted for another. In the remote past, iron took the place of bronze. More recently, plastics have supplanted metal and rubber, synthetic fibres like nylon and polyester do duty for wool and cotton.

At the same time, advances in technology also often amplify. The plough is more powerful than the hoe, the lathe or milling machine more than the chisel, the word processor more than the conventional typewriter. The magnitude of technological substitution and amplification grows over time as we apply the fruits of new knowledge and new discoveries. Today we are entering the threshold of yet another era of advance which will combine both these elements in the massive application of robots.

Robots, of course, have been with us for a long, long time in science fiction. Today, however, we can foresee a not-too-distant future when the real robot population could exceed the human population. In such a future, robots are expected to take over many work roles that could heretofore be performed only by humans. Such an eventuality obviously brings up visions in the mind's eye of a future beset with unemployment.

Yet, when such a future prospect is minutely analysed and telescoped, using the techniques of anticipatory science research, another possibility appears more probable — a future with constant new job creation. Rapid job creation amidst a robotic environment, however, also means rapid job displacement and job obsolescence.

There is a third benefit that society reaps from technological advance: the ability to do what was impossible in the past, thereby creating more jobs than are displaced. In fact, growing expectations for a deficit of people are expected to emerge as a result of massive application of robots. Such an alternative future comes about from the created new work roles rather than

---

[*] Present address: Anticipatory Sciences Incorporated, Minnesota

from scenarios of lack of work due to job displacements. But we can also expect massive and continuing changes in the infrastructure of society as the nature of jobs changes ever more rapidly.

In the Information Age, the Computer-Robot Revolution, it seems likely that the established professions will gradually be displaced, their power eroded. This vulnerability of the professions is tied up with their special strength — the fact that today, as in the past, they act as exclusive repositories, appliers and disseminators of specialised knowledge. This is true for all professions, whether their knowledge concerns the symptoms of illness and the keys to treatment which are currently in the hands of doctors, or the weird permutations of tax laws and changing economics on which accountants thrive, or the tangle of legislation which makes the practice of law so formidably restrictive to the average person. We must not undervalue the professions or the complex information they handle on our behalf, for they have served us well in the past and continue to serve us well. At the same time, we must recognise that they are the end products of a process of labour specialisation which began a long time ago and which came into being because social evolution made life increasingly complicated. As the Information Age gets into its stride, such knowledge will become far more widely and easily available and as a result could well diminish the awe in which we have traditionally held the professions.

In the beginning, information was recorded in such forms as marks in clay, scratches on cave walls or engravings in stone. Then came paper, and later moveable type for books. Now, the forecasters say, books are on the downturn, to be replaced with paperless electronic information storage and display — at a time when the wisdom they contain is more valuable to our survival than ever before. As electronic paperless systems increasingly come into use, books will bequeath their legacy to magnetics and silicon chip technology, and our words will be contained in the molecules of crystals dreamed about in past science fiction. Imagine the new opportunities when the totality of societies' amassed knowledge can be electronically available to us in the real-time of our actions to assist us in whatever we do!

With electronic assistance, professionals could well be largely displaced from the in-line delivery of their profession. What will future professionals then do? Perhaps many will turn toward spending more of their working life in increasing the societal knowledge base in their expert areas, thus putting society on a more rapid growth and change trajectory, since new knowledge could be thus developed and utilised faster in such an environment.

Will not such "expert" people-amplifier appliances change the total infrastructure of society, including educational, government and many other institutions, science and much more? Such technology advance, greater than for any equivalent period in the past, can thus be expected to continue to create jobs faster than the application of new technology displaces them. The application of new technology raises productivity by allowing labour, energy, materials and capital to be applied more efficiently. Therefore, society's real problem is to release the old, inefficient jobs more quickly: that is, to displace jobs faster so that resources can be released for new job creation.

But our intuitive reaction, when worried about jobs from the micro-view of a farmer, clerk, truck driver, or doctor, is to do everything possible — go on strike, demand government bail-outs, to quote two contemporary examples — to hold onto the old jobs. In this situation, society establishes policies to inhibit job displacement and in doing so also prevents the creation of new jobs. In the long run, therefore, such policies reduce jobs, thus causing unemployment as costs continue to climb, forcing the eventual employment of new technology in order to raise productivity. Whereas, by establishing counter-intuitive policies for short-term job displacements in the micro-system, coupled with incentive policies for job creation in other micro areas, the end result for both the short- and long-term future is growth in employment for the total macro-societal system.

From a general system historical viewpoint, micro-system policies and intuitions tend to focus, reduce and close the societal system by narrowing the alternatives, reducing jobs, and reducing the quality of life and standard of living by establishing laws to control job displacements. On the contrary, *macro*-system (holistic) policies and intuitions open the societal system to growth in alternatives, jobs, quality of life and standard of living by establishing incentive laws for job/industry creation.

Further, when a *micro*-system viewpoint is taken, controls and laws are established to create, for the long-term, the opposite of what is intended, for example, unemployment rather than jobs. Whereas, by adopting a general systems *macro* approach, jobs are created with long-term growth in employment for society as a whole. During this process, job displacement does occur. For the long-range future, therefore, the problem is not unemployment but job displacement. Job planning and preparation and job education — some approach to life-long education — is clearly required.

Alarmed by the newly developing office of the future and the factory of the future, the Luddites are again raising a hue and cry over rapidly advancing computer and robot technology and the possibility of its creating large-scale unemployment, overlooking the fact that as more robot-like machines take over certain jobs they also amplify others. Further, as industry attempts to pull itself out of its productivity slump with new technology and to find ways to cope with the energy crisis, many workers begin to believe in the Luddite theory that technology advances create unemployment.

The remainder of this paper investigates robots and reasons why the neo-Luddites will again be proven wrong, as in the past, as the wave of new information-age technology creates a myriad of new work roles and jobs. We cannot disregard the fact that there will be short-term micro-time problems with job displacement. Nevertheless, as will be shown, the future application of advanced technology to increase the amount of work that can be done by each person on a job will not produce unemployment but rather job displacement. The individual will need to be rewarded to accept newly-created jobs and work roles. This expectation is precisely the opposite to that which motivates current "public planning" and the public policy generated as a result.

The scenario for the future is as follows. Society is creating new knowledge worldwide at an exponential rate. Currently the total knowledge base is doubling every five years and this rate will accelerate as time goes by. Two things will happen when the fruits of this knowledge are applied as technological advance. First, the new knowledge will be used to allow society to do what it must continue to do, but with greater efficiency — and displace certain jobs. In other words, fewer resources — energy, material, capital and people — will be required. Simultaneously, society will acquire the knowledge to do things which were previously impossible, things which will create new jobs, improve the quality of life and the standard of living for individuals and raise the level of civilisation in society as a whole.

This will not happen all at once. The early history of many inventions, even those whose revolutionary nature was immediately recognised by front-page publicity, shows that there was a slow, evolutionary development before any real impact was felt. One striking example is the laser, which was often referred to in its early days as "an invention looking for an application". The robot is another case in point. "Robot" was added to the world's vocabulary by the Czech playwright, Karel Capek in his 1920 play *R.U.R.* (Rossum 's Universal Robots), a satirical work about the mechanisation of society. The word is derived from the Czech *robotnik* meaning "serf" and *robota*, "compulsory labour". In *R.U.R.*, Capek visualised a "manufactured or machine-like person" capable of doing what human beings do. Ever since the robot has derived considerable notoriety from science fiction and more recently has been given leading roles in movies like "Star Wars". Only now is it receiving serious consideration as the answer to failing industrial productivity.

Robots should not be confused with automation. The technology exists, so that a prototype new industrial microprocessor-based robot could see, think, talk, learn and respond to voice commands — but it does not look like a human being. Rather, industrial robots are automated arms. Robots are rapidly finding a place for themselves in most phases of industrial activity.

Robot technology has been dubbed the science of "robotics". A better, more revealing name would be "robotronics" to emphasise their make-up of electronic circuitry.

Until now, productivity has depended primarily on advances in management, science, technology, people and policies that were designed to ensure long-term gains. Increasingly, productivity is coming to depend on robot advances. Robotics is expected to become a domestic US industry with a value exceeding $2 billion by 1990.

At the moment, the USA has the electromechanical and microprocessor technologies to maintain a worldwide edge in robotics design. But in the application of robots (not their design) the Japanese are leading. The question is whether, in this decade, the USA will gain the lead in the use of robots. Current trends indicate that the rate of growth of the robot population will be faster than that of the human population and could outstrip it by 1995. "Expert" systems are beginning to become available. Although still primitive in nature, they are expected to evolve rapidly. Is it not therefore time to map out the alternative futures they could imply?

Robotic devices that amplify people, allowing us to do with information and knowledge what experts do, are "brain amplifiers" that will create a new electronic amplified human culture — a new group of amplified people. Further, it is expected that such "expert" machines will eventually also be able to converse and exchange information with other machines. When this happens, such robots and people amplifiers will soon be capable of operating through electronic communication channels (wired or wireless) in co-operative roles — to help us and society. Such expert/robotic machines could become a future "ethnic" group of active, sensing, knowledgeable and co-operative electronic machines. Hence "ethnotronics", the word which combines ethn(ic) and (elec)tronics, coined by Professor Arthur Harkins of the University of Minnesota to describe this future category of robotic automatons.

Ready-made and fully equipped mini-factories are now on the agenda of the near future for helping to solve the problems raised for industrial companies and offices by the need for constant change and adaptation. These would be assembled on-site from fully fitted components and be ready for machinery installation within a few days. The availability of additional components and a design which allows piecemeal updating would ensure that further space and capacity requirements could be met whenever they were needed. The first units, already becoming available, are intended for permanent use and meet the relevant regulations. Yet they can also be dismantled and moved to another site quickly if necessary.

Such units are designed to complement and update conventional factory buildings, especially when long-term location is uncertain. It is expected that future institutions will be able to specify their needs at any given time by selecting from a wide range of floor, ceiling, insulation and equipment options. Most will probably require a modular incremental floor area of 500 to 1500 square feet, although larger workspace units will also become available.

Components are delivered to the site with all fittings already in place, and are simply and quickly put together. Partitions, workstations, washroom equipment, piping, water, heating, wiring power outlets, lighting and extractor fans are all factory-fitted. Even carpets, desks, chairs, filing cabinets and machine tools can be installed before delivery. Site preparation is limited to simple concrete foundations and main service links. The units could be bought, rented and/or leased.

Later, this "future history map" with its mini-factories and mini-offices, could include programmable microcomputer technology of logic, sensors and actuators for creating "smart robotic factories and offices": systems which self-adapt to changing need with self-contained machines which co-operate with one another to perform (or assist in performing) the intended function of the mini-factory or office.

Next to come will be mobile micro-factories and/or mini-factories and offices delivered complete with resident robots, factory-installed and ready for work.

Thus a scenario for ushering in a future era where future robot-manned factories and offices could be hired, fired or laid-off (just the way people are today) is already envisaged as a possibility.

INTERMISSION

The Population and Other Explosions

10

Make Room ! Make Room !

H. Harrison

Kestrel Ridge, Co Wicklow

The film "Soylent Green" shown at the Sperry Univac Seminar for the UK Press was introduced by Harry Harrison, author of *Make Room, Make Room*, on which "Soylent Green" was based. Although intended to be private, Mr Harrison has allowed us to publish this version of the vigorous commentary-at-large which he delivered on that occasion (Eds).

Of all the people here, including the employees of Computer Product X, I am the one who worked on it first. I was a technician on the Sperry Mark V computing gun-site in 1943. This was a very handsome object, all wheels and gears and cam followers. Our biggest problem was the backlash on the gear train. So I have been associated with the company for quite a while. I won't mention the company's name, though.

My topic is over-population. I am going to discuss that first and afterwards I am going to answer all of the problems that were raised earlier by the Panel. Why not? No-one else appears to be doing it. I notice that the Panel waffled on them.

First I am going to tell you about the fine film "Soylent Green". You are going to see a film which is a monument to Hollywood. In the early 50's there were no books at all about over-population. There was literally nothing. It was well before there were any popular non-fiction books on the subject. You have all seen the charts with that population bit! When I had an idea for the book there literally was nothing popular about it. All of the science fiction novels took place many years in the future. I had the very simple idea of setting the book in our own lifetimes — 20 or 30 years ahead — and show what is going to be.

But dystopia, this is what science fiction does so well: the admonitory finger. We shake it very nicely. So I said "We will look very closely into the population growth in the future". Seven years later the book was finished. It had the spectacular success science fiction usually had — sold four or five copies in total secrecy. Some years later I had a call from a firm of lawyers in Hollywood. They said, "Listen, we're interested in having an option on one of your old books". I said, "Oh, that's very good". "And we are thinking of buying an option to make a film, possibly, if you sell it cheaply enough." I don't remember the name of the firm but I remember their trademark. It had a big "U" over a wood screw. It looked like Screw-You Productions.

You may think that you know high finance and important journals and all that. You have never been near the real twisters in the world. They don't want to give you any money, they want to keep it for themselves. This company, as soon as they bought the option of my book, sold all the rights to MGM for one dollar. It turned out it was MGM all the time. And the producer there, Walter Selzer, and old Chuck Heston, they had a production firm. They wanted to make a film. The secretary (always ask the secretary) of the chap in charge knew everything — she said, "Oh yes, five or six years they've been trying—" Well they didn't tell me about that. They were flogging *my* book for five or six years to MGM.

So they took it to MGM and MGM said: "Over-population? We're not interested in that, not over-population. Sorry about that." They went away and they got a hack to write a screen play (whose name I will not tell you — perhaps it was Stanley Greenberg). He may be the world's worst writer. The writers are queueing up for the job. He said, "But MGM doesn't want to do anything on over-population — not important enough. So I'll do something on cannibalism." He literally invented it. If you read the book there's nobody eating bodies in there. In the film, you see it in the first reel. MGM said, "Yes, my God, cannibalism. That's socially important. They'll eat that up."

So they had me down there and one clause in my contract was that I couldn't say one word about anything. But they were financially right. No author in the world will allow anyone to screw his book up completely. They showed me a screenplay. It was all wrong. I thought I'd straighten these guys out. And they said "Harry, no money".

Walter Selzer, my old buddy, was coming round and saying, "How are you Harry you son of a bitch? You're costing us a lot of money". "Good," I said, "this is the best news I've had in a long time." Because I wrote about 19 letters. But I still wasn't being paid. I said, "Congratulations to you and your script writer. You have bought this book for this outrageous sum because it takes place in the near future. That's what it's all about. It is about the world in 20 or 30 years. But this dummy has not dated it in any way whatsoever. It could be a million years in the future."

So Walter Selzer said, "Hell, it's going to cost us a lot of money. We got Chuck Braverman in — you know Chuck Braverman?" I said "no". He said, "You know Chuck Braverman. He did the history of the world on television in two minutes."

"Oh *that* Chuck Braverman. How could I have forgotten that Chuck Braverman?" As you'll see in the film tonight, he did the opening credits which they'd forgotten to write into the script. He did it only with stills. Music over. No voices. They intercut a lot of pictures. They showed a Wild West, the old TV cowboys and Indians and farmers breaking the sod and building up to waggon-wheels and cars and then they switch into New York in the year 1999. Very nicely done.

Then, still not being paid, mind you, I went down to the set where they were shooting this picture. What joy! "We've set the set Harry. Great, this is real design. This is for the meatleggers." The meatleggers! Meat's in very short supply in the future, you know. They were selling dogs' legs and things. So here is this meatlegger — like a bootlegger selling meat.
"Look," I said. "What's this?"
"That's the meatlegger's shop."
"What's that on the counter?" It's America, mind you. It's not Britain or tired old France or broken-down Italy, it's America. "So what's that?"
"It's the plastic bags they put the meat in."
About 480 plastic bags there. I ask "So where the hell do you get the plastic bags from? Petroleum, kid, it ran out. Do you know what goes on outside the United States?"
. "No," he said.
"In Italy or France" I said, "you go shopping and take a bag with you."
"They don't give you bags?"
"No, they don't give you bags."
"How backward can you get!" They threw out the plastic bags.

Edward G. Robinson's there, and I keep on seeing a lot of things going on, you know. I give out copies of the book, that's always great. The people doing the actual film work, the technicians, in Hollywood they are good people. The financial people are just like what President Johnson said about President Ford — he couldn't walk and chew gum at the same time. These guys know how to make money and screw people. But they rely upon technicians to make good films. And these guys are really good: they are interested, bright, alert people, good people. So I said "Read this book".

They did a lot of stuff on the set that wasn't in this rotten screenplay by this writer Stanley Greenberg, whose name I forget. Edward G. Robinson comes up to the director, Dick Fleischer, and says, "Dick, I read the script and I don't understand my role." With good reason. There was nothing there to understand. Robinson was a very good actor, a very good man. The tragic thing was that he died before the picture was released. And in the film, which you'll see, he dies. We were all very upset about that, but you couldn't

just take it out, it's vital to the film. So Robinson and I had lunch and I said, "Look. This thing takes place in 1999. You are the only person in this film who has lived in the world that we now know. Who has seen food, meat, beef steaks. Who has lived in a decent world. In fact, to tell you the truth, you are me. In the book, I am the old shag who wanders around there. My age, my military background, everything. The spectre from the past. Living in this horrible present." I told him about that and he said: "Why that's a very good idea. Why didn't they tell me? It wasn't in the script."
"I know it wasn't in the script. There's nothing in the script."

It was a closed set. Which means literally no guests, no visitors, just the technicians. There were about 35 people there. The grips, the microphone booms, best boys and everything. These guys as usual were bored to hell — you know, picking their teeth, yawning. And they shot the key scene which you'll see about halfway through. And the key scene runs for two or three minutes. They actually had to memorise lines for this. It's very hard to do for some actors. But they shoot the whole scene. Then do intercuts afterwards. They did the key scene and Robinson muffed a line. Robinson said, "Listen. I'm 79 years old. I like to waste a little bit of film. Right, right, go ahead." So they did it a second time. And the third time he took this really dreary scene, which you'll see in the film, badly written, nothing, and for once in his life, old wooden face had to actually act a little bit — eating food, reacting. And it's not in the script. They're not saying anything, just Robinson acting and inventing the role on camera. They went through this whole scene, finished it. Fleisher said "Cut" and all these bored technicians actually clapped. It's very rare in the cinema, let me tell you.

What you are going to see is a sort of half good film. Done by nice people. Done well. And it is also a film that is the essence of science fiction — the good stuff. Not the sort of stuff other people write, the stuff I write. What it is is background as foreground. The world that the story takes place in is what the film is about. Not the stupid things these people are doing in the foreground. And remember, many people who saw it and said, "It's a pretty bad film, you know, I didn't really like it", about a week later came back and said, "You know I woke up the other night. I dreamt about that film."

This is the hortatory thing that good science fiction can do. A technique that goes right back to Wells and Verne. It dramatises the situation. We explain the unexplainable. We solve all your problems for you. Your good science fiction has a residual shock content. It doesn't have to have much else up front. Except emotion. My old friend Van Vogt wrote a book called *The World of Null-A* and in it he had a device (this was written way back in the 40's) which was an answering machine or a speaking phone book on the desk in the hotel room. And one of the more serious literary reviewers, Damon Knight, said "This is nonsense. You can't construct a machine like that. You can't put that much memory in a machine that small. That's just nonsense." Well Van is mad and he was right. Damon was very accurate and he was completely wrong.

This talk today brought to mind London years ago. Do you remember Piccadilly Circus having a great big sign up one side, on the north side, EXPORT OR DIE? I was walking with Brian Aldiss one day and I said, "Brian, what happened to the sign?" He said, "We died." What's the answer for Britain? There are a number of solutions. Declare war on the United States — and lose. And get reparations. But it *could* be no joke. What if we win?

That's one answer. Let's consider some other ones. I'm very serious about this. Let me give you an example. I have a friend who's a Greek shipowning millionaire. Now *that* is the hardest nosed type of person in the entire world. They can teach us all a lot. I was on his ship once in Rotterdam and there was a lot of vibration in the prop shaft. We went to look at it. There is a little motor, a motor about as big as a watermelon rotates the propeller about once every five minutes. We were in ballast so the propeller was out of the water. The ship's engineer was an old German and he showed that one of the tips of the blade was bent, they had touched the bottom in Rio de Janiero in the river. The owner asked, "How much does a new bearing cost?" "Eight hundred pounds," he was told. "How much?", "Eight hundred pounds." Off we sailed. Across the Atlantic. Because the sums were working out the proper way. We vibrated and wrecked the bearing — but did not go into dry dock. And that's the way you make money if you are a Greek shipowner.

People asked me why do all the grain ships head for Rotterdam. I'll tell you why. The Germans destroyed it. They came down and levelled the thing but they missed London. Too big, the defences too good. If only the Germans had blown up the London docks they might be modern today. About 10 years ago *The Observer* showed a picture of a steam winch in the London docks. Wooden docks built in 1895 were still being used.

That's the technology we have to abandon somehow. If we could. In Rotterdam they blew the whole thing up. The Dutch in their own simple way rebuilt the town, a very lovely town. They put in floating grain elevators in the harbour. Now, if you want to unload your grain anywhere in Northern Europe, other than Rotterdam, you pull up, you pay your wharfage fees. You've got a shovel. Every day you're paying for what gets shovelled into the freight cars. Not in Rotterdam. You tie up in the outer harbour. No wharfage fees. And there you have a floating grain elevator. Inside are two great big vacuum cleaners. Like big Hoovers. There are two men who work 24 hours a day. They pay them overtime. And they walk up and pump the whole thing in about 20 hours into the elevator and away your ship goes.

And what happens to the grain? You might very well ask. I'll tell you what happens. Down the Rhine, all over Northern Europe, come little flatboats,

little barges, with mum and dad running the thing. They come up there — they've got time on their hands, they're not in a big hurry, the things are not very fast — and the grain is blown down into the barges. Any kind of cargo, anywhere in Northern Europe, goes through Rotterdam. For the simple reason that the old Dutchies got it right. If it's not grain, they do cement. Sand. A very new invention there. They call it an Archimedian screw. They put the thing in and it takes everything out. So Britain can learn by that. We need more Archimedian screws. Here's a few more things we also need.
1. Declare war on the United States.
2. Blow up the London Docks.
3. Abolish the class system: that comes next, you know.
4. Get rid of the private schools — that has to come.
5. Put in comprehensives. People will have them, like it or not. They have them in the States, no problem. Abolish the old nonsense of private education, spending money on your children when you have already paid taxes for their education. We want a lot of people climbing up each other's backs. We want life and death. American executives die at 42, or thereabouts. Of coronaries. English executives go on to 89. So — more heart attacks — and competition.
6. Level Oxford and Cambridge; make them into museums — or turn them into technical schools. Hire the staff of MIT to come over and re-jig the thing completely.
7. No more product research. Let someone do it, then license it like the Japanese. If you like research, do blue sky. We have to have that. But *really* blue sky. A few people here know John Pearce, Dr Pearce from Bell Labs, a very lovely guy and a fine science fiction writer as well. We were sitting in Bell Labs one day and I said, "What are you doing over there?" He said, "Well, over there is Product Development, where they drop telephones four million times. If they break they make a bit stronger telephone." I said "I understand that. But what are you doing here?" He said, "Nothing at all. Blue sky. We give anyone money if they have a way out, new idea. And they do it. But don't tell them upstairs. That's all we do. Machine translation. Dot recognition . All that sort of strange thing." I said, "How do you live?" He said, "Well once a year, on the average, one idea comes up and makes a lot of money for Bell Labs. And empirically it works." So *only* blue sky in research please: scrap the rest.

So now we have a plan. Level the public schools. Have a lot of blue sky research. Buy from the Japs and the Americans. Adopt their monetary class system, abolish the British one. You know, in Britain everything's sex or class when you come down to it. We know where the action is. Keep sex, abolish class. That's the answer. Any questions about how to do that? I'll be happy to take questions from the floor on the mechanics of this process.

Are there any questions? Are there any answers? One thing about the old science fiction, we have difficult questions, easy answers.

We are a vanishing breed. I mean science fiction writers are, they're vanishing very quickly. The good ones are. And I'm very unhappy about it. But we've served our purpose. The whole world's a science fiction world and all the problems are very simple to answer if you phrase the question right. The question then demands an anthropological answer: Where did culture come from? We invented culture. And we can change it. If you invent it once, you can change it once.

I'm a good American capitalist — but I lived many years in Socialist countries, in Denmark particularly where socialism works. Marx was wrong. They do blend. There is no black and white answer. You can have capitalist socialism and socialist capitalism working together. I remember in New York years ago, a British MP was on a radio programme. The interviewer was Henry Morgan. Morgan asked him, "Well, what political party are you in?" He said, "I'm a Tory." And Morgan said, "Is that like a Republican?" "No, he said. "We have Labour, which is sort of Left and the Tory party is to the right but both of them are far to the Left of your Democratic party." We can live with Socialism, we live in Britain. Let's face the fact that the government has to do something besides sell council houses and encourage unemployment. That's not what they're in there for. They weren't elected for that. And there are other things they can do. One thing is face reality, including the reality of R & D. They could send out everybody all over the world to find the D. Bring it back in. Get rid of the class system. Change the culture. Build the paradise Britain could be — a scientific utopia at last.

PART III

Impact on Life and Work

11

The Emerging Challenge

Ian Lloyd, MP.

House of Commons, Westminster

Members of the lower House generally address three kinds of audience. The *converted,* the *inverted* and the *preverted.* The converted are those who come to have their convictions reinforced. The inverted are those who display their convictions with all the enthusiasm of an angry hedgehog. The preverted are those who have been perverted by ideology, who invite you down because they are confident they can stare through your intellectual clothing and derive some cynical amusement from the unconvincing skeleton of logical argument which they discern beneath the political camouflage. It is rather important to keep these three audiences very clearly distinguished. The mixture of cajolery, persuasion and attack is very different for each one.

The readers to whom this paper is addressed do not fit easily into any of those categories. All know a great deal more about information technology and computers than I do. They include several whose ideas I purloin with total lack of shame in my persistent, if somewhat forlorn, efforts to bring the message of information technology to my political colleagues. Teachers, these days, are prone to refer to the "chalk face", thereby seeking some identity with coal miners and, perhaps, to convince us that the output of an ounce of chalk deserves to be rewarded by the community in much the same way as that of a ton of coal. But here I am addressing two very unusual groups. Most of those who are talking to you can be said to be working at the "silicon face", whereas those who are listening labour diligently at the "type face". But perhaps that is obsolete technology and from now on we should refer to the scene of their endeavours as the "video face"!

Whether we work at the video face or the microphone, whether we use a pen, a light pen or a laser, the one thing we certainly have in common is the emerging challenge which envelopes the whole of our society in this remarkable year, which saw the prodigious achievement of solar powered flight across the Channel coincide with the collapse of social order in parts of several of Britain's major cities.

The title — "The Emerging Challenge" — is a broad one. I expect that each of you will have his favourite candidate and that you will disagree as much about candidates as you will about consequences. But I would be surprised if there was not general agreement that the title which Barbara Tuchman chose for her brilliant book about the 14th Century — *A Distant Mirror* — was well chosen in view of her belief that the 14th and 20th Centuries have much in common: violent change, mindless and indiscriminate violence, the appearance of new technologies, great intellectual controversies and dramatic population changes.

It will perhaps be useful if I endeavour to analyse the challenge which I see emerging in a number of different contexts. I am taking for granted that the challenge and the opportunity presented by microelectronics is common ground, even if we find ourselves at different ends of the spectrum in which this phenomenon is perceived. I propose to try and set the scene in the political, social and industrial context and to evaluate some of the problems. The problems I discern are not necessarily the most important; but they may shroud others which are. I shall be mentioning Japan, but I do not feel myself to be an authority on that country, not having visited it since early 1977. In terms of modern Japan that is a very long time.

The phenomenon or unit of measure which I find common to all these problems is disparity. We are familiar in Britain with disparities in income and wealth, about which as a nation we have an almost neurotic preoccupation, a preoccupation which our major schools of economics have spread, via the gospels of Marx, Laski, Tawney and others to the Third World.

That has created an acute consciousness of what is, in fact, an entirely different phenomenon, the disparities in national incomes per head. We are now becoming more acutely conscious than before of disparities in *natural* economic endowment, thanks to phenomena such as Arabia's oil, South Africa's platinum, asbestos and gold (amongst other riches), and more recently Britain's North Sea. We are beginning to become conscious of disparities in such totally unalterable endowments as available sunlight and indigenous coal. Both these will lend themselves to redistribution mechanisms.

We are also becoming conscious of disparities in scientific, technological and innovatory capacity. Though these lend themselves to redistribution by entirely different procedures, there is a suspicion abroad that those who have created these machines of technological evolution will not easily or rapidly be overhauled by those who have not.

Considerations of this kind carry us rapidly to the central preoccupations of the Brandt Report and the kind of arguments which lie at the heart of the philosophy known as the New International Economic Order. I have been fairly close to that order at one or two international conferences and I find little to distinguish it from the old saying, "what's mine is mine, and what's yours ought to be mine too". But there are serious and important problems which disparities between geographical areas require us to address if social and international tensions, however irrational or illogical their basis may be, are to be kept within the limited scope of political initiative and imagination, both of which are extraordinarily fragile mechanisms. It is Bertrand de Jouvenel who has reminded us of the real dangers lurking here.

"Nothing is more dangerous for psychological equilibrium than the launching of heady promises incapable of implementation. It is one of the tasks of those who envisage the future to zone off the unattainable. Many pleasing prospects are irreconcilable with likely human behaviour; the sociologist and the political scientist must here weed out the improbable, just as the economist must cut, in view of their investment costs, some of the technological forecaster's visions."

One of the most challenging and dangerous of all disparities, of which we are all acutely conscious, is that of military power. The civilised world (and much of the uncivilised world, if one dare draw such a distinction) squanders a high proportion of its wealth on maintaining this tension. We are all much more skilled at embellishing the mirror image of risk and threat than we are at illuminating the growing areas of interdependence, common interest and common danger. If the UN were not such a hare-brained organisation, I would strongly support a proposal that the major powers should agree on a self-imposed tax equal to a rising percentage of their military expenditure, the proceeds of which would be devoted to international projects of general benefit to the human race. But I fear the human race is simply not capable, yet, of handling funds on this scale in a manner which gives such projects immunity from political interference, drawing its motive power not only from the inclination to meddle but from the principle of *juste retour*.

I have mentioned, in a general sense, disparities in scientific and technological capacity. There is an important sub-set of this which is the disparity in the capacity which different nations and communities have to perceive, develop and exploit information technology. This may well provide its own counterweight, but in the critical period of transition which we are entering it will be important that the institutions which can exploit information technology to the full should not be inhibited by the cries of anguish that will be heard from those which do not or cannot.

There are two other major disparities which I would like to mention before I endeavour to draw one or two conclusions and suggest one or two courses of action. The first is a disparity which has not, so far, found itself in the line of sight of the many weapons to be found in the egalitarian armoury.

That is because the target is probably rather hard to hit unless one has the intellectual equivalent of an infra-red night-sight. I am referring to disparities in resilience and adaptability. In a revolutionary age this is a critical resource for any community.

I would not like to suggest, without a very thorough examination of the problem, the extent to which these qualities in any society are the product of *individual* character and resourcefulness as opposed to *institutional* flexibility, incentive and drive. But what is quite clear at the moment is that the United Kingdom is acutely aware of the need for a more rapid response to the emerging challenge than we seem able to generate. I am quite convinced that the emergence of a new political party is primarily a reflection of the general concern which the nation has over its inability to proceed rapidly and effectively from the calm logic of analysis to the noisy clatter of direct, convincing and effective action. I believe the diagnosis to be correct, as is the nation's instinctive judgment.

That is not to say I am publicly abandoning my own political beliefs. Rather I am stating my conviction, held ever since I entered politics, that it is ultimately the party — or, to be more flexible, political force — which recognises these imperatives and provides a convincing and relevant philosophy of change, which will exercise power in the late 1980's and early 90's. If no party or institution does so, including the Social Democrats, then in my judgment the political process will continue its headlong progress down the cul de sac named CHARADE, and the institutions we serve will become increasingly a mere symbolic representation of power that has moved elsewhere.

On this subject, de Jouvenel again has something to tell us, although the conclusion is a bit disturbing:

"It seems that the exercise of power, which is like a great stretching out of the hand, is accompanied by a shrinking of vision. Perhaps the reason is that the hand is not merely the muscle for manipulation, but also nerve for the sense of touch, so the immediate pressures the hand encounters or provokes inform the governor's brain and there extinguish the eye's information, vision. Be this as it may, the man with the least foresight is, other things being equal, the man in the seat of power."

That disturbing observation brings me to my last disparity, disparity in conceptual models of the real world. In recent years I have become acutely conscious of how much the political process is dominated by this phenomenon. The most influential is the model disparity that is due to information differences. The looter in Liverpool who, as one commentator put it when endeavouring to draw comparison with the Watts riots in Los Angeles, "essentially wants a free colour television": the shopkeeper, the man who insures the shopkeeper, the community worker, the local authority who raises the rates to back him up with services, the insurance market, the local police, the Chief Constable and the Home Secretary all have a very different model of the situation.

As new levels of perception are attained in the hierarchy, so the constraints on self-interest increase in number and importance. But what has changed in our society is complexity. The significance of a "little local difficulty" in a mediaeval village was far less than a similar event in a major modern city, magnified as it is by the most socially infectious technology that man has known — television. Most models of society are based on the inverted pyramid of self-interest. One of the major contributions of information technology must surely be to improve the procedures which ensure that when there is perceived disparity between the local model and the national decision (as is increasingly probable) there will be confidence in the procedures and those who operate them. For change generates insecurity if the model disparity is too great and insecurity leads on rapidly to fear, rigidity, inflexibility and finally loss of confidence, aggression and violence.

In this context great disparities are displayed by political models, which tend to rely on powerful self-reinforcing mechanisms, rejecting information that does not reinforce and accepting that which does irrespective of its merit or relevance. Although conflict is resolved more often than the media may suggest or the public perceive, major political philosophies and systems tend to be intellectual black holes which finally collapse under their own weight. Unless they are constantly refreshed by new models and new model sub-systems of the real world, which is changing at an unprecedented rate, our present political philosophies will become very vulnerable. If the fashionable word "pragmatic" means anything then it describes precisely that process of refreshment.

Let me illustrate this by a few comments on the famous "limits of growth" controversy. It is much easier to forecast the exhaustion of any raw material than the likely technical solutions, adaptations or behaviour modifications which will falsify a prediction of impending disaster. But the models generated by fearful environmentalists can often be highly pessimistic; and if governments over-react to presumptions that one or other raw material is about to be exhausted (e.g., oil and gas), the economic consequences can be devastating, the social consequences unpredictable and the political consequences unmeasurable on the Richter scale of human reaction.

It is at least arguable that the revolution of rising expectations has been aborted by environmental restriction, bureaucratic intervention, entrepreneurial lethargy and institutional arthritis. When the technological pessimism underlying these ecofrantic attitudes is eventually revealed by events, those espousing these causes may have to carry a great weight of responsibility. The difficulty is that we cannot say they are wrong, for their arguments are swathed in convincing plausibilities and half truths. If we admit they are right, the challenge to political leadership and process, especially in the great democracies, would exceed anything we have experienced outside time of war.

The questions we are left with are not easily answered:

- Which of these challenges is the most serious and threatening?
- Which can or should be reduced by constructive action?
- Where, with or without information technology and computers, might we hope to break out of the vicious circle of human intransigence, ignorance reinforced by vested political or economic interest, cynicism and, indeed, despair?

Earlier I mentioned Japan, for the industrial efficiency of that country is now becoming a perceived threat to much Western industry. I do not believe that Japan is the most important challenge to our complacency. Japan's performance is the result of a superior response, in many ways, in that country to the same array of challenges which we are all facing. Let me give three examples, one trivial, one far reaching and one pertinent to this conference.

The trivial one is a plastic bag from Sony which is ornamented with the slogan: RESEARCH MAKES THE DIFFERENCE. The far reaching example is represented by the fact that Japan's energy consumption in steel manufacture is the lowest in the world. Most of that performance has been achieved since the onset of the first "oil shock" as the price crisis is known in Japan. The consumption of oil, diesel, LPG and other petroleum-derived fuels has been reduced to *half* 1973 levels. Thirty out of 44 blast furnaces have stopped using oil and top-recovery-pressure turbines, using pressurised gas from furnace tops, are now producing 320 mW of electricity.

The overall result is impressive. If we take the energy consumption per ton of steel in Japan as 100 in 1979, the figures for West Germany are 115, France 120, the USA 144 and the UK 156. No subsidy of energy costs can or should be asked to provide a solution to a disparity on this scale. Moreover the Japanese steel industry has published its target, which is to reduce energy requirements per ton of crude steel from 5.5 in kilocalories per ton to 5Kc.

The pertinent example is, as many might expect, the fifth generation computer strategy. I have read the JIPDEC description. It is technically vague and uninformative but I sense that the Japanese believe that, with sufficient R & D thrust, computers can be given a push beyond the improvement which greater chip density and reliability might give to reach a new level of comprehending and communicating power. If they do achieve this, as I suspect they may, it will be because they seem to have discovered a way of combining essentially Western skills and technology with an efficiency which we ourselves cannot match, at least for the time being.

I do not, however, believe that this lead is necessarily predestined or irretrievable. Either Western Europe or North America alone has the scientific, intellectual and industrial resources to define similar objectives and achieve them more rapidly; but NOT if we continue to accept the institutional restraints and sub-optimised solutions that we have adopted so far. It is for these reasons that I am somewhat depressed by such documents as a recent Confederation of British Industry paper entitled *The Japanese Challenge,* with a sub-title, *Plain Speaking to the Japanese.* The CBI argues that Japan is "exporting unemployment as well as goods to Europe". This is dangerous nonsense. Imports do not establish a bridgehead in competitive markets unless the indigenous industries have exposed a flank. What you usually find is that:

(a) The investment pattern has been totally inadequate
(b) The R & D percentage is grotesquely small
(c) The productivity growth rate has been negligible
(d) The market judgment has been faulty and/or a change of market scale or size overlooked.

Was it Mort Sahl who said "we have found the enemy and he is us"? The plain speaking should invariably be to ourselves.

As a nation, we are not good listeners. British governments were warned about the robotics challenge in 1977 (at the latest). The Secretary of State for Trade and Industry confessed in public at the despatch box in 1979 that he wondered what the term meant! In 1981 the Prime Minister is lending her personal authority to British robotics demonstrations, but can we now, seriously, expect to catch up? Yes — if!

I suspect, however, that a preoccupation with Japan would now be dangerous. Recently I returned from an intensive two-week examination of what the USA is doing in the field of energy conservation and alternative energy systems, particularly solar. Before leaving, I spent a fascinating day talking to some of the front runners in computer education in schools. The progress in some areas is staggering and it would surprise me very much if the US did not overtake Japan in a number of significant areas during the 1980's and 90's. Bully for the Anglo Saxon world! But I very much suspect that by the end of the 80's these rat race judgments, based on frontier psychology applied incorrectly to an interdependent world, will be irrelevant. The OECD countries, at least, which include Japan, should perceive that they face an identical challenge and that the response is likely to be inadequate if we cannot develop, fairly quickly, satisfactory procedures to generalise the research, the benefits, the solutions and the mechanism which create efficient economies in fuel and raw material. The key to all lies, of course, in information technology.

I end, as I began, with Bertrand de Jouvenel:

"In a regular system men deliberately enclose themselves in a Universe of restricted possibilities... In between the unachievable and the unchanging stands the ample zone of feasible futures."

We must expand that Universe with greater courage. We must enter the danger zone of feasible futures by drawing more effectively on the resources and skills which we either command or can, with imagination and will, create.

12

Training for Multi-Career Lives

Philip Virgo

National Computing Centre

Abstract

Most of the basic skills needed over the next hundred years can be predicted with reasonable certainty but many of the precise trades and professions cannot. "Age-Related Careers" is an employment strategy which can handle such uncertainty. Fundamental changes to the education system are necessary. Information Technology makes these possible at economic cost. Encouragement and favourable publicity are more effective weapons of persuasion than coercion.

Introduction

Some time ago I heard Ian Lloyd say that our greatest requirement from the so-called Microelectronics Revolution was automated abattoirs for sacred cows. Nowhere is the slaughter of sacred cows more necessary than in our education system. Its inability to cope with change must not deny us the benefits which the new technology is bringing to other societies. I shall begin with some comments on the role of the education system in the past, and how it must adapt if we are to have any worthwhile future.

We can predict with reasonable certainty most of the basic skills we are going to need over the next hundred years or so. Where we cannot, we need a strategy to handle uncertainty. I will propose the strategy of "Age-Related Careers" and will then discuss some of the fundamental institutional changes that will be necessary and how the new technologies can help.

In conclusion, I will identify some of the obstacles we must overcome on the way and how those in the information industry can contribute.

The Role of the Educational System

Two hundred years ago was the take-off period for Britain's first industrial revolution: the take-off that transformed England, Scotland, Wales and Northern Ireland from an economic condition akin to that of modern India, famines and all, to one akin to that of Hong Kong today.

There may be extremes of poverty in Hong Kong but few actually die of starvation. The last English famine in which whole villages died was in the middle of the 18th century. The last Scottish famine was in the 1820's.

There are many myths about the consequences of that revolution but few about its causes and course. An ambitious and underprivileged (but also undertaxed) class of entrepreneurs in an unregulated, unplanned environment, sought to buy social respectability by making money out of providing the materials and munitions to enable Britain to fight each of its continental neighbours in turn. In doing so they managed to create a forty year long investment-led boom, ending only with the post Napoleonic War slump in the 1820's. Then another long boom followed as railway mania gripped the country, fostered by the same group.

We have read much about the evils of 19th century education: it is worth thinking about the education system in the 18th century, the education of the men who made the first industrial revolution. Since the Royal Navy was the only service fit for a gentleman of courage (the Army was discredited as a continental-style threat to civil liberties), and since the specialist naval academies of the 19th century had yet to be founded, elementary engineering and scientific mathematics ranked higher than latin and greek in the education of a gentleman. Meanwhile, the Quakers and Non-conformists of the Midlands and North West, excluded from grammar schools and universities, ran more Trade, Commerce and Artisan schools than the rest of Europe added together. The poor condition of the English grammar schools and universities was no hindrance since only clergymen looked to them for inspiration.

In the 19th century, with the founding of naval academies, religious tolerance and the new found respectability of Army and Empire, the picture changed dramatically. The children and grandchildren of the men who made the first Industrial Revolution could enjoy the clergyman's education of latin, greek and theology in reformed grammar schools and universities. Trade, commerce and engineering were relegated to the ragged aspirants of the Workers' Educational Association despite the complaints of boring foreigners, like Prince Albert.

Meanwhile the rest of Europe, with no world-wide Empire to administer and having to innovate rather than live off past innovation, learned from the Quakers and the Non-conformists and made no such mistakes. Thus the seeds of our century long decline were sown in the classrooms of Dr Arnold's Rugby rather than on the playing fields of Eton.

Now that we have spent our inheritance and must once more earn a living, we can do a lot worse than to look again at the institutions of the 18th century. We must recognise that education should not be a joy for the few and a trial of youth for the many but a lifelong experience for all, as and when the opportunity arises. The young should acquire a desire and an ambition to "improve" themselves and should associate learning with reward, not with examination trauma.

The men of the late 18th century shared many of our problems. They knew the world was about to change but did not know in which direction: unemployed anarchic bloodshed alternating with tyranny as in France, or hard-working republican virtue as in America. Some thought the steam engine would usher in an age of leisure (or mass unemployment), others were confident that work might change (from brawn to brain maybe), but that it would still be necessary and that the basic skills needed were likely to be much the same.

The latter were right. Two centuries later we are still looking forward to an age of leisure. I venture to predict that in two hundred years our descendants will still be looking. Meanwhile, it is our duty to do at least as well, and preferably better, than our ancestors in preparing for change.

Future Skill Requirements

We shall still have to work for a living but the nature of that work is likely to change and we cannot predict many of the changes with much certainty.

We can no longer afford to spend one or two decades of detailed preparation for a single life-long career progression. Instead we should aim, like our ancestors, to impart those basic skills almost certain to be in continuous demand and to build a system capable of responding rapidly to change, and disseminating new skills to *any* age group when necessary.

This is all the more important since our education systems appear incapable of supplying the skills currently in demand, let alone new ones. Where we can predict major new industries, such as computer assisted video entertainment and learning, mass produced electronics-based medical aids, biotechnology and telematics, we, unlike the Japanese, are incapable of delivering the appropriate career preparation or retraining. We even appear to have lost the ability to impart the basic commercial skills necessary to create fast-growing new businesses. If we do not change our educational systems to produce generations capable of competing with the Japanese, the Germans and the Americans, we shall lose out on the millions of wealth-creating jobs potentially available. In consequence, we will not have the resources to support the idle decline, like that of 19th century Spain, that will be our lot.

For some of the new industries we can specify the technician training requirements in fair detail: for video they are akin to film production on a very tight budget and time schedule, for biotechnology they are a cross between process engineering and brewing real ale.

But our training facilities are far too thin on the ground. We need packaged course material for mass delivery but no commercial organisation will invest money in developing such material when it will be pirated as soon as it is supplied. Copyright reform is essential.

We can also list the basic skills that everyone will need for the office, factory and home of the future.

In the office of the future with its video workstations, electronic filing systems and telecommunications links, technical literacy and dexterity will, of course, be necessary. However, the ability to think clearly and express oneself accurately and concisely, to get sensible answers from the all-embracing information databases, will be even more important. The GIGO principle (garbage in leads to garbage out) has its counterpart in information science where a woolly question will produce a meaningless flood of irrelevant data. The problem with modern management is already too much rather than too little information, and computers often do not help. If the West Yorkshire police had had computerised information systems they might still be looking for the Yorkshire Ripper. The uniformed policemen who finally caught him would have been too busy helping administer the database to leave the police station.

Without old-fashioned linguistic skills, as tested in a "comprehension" exercise, and without the ability to frame an intelligent question and to recognise a sensible answer, the new Information Technology can all too often make things worse rather than better.

Similarly, the ability of the technology to perform instant statistical analyses will make essential the knowledge of how much or now little those statistical analyses mean. However, to Reading, Writing and 'Rithmetic we need to add three new skills. The first is the concept of simulation. It begins with the concept of a computer model analogous to the real world in the way that a meccano crane or a model railway is to the real thing but should lead on to the understanding of how computer models can be run backwards from the desired ends so as to identify and test the logic, assumptions and premisses which lead to that end. This may well have a dramatic effect on the way we think, since in many modelling exercises the significant variables turn out to be unmeasurable, or based on hunches — value judgments or even moral principles where mere logic is of limited value. A case in point is provided by the so-called "social" costs which befuddle public enquiries and motorway or airport planning exercises.

The second new skill is problem structuring and solving, and in particular group problem solving of the kind used by the class "cheat" who knows which classmate's homework to copy for each subject. By definition, this skill is selected *against* by our educational system and thus its most skilled practitioners frequently end up working against society as rebels, criminals or parasites rather than in the key management posts which they should occupy.

Thorough and imaginative approaches to group problem identification, structuring and solving are going to be essential in the factory of the future where quality control will be one of the main occupations. Ensuring that complex computer-controlled products are functioning correctly, and that the specification of the control program is adequate under all circumstances even the most unlikely, may well become the most labour-intensive part of the production process.

Outside the factory the maintenance men who are to service the multiplicity of devices from automatic doors and light sensitive blinds, to mass produced powered limbs and living aids for the elderly and rheumatic, will need similar skills since remote or automatic fault diagnosis will often be inadequate.

Even in modern Britain with the lowest proportion of self-employed and small business proprietors of any country outside the Communist block, the basic commercial skills of running a business are needed by more than one in eight of the population. If one accepts the thesis that most of the new jobs are going to be created in small businesses, private sector personal services and the informal economy, and that in the future more than one in four of the population will, at some time in their lives, run their own business, a revival of "commercial" and "business" studies as subjects to be taught to all in school is necessary. Their current absence from the curriculum condemns the school leaver to servitude, unemployment or, at best, several wasted years learning for himself what he should have been taught at school. If education is truly a preparation for life, this absence cannot be defended outside a Communist society.

The impact of technology on the personal service jobs, from street cleaning to street walking, will be negligible. Gardeners, window cleaners, plumbers, cooks and so on will be needed as much as they are now.

At the other end of society, however, the changes may well be traumatic as expert systems render obsolete the book-learning and machine-like logical skills of most lawyers, accountants and consultants.

The robot that can sweep a factory floor or weed a garden is at least a century off. But most of the work of the Inland Revenue, most administrative accountancy, the routine conveyancing that keeps most solicitors in business, even some of the complex diagnoses that elevate the Harley Street consultant above the local general practitioner, can already be done faster and more accurately by computer. In twenty years perhaps the local tax office will give an instant response to your query and the general practitioner will no longer refer you to the hospital for analyses and diagnoses but will do them himself with the aid of his surgery expert systems backed by links to national epidemiological and other databases.

There will be a great many skilled professionals checking the systems and equipment used, but status will pass to the man doing the job that no mere machine can do. Caring for an incontinent cripple will be a more valued task than diagnosing some rare cancer or tropical fever.

The possession of book-learning or logical reasoning ability will lose status just as literacy did when everyone could read and write. The human touches of sympathy and creativity will be the hallmark of the high status job.

The trauma of this *reversal in our hierarchy of status* cannot be overestimated. At one fell swoop it removes the rationale behind most of our educational values, with their emphasis on memorising large quantities of verbal information, from irregular verbs to the naming of parts, the ability to follow complicated logical processes, quote obscure documents or recognise unusual sets of symptoms. It removes the main justification for the examination treadmill to which we chain our adolescent youth in a set of puberty rites crueller than those of primitive Africa. At least in Africa they do not label any of the participants as failures!

Rather than develop the learning skills of the few, we must train those of the many so that they can use the artificial intelligence and memory aids that will be available for all. Thus machines will take over the menial logic and memory tasks, leaving us humans with the interesting problems of judgment and the many interpersonal and service tasks which they may aid but cannot take over.

These changes are going to take time — certainly decades, possibly even centuries. But they are going to be fundamental and many new trades, skills and professions are going to be required on the way. However, unless we recognise and accept the transience of many of these new trades, we are going to condemn future generations to the fate of the handloom weavers. The handloom weavers were called into existence by the availability of cheap yarn, but were reluctant or unable to change trade when machine weaving became practicable. Their fate gives a stark lesson that a single career change may not be enough in an age of fundamental structural evolution.

The handloom weavers' modern counterparts could well be the commercial programmers and analysts of today. Called into existence by the availability of expensive computers which had to be used efficiently, they may well be reluctant or unable to change trades when packaged software on cheap computers has made their particular branch of computing skills redundant.

Age Related Careers?

Given the uncertainty as to the duration of requirement for specific trades, should we not prepare our school leavers for those jobs known to be in current — but possibly temporary — demand, while reserving certain careers, where demand is likely to be constant, for older generations who, because of family commitments are no longer so mobile, who may take longer to retrain and who must therefore plan further ahead?

— Flexibility for the young
  15-30: Mobility with Transient Skills

— Security for the family
  30-45: Executive/Managerial

— Academe for the mature
  50-80: Education/Social Service.

Thus the school leavers would be prepared for the currently fashionable jobs and those jobs requiring rapid learning or geographic mobility. As the individuals mature and seek to settle down they would retrain for a more stable executive or managerial career. Social careers, such as educating or caring for others, would be reserved for those with experience of all the vicissitudes of life.

Make no mistake, the very concept of a multi-career life, let alone the suggestion of age related careers, is at variance with our trades union, social security and pensions structures, let alone our educational systems. It is also incompatible with the Graeco-Roman ideal of Plato's "Republic" of one education for one career for life.

It is, however, similar to the way many non-European societies, including that of Japan, are organised, with veneration for the growing wisdom of age and the tasks suitable for different age groups.

Rather than expound analogies and principles I will attempt to describe the careers of an average school leaver of 1990.

John Dent, cousin of Arthur Dent, has no academic interests. On a School Project in Wales he once had to be manhandled out of a museum at closing time, but that one symptom of deviant enthusiasm was quickly cured. He is reasonably dexterous, likes making things in the engineering workshop and crashing other people's computer systems.

In his last year at school he does a course on Numerical Control Programming which includes part-time work in a local engineering company which he joins as a trainee robogate supervisor.

In his spare time he is active in the local branch of CAMRA (Campaign for Real Ale), gets interested in the mechanics of brewing and when the demand for robogate supervisors tails off and salaries start to lag, takes a Biotechnology Production course at the local tech. He is now in his mid-twenties. Failing to get a job in a real ale brewery he settles for a metal recycling plant near Scunthorpe rather than work for a synthetic beer factory.

In his late twenties he gets married, stops drinking and starts to study Production Control and Finance on an Open Tech course. It is heavy going, and he does not qualify until his mid-thirties, when he manages to get a job as deputy production controller of a cattle feed plant in Cheshire. He has worked his way up to production manager when he realises, just before his forty-fifth birthday, that the plant will have to close because it cannot be adapted to meet the latest pollution control standards.

Unwilling to move, he takes a teacher training course and secures a part-time post at the local school teaching basic numeracy and industrial skills. He is elected to the local council, and with his attendance money and his wife's earnings as a paramedic running the body scanners in the local group practice combined health centre, operating theatre and cottage hospital, he decides he can afford not to take another full-time job. In the school holidays he takes to studying Welsh History and at 55 graduates in Celtic Studies from the Open University of North Wales. At 60, when their last child leaves home, he and his wife buy a derelict hill farm in mid-Wales and he opens a holiday centre specialising in the development of the Welsh Longbow, in use and in literature.

Note that John Dent retrains four times, none of them at his employer's expense because each time he is going into a very different career. Each time, partly because he is getting older and has more family commitments, it takes him longer, until his final academic cum leisure cum retirement post. Note also that after his youthful job mobility, at 45 he settles for a collection of part-time sources of income, including teaching and social cum political activity, rather than disrupt his family life and move again.

This kind of multi-career life requires major changes to our trades union structures, pension schemes and social security schemes to permit multiple job changes without loss of pension rights and to permit part-time work as a norm. However, I will now concentrate on the changes it demands of our education system.

Institutional Changes Needed

Unacademic John Dent spends more time in the educational system, both for business and for pleasure, after he has left school than even today's academic high flyers. Therefore, unlike current and past generations of school leavers, he must enjoy it. I understand that one cannot drag London's adult East Enders over the threshold of anything that looks like a school but house the establishment in a Portakabin or a Shack, give it a different name and ethos, and dissociate it from memories of pain and boredom, and they are often as eager as any child to learn new skills.

It is essential that the initial educational experience should be such that the student learns how to learn in a way that makes him associate education with reward and relevance, while at the same time he acquires the basic skills essential to all career structures.

Given that most new jobs are being created in small businesses with neither the time nor the money to train school leavers in changing skills, and given that the schools have 10 years of the individual's best learning years, the school leaver should already have acquired most of the vocational skills and training necessary for his first career. This first career is likely to begin at 16 or 17 and to involve a job in close proximity to the school. Therefore, much closer links between schools and local businesses are necessary. Whether these are fostered by cross-secondments, use of part-time industrial staff for vocational training in schools, the recruitment only of teachers with outside work experience or sandwich courses for children, the current isolation must be broken down.

Retraining at reasonable cost, social cost as well as economic cost, should be available at any stage of life, independent of the desires, means or needs of the current employers.

The kind of availability needed is possibly illustrated by the fate of an American steel company which gave notice of a closure in a town where there was little alternative work for steelworkers. The sellers of retraining courses descended on the town like locusts, and although the company rescinded the closure notice, two years later it had to close because of shortage of labour. The workers had taken the message, retrained at their own expense and left for better, more secure, jobs.

We should not concentrate resources on those who are easiest to train, like the teenagers, at the cost of throwing later generations on the scrap heap, nor should we squander resources on the untrainable or those who wish to acquire skills not in demand at someone else's expense. When the taxpayers' money is to be spent, priority should be given to retraining taxpayers or training their children for jobs in known demand. Exotic or esoteric subjects should be studied at private, not public, expense.

A major shift in resources away from the 14 to 21 examination treadmill will be required, as will a massive shift from non-vocational to vocational education and from "offering" courses to meeting demands. Non-vocational education will largely become a leisure activity paid for by mature students out of past earnings rather than a middle class puberty rite at taxpayers' expense.

For many subjects the student age will rise from under 21 to over 60. Perhaps we should be considering the conversion of redundant universities to recreation and leisure schools or to industrial training centres, depending on their location and facilities. It may be that in 20 years' time we will again have in Britain a dozen or so proper research-based endowment funded universities and, hopefully, at least a dozen first class colleges or institutes of advanced technology funded largely by industry.

Second rate institutions, where university status and academic freedom have too often been an excuse for woolly thinking, inefficiency and futility, will no longer be supported with public money. Good researchers and funding will be concentrated in centres of excellence. Competent teachers will be paid more to train for specific professional skills in polytechnics and colleges of further education, possibly linked in an Open Tech-like framework. The concept of the university as a home of learning and research for young and old alike, rather than an imitation polytechnic for adolescents but without the polytechnic discipline of defined educational objectives, will reign again.

Maybe that is a pipedream; however, a revolution in teaching techniques will certainly be required since current methods rely too heavily on the ingrained awe and academic docility of examination-broken youth for them to work with the cynical maturity of the adult trainee. This, together with the emphasis on learning how to learn rather than mastery of any particular subject matter, may well lead to teaching and lecturing in most subjects being reserved as a second or third career so that mature students are taught by their peers. Given the use of packaged material, mastery of the subject will be less important than understanding of the learning experience, the ability to manage the learning environment and motivate the student by sympathy, guidance and understanding — those attributes which the expert in his own subject has all too often lost. Teacher centred methods must be replaced by learner centred methods.

Can New Technologies Meet this Challenge?

At the simplest level, audio-visual techniques enable the best lecturer or demonstrator to address an audience of thousands rather than a few dozen.

A good video is very much more effective than an average teacher in one-way communication such as a lecture.

Freed from the pressure of the timetable to prepare material, the teacher can act as a tutor rather than a lecturer, advising which sources of information the individual student would find most helpful or relevant: videos, books, computer-based simulations and so on.

The simulations which are at the heart of many computer-aided learning packages appear to improve greatly the motivation of students of all types. Good packages speed the assimilation of knowledge and understanding, facilitate the practice of techniques and of recall. They can also make formal examinations and the associated trauma unnecessary by testing the student's understanding at each stage before he can move on to the next. Thus at the end of a CAL packaged course, each student has reached the same level of understanding, some more quickly than others. Packages enable the teacher to concentrate on his students as individuals, especially on their interpersonal abilities: for example, in group situations where the computer has set a task which requires a number of students to work in concert. The computer can be left to manage the task while the teacher concentrates on developing those skills and qualities which the computer cannot, such as consideration of the feelings, motives and abilities of other people.

Learning can also take place to suit the student's choice of time, place and pace. Thus the part-time student can study the theory of genetic engineering in the village school by night, using video and simulation packages with teleconferencing facilities for tutorials, while the pregnant teenager does mathematics and babycare at home with a visiting teacher to keep up her morale.

Our current education system is "schooled" into subject areas, while life is not. The ability of the expert system to manage complexity makes it ideal for controlling multidisciplinary study projects, crossing subject boundaries in a way which few teachers have the ability or knowledge to match. An example might be the complex interactions between economic growth, nutrition standards, mortality, mores and birth rates in the first industrial revolution in the UK or in the developing countries of the third world today. The medical ignorance of most historians, the cavalier way in which theoretical economists regard most historical evidence, the woolly thinking of most sociologists, and the narrow interests of most medical men, make this an area abounding in myth and nonsense. Such packages could be invaluable in broadening the outlook of our narrow specialists in both teaching and research.

Packages are labour intensive to specify and prepare, and require much planning and discipline in assembly and testing. However, two years and a million or so to assemble quality packages which can then be mass produced on discs or transmitted over the air or down telephone lines represents an expenditure of far less time, money and effort than retraining several thousand teachers over a decade or two. The comprehensive indexing of packages, learning and research should enable duplicated effort to be avoided, except where teams are sufficiently confident of the market need and their own competence to compete deliberately.

Given the PhD rat race and the scramble to publish, the effects of worldwide indexing and updating and the exchange of information over teleconference links could be interesting. Will it actually lead to the free interchange of knowledge for the benefit of all, with an end to the desperate race to publish first in a prestige journal, leaving the losers to save face with duplicated variations and glosses in a plethora of obscure publications? Probably not, unless reinforced by turning off the tap of taxpayers' monies, or the fear of public ridicule which can sometimes shame the most obstinate into changing their ways.

Problems the Information Industry can Help to Overcome

The Japanese, like the Americans under Kennedy or our Victorian ancestors, succeed because they think they can. We are failing because we expect to. We do not suffer from a lack of resources but from the fragmentation of those we have, the refusal to consider solutions we did not invent for ourselves, bureaucratic procedures and institutions which do not believe they can cope with change, an idiosyncratic examination system which reinforces the status quo and recruiters who have, for all too human reasons, given up trying to influence the systems they have to work with.

In all these areas the fear of public ridicule can be a potent weapon. Fear of the public exposure of wasted resources can often persuade a local authority to bring together further education, polytechnic and school resources to solve common problems in situations where rational argument gets strangled with red tape. The "not invented here" syndrome can equally be countered in a time of financial stringency by forcing the public cost-justification of each attempt to re-invent the wheel.

Institutional resistance is harder to overcome. Of course, an authority with a large architect's department and a militant bunch of maintenance men and caretakers will seek to spend more on buildings than on books or teaching aids. Of course teachers will seek to impart to others the subjects they know. Of course examiners will seek to preserve the status quo.

Consumer revolt, whether on the part of parents, taxpayers, students or recruiters, is one weapon capable of overcoming institutional resistance in the long run. But it can be a very wasteful mechanism. Waiting for *Encyclopaedia Britannica* or *Time-Life* to fill the gap with packages sold direct to parents or mature students is not the best way, unless we really believe that American methods are so superior that we cannot catch up.

Subversion is likely to be far more efficient. Demonstrating to the teachers that copying material produced elsewhere, perhaps even paying copyright fees, that prostituting academic freedom in return for gifts of equipment, books and visits, that adopting commercial rather than academic norms can greatly ease their problems, will encourage them to change the system from within. Demonstrating that interesting relevant packages can make a class of unacademic delinquents an acceptable challenge rather than a futile trial of strength will encourage the teachers to fight the waste of resources on bricks and mortar and get the money to be spent on teaching aids and material instead.

In Japan, the universities are showered with gifts of money and equipment by employers, not because they value university research — they do not — but because they want recruits trained to their standards. Our employers must adopt similar tactics, not just in dealing with universities but with schools and colleges at all levels. Because of the difficulties on both sides and the cultural gulf that exists, they need all the encouragement they can get through publicity and praise for successful case studies of co-operation (as in the Japanese press): case studies which emphasise the direct selfish benefits to both parties as much as the long term benefits for the students. The Marconi-sponsored MSc course at Southampton is one example; I am sure Sperry Ltd can cite examples in which they have taken a similar lead.

Finally, recruiters who buck the system and re-test applicants or select for deviance, rejecting the validity of examination results, or who offer inflation adjusted pension transfer rights or payments to independent pension schemes should receive praise and publicity for their initiative in helping to change the system. The docility of the recruiters merely serves to reinforce the complacency of the examiners who are convinced they are imposing the correct quality control procedures on the rest of the system. A revolt among the recruiters, fomented by the press, could well be the fastest way of securing rapid and far-reaching change.

Conclusion

Much of this thesis may be wrong (forecasters such as myself are very content if they are right more than half the time). One thing of which I am certain is that rapid and far-reaching changes in our educational systems at every level are essential. I am also certain that throwing money at the system will probably serve to delay those changes, while financial crisis and constructive publicity for the alternatives may well help to promote them.

13

Technology and the Future of Work

Sir Ieuan Maddock

*St Edmund's Hall, Oxford**

It has become conventional to regard "work" as not only the means of producing the goods and the services we need but particularly as the means by which individuals acquire the purchasing power necessary to obtain some proportion of these goods and services. Most economic analyses show a loop diagram relating output to the various inputs (capital, labour, utilities, raw materials) on the one hand and the recycling of income through purchases, investments, accumulation etc. on the other. Low unemployment, high productivity, high use of capital equipment, are invoked as formulae for economic advance (or recovery).

Yet there are examples in history which show that there is no fundamental relationship between the working capacity of individuals and their ability to purchase. The very high civilisations of the Egyptians, Greeks and Romans prospered without "working" being associated with "purchasing" — the slaves did the work, the masters did the purchasing and consuming. Indeed it has been argued that the advance of cultures of all kinds coincides with a large leisured class, free from the burden of working to survive and therefore able to pay more attention to more abstract or aesthetic things. However real this relationship might be there can be little doubt that in the 18th, 19th and 20th century work has been linked with purchasing power and affluence, and unemployment equated to misery and deprivation. So strong have these links become in people's minds, that the provision of employment has become a greater priority than increasing the total availability of goods and services. It is regarded as better to continue inefficient and uncompetitive enterprises because they provide purchasing power, albeit a small one, rather than to improve efficiency, and the ability to compete in home and foreign markets.

As technology has advanced, it has become progressively more difficult to maintain this stance. Modern capital facilities (electricity, gas, oil, chemicals, man-made fibres, food processing, telephone etc.) are able to supply most of

* Now Deputy Director, International General Electric USA.

the goods or services needed without great use of labour. Reverting to the example of the early civilisations and the use of slaves, the modern slave is the machine and man could progressively be the master.

The tempo of technological development becomes ever more rapid and the range of potential "technological slaves" becomes progressively wider. This paper discusses some of the powerful influences which can now be seen to be operating, and speculates on the future pattern of work in the UK.

The Growing Constraints on Work

Figure 13.1 shows in a schematic way six powerful forces which now influence and in the future will dominate the pattern and scale of work.

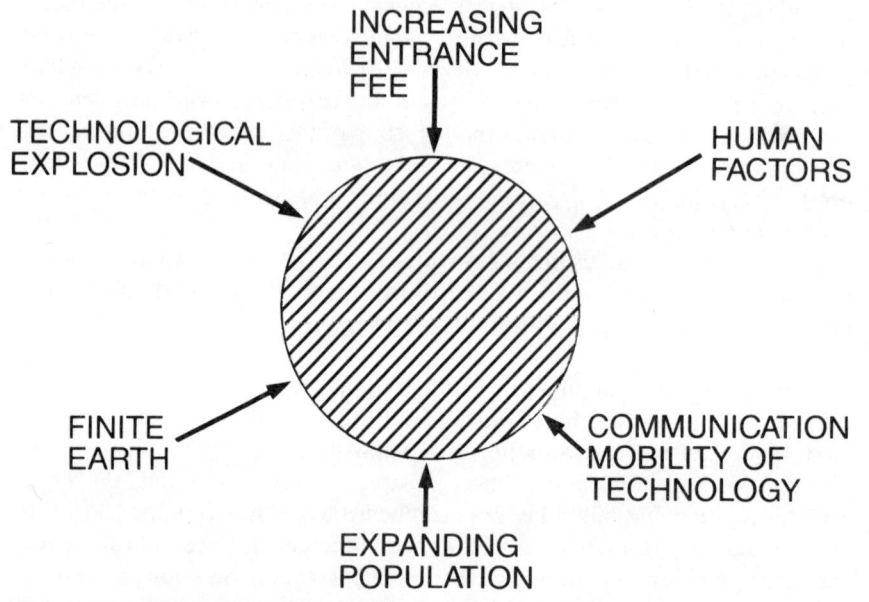

Figure 13.1. Six forces affecting future work patterns

The Technological Explosion

Every single branch of technology has advanced at great speed in recent times, and even more dramatic have been the effects of the interplay between different disciplines.

As a measure of the rate of progress one can look at a few simple indicators such as:

(a) How far a person could travel in a day;
(b) The number of people that could witness an event (e.g. sports) at the same time;
(c) How far and how frequently man could communicate with his fellow men;
(d) How many people could be killed by a few warriors;
(e) How many calculations could a man perform in an hour.
These are shown in a notional way in Fig. 13.2.

For many thousands of years man could only travel as far as his feet would carry him. He naturally settled into a way of living which suited this limited range of communication. The basic social and cultural unit was the tribe or the large family, and each unit inevitably developed different physical characteristics, a different language and a different pattern of behaviour. Later he found that he could harness the carrying power of animals, he discovered wheels and he found ways to travel on water. These greatly extended his ability to communicate and a generation is now growing into maturity to whom a direct (i.e. realtime) view of a sports event or political drama in some very remote part of the globe seems an ordinary and unremarkable event.

In a similar vein it is possible to trace the advance of armaments. The whole of history is dominated by human conflict and of the domination of one human group by another through the process of conquest.

Over a very long period the character of warfare changed relatively slowly, enabling each generation of warriors to learn from their forebears and to add their own cautious innovations. This left plenty of scope for individual characteristics, such as skill (swordsmanship, riding etc.) bravery, cunning and leadership. But towards the end of the nineteenth century the pace accelerated to the point where the attitudes of the "last war" were no longer relevant to the "new war". Cavalry charges into a hail-storm of machine-gun bullets, fixed defences against mobile tank regiments and, more recently, civil guards confronted by the obliterating power of high explosive and incendiaries were proved to be disastrously out-dated. By now we have moved to the numbing concepts of vast mobile deployment of intercontinental ballistic missiles, each with a "scatter array" of thermonuclear bombs which in combination are able to extinguish the whole of the civilisation that man has taken thousands of years to create. Yet people talk about these in terms of "strategies" and "tactics" which savour of the mediaeval encounters.

On a less destructive plane and possibly on a positively constructive plane is man's ability to communicate with man and to control the society he wishes to live in. From the days when Caxton produced his press to the early part of the 20th century, the main means of mass communication was the printed word which not only provided the vehicle for a great growth of literature, of law and of social order but also, alas, a means of spreading seditious information and political dogma. But since the early nineteen hundreds we have seen the growth of the telegraph, then the telephone, of radio, then television, to the point where in the so-called developed nations over 90% of the population are in instant contact with each other. The formerly remote, mysterious and therefore revered figures of Royalty, Politics, the Church, have become familiar and, in consequence in some cases, fallible human beings. Parallel with this has been the growth of the abilities to record, to analyse, and to process facts. In the span of less than three decades the ability to collect, sift, refine and manipulate data has increased a millionfold and promises to continue at this growth rate for the remainder of this century.

The Finite Earth

One of the inevitable consequences of the rapid acceleration of man's ability to control and exploit the resources of nature has been the great leap in the demand for minerals, water and coastline until now it has become evident that there is a finite limit to their availability. This is the first generation of the human race that seriously has to contemplate the exhaustion of the planet's resources and to have not only to speculate earnestly about some of the consequences of impending shortages, but to have even been driven to legislate against the wasteful use of one of the most strategic materials — those that provide energy. Much as one can criticise the methodology of the work of the Club of Rome and "Limits to Growth" it must be warmly acknowledged that this early work did a great service in alerting mankind that there was a real problem, which called for urgent attention from the governments and the large corporations of the world. To carp at the dramatic terms of their presentation or to criticise some of the naivety of the forecasting techniques is only to underestimate the value (and indeed the courage) of this work.

The resource that has received most of the attention in recent years has been energy. It has become fashionable to display graphs similar to Fig 13.3 which show a constantly increasing demand for energy (tons oil equivalent) set against the capacity of the various energy sources to meet this demand. Whatever the degree of optimism or pessimism displayed by the various forecasters, frequently coloured by their dedication to one or other of the sources, a gap between supply and demand is likely to appear in the late 1980s and this gap rapidly becomes a chasm as the end of the century approaches. This can only be avoided if there is a dramatic and continuing

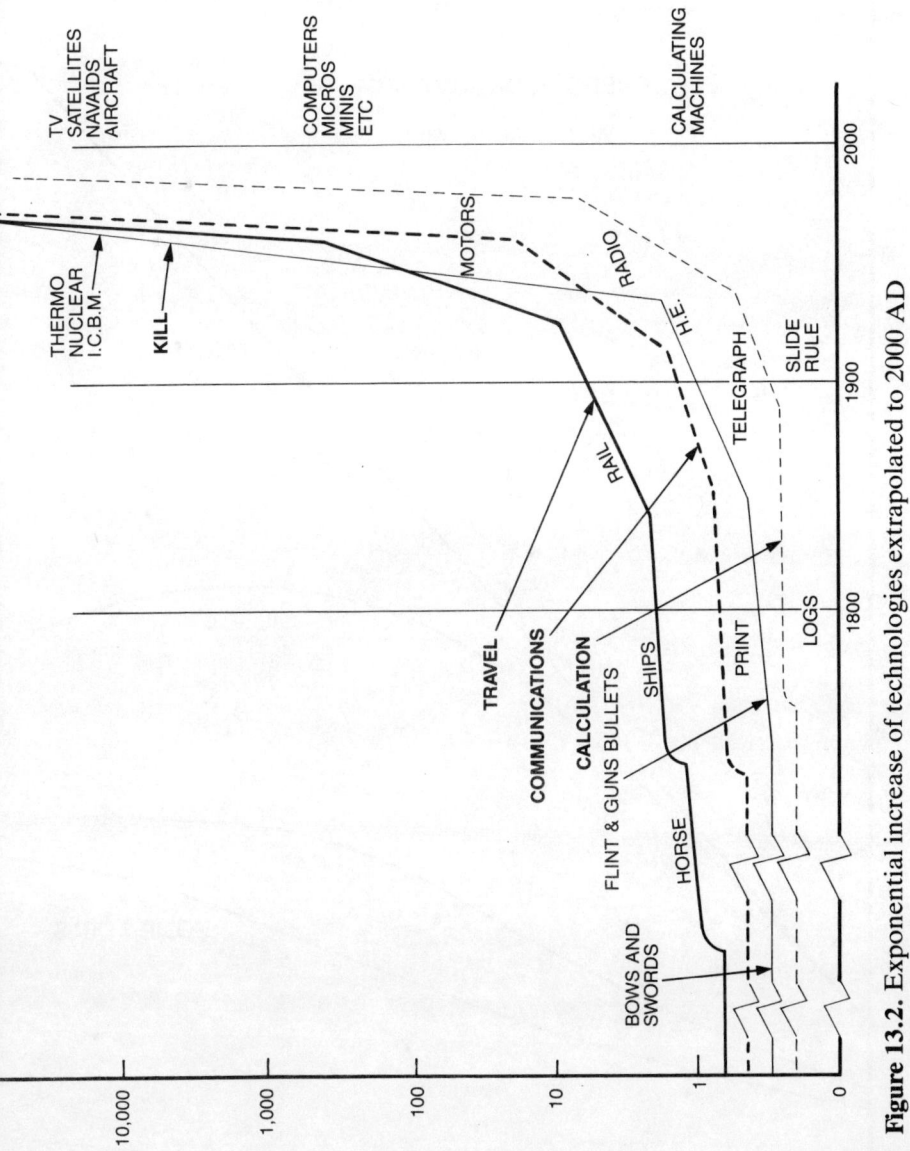

Figure 13.2. Exponential increase of technologies extrapolated to 2000 AD

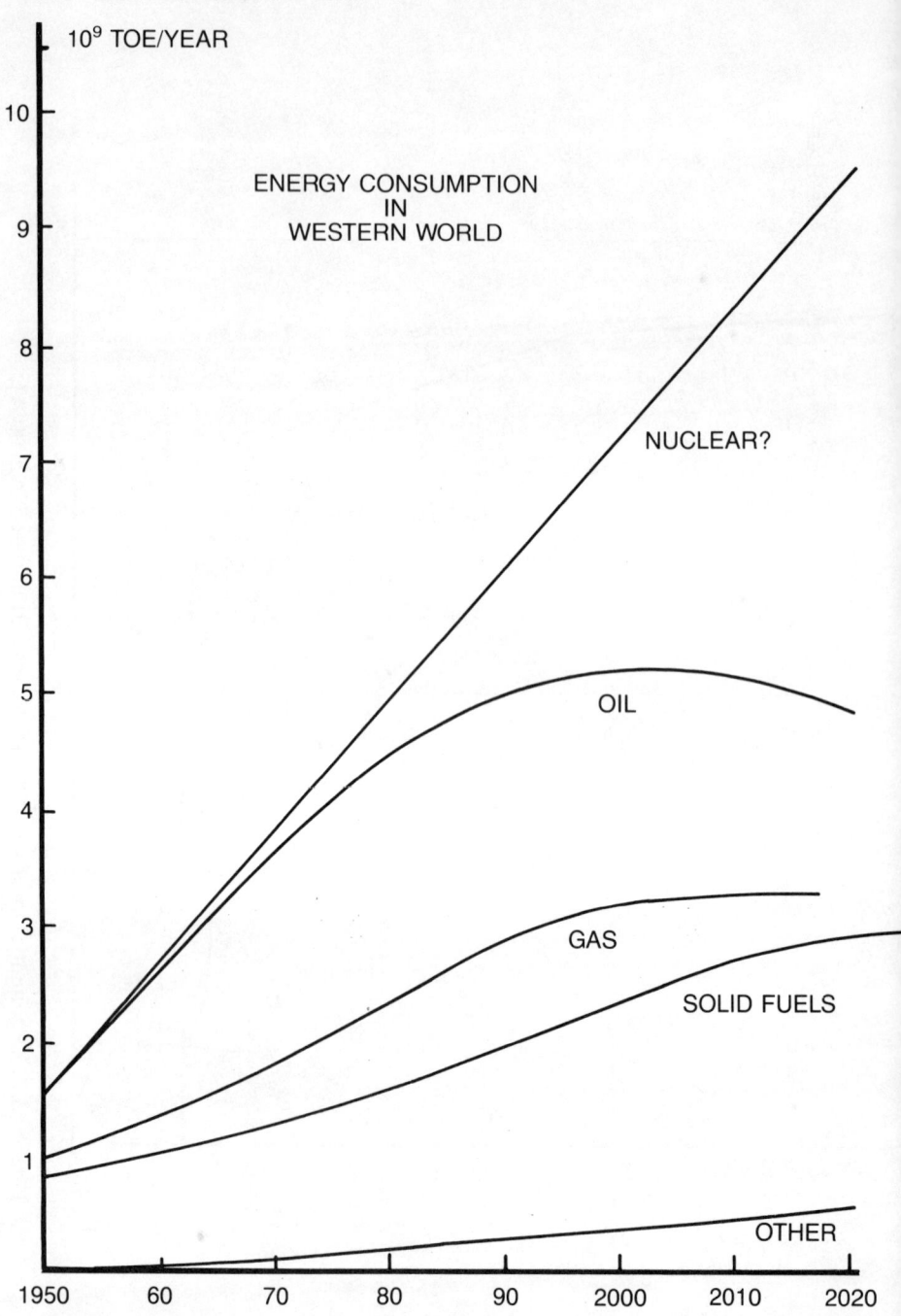

Figure 13.3. Recent and projected energy consumption (in tons-of-oil equivalents).

drop in the rate of consumption of energy or if a massive new source (or sources) of energy was to emerge. This — it is frequently argued — can only be by the production of power on a gigantic scale from nuclear sources. That the current technology could enable this to be done is beyond doubt but the problem of satisfying public concern about safety and about safeguards against the proliferation of nuclear weapons is already proving to be very difficult and it is becoming more problematical each day. To dismiss the objectors as "foolish" or "ill-informed" is short sighted and insensitive. For reasons which are argued below these very natural and justified human factors must be taken into account in any assessment of any new technology or in the potential development of a new resource.

There is no energy "crisis" if this is taken to mean that all of the energy sources will suddenly "run out" at some critical date. Nor is there an impending cataclysmic shortage of key materials. For example, the earth receives an average of around 100 watts per day for every square metre of the surface of the whole globe. Every hectare of land receives enough solar energy, on average, to supply continuously over 30 kilowatt electric fires. To talk of a crisis is therefore unrealistic and the problem facing mankind is of a different character. Over a period measured in millions of years nature has been storing up some of this constantly available energy, using the process of photo-synthesis which was then followed by various biological processes which ultimately led to the production of oil, gas and coal. Up to now man has been spared the task of accumulation and of storage by being able to use the fruits of these processes which happened in geological times. When there is talk of energy shortage it is only this stock of pre-collected and pre-stored energy which is being depleted. The challenge now is how to collect the abundantly available solar energy and how to store it by methods which are economical and also are environmentally acceptable.

These methods as and when they appear (as they certainly will) will demand more positive effort by man and it is a high probability that, within the next few generations, energy will become a very expensive and a precious resource. Man will have to acquire much less spendthrift methods of using energy and fortunately there are now signs of positive, albeit long overdue, steps to do this. However until these alternative sources and their much more thrifty use have grown to such a level that they collectively have some major effect on the energy balance, the countries and organisations that have control over the fossil fuel resources can be expected to take maximum advantage of their good fortune. OPEC will continue to exert a great influence on the development of the world's economies for decades to come.

Nor are the key materials of the planet "running out". Most of the elements which were in the crust of the Earth a thousand years ago are still

174   IMPACT ON LIFE AND WORK

around — but now a substantial amount is distributed in microscopic quantities over the surface (due to combustion processes), in garbage heaps, in ancient and forgotten structures, or absorbed into flora and fauna. The original order which nature had contrived by a series of accidents which gave rise to metal ore and chemical rich deposits has been replaced by disorder. Just as in the case of energy, the problem which now faces man is how to produce new order out of his own disorder. There is a great deal that can be done, but again it will take far more deliberate effort and therefore increased cost to do this rather than the relatively simple exploitation of nature's own ordering. Until the economic/social/political machine has evolved to the point which makes re-ordering of resources a natural way of life, the countries which have control of some of the most vital materials will be tempted to form their own OPEC type organisations. Fig. 13.4 gives a list of some of the key materials which will have become problems before the turn of the century, and where limitation of supply and consumption will have become a powerful political and economic tool. It is inevitable that there are other potential "OPECs" that could arise from growing shortages of key materials.

Expanding Population

One of the most powerful effects of increased communication has been the improvement of medical services and hygiene in the countries which had been slow to develop. The interplay between high birth-rate and improving expectation of life is shown in Fig 13.5 and this inevitably led to rapid growth of the global population — primarily in the late developing countries (LDCs) (see below). There is evidence that as the literacy, numeracy and affluence of a society grows, then the birth-rate drops and can ultimately reach an equilibrium with longevity. Various demographers have studied this interplay and their results — not surprisingly — differ over a wide range, but they are all agreed that up until the end of this century the world population will continue to grow rapidly (Fig 13.6) and that a further 1.5 billion human beings will be added to the existing population by the year 2000. Mankind took the whole of the prehistoric and historic past to build a population of the first 1.5 billion, a figure which was achieved by the beginning of this century. The entire global population in the time of Queen Victoria (and the high-noon of the industrial revolution) was less than the increase which will occur in the next two decades. The extra demand for food, clothing, shelter, communications, energy and culture will have to be met, all within a single generation. This is both a challenge and an opportunity.

The curves in Fig. 13.7A show one of the estimates of the ultimate population figures for the late developing countries (LDCs) and for the

PROBLEM MATERIALS BY YEAR 2000

MATERIAL	SOURCES
Aluminum	Australia, Guinea, Jamaica
Copper	USA, Chile
Gold	S. Africa, Canada
Lead	USA, USSR, Australia, Canada
Mercury	Spain, USSR, Italy
Natural Gas	USA, USSR
Petroleum	Saudi Arabia, USA, Kuwait, USSR
Tin	Thailand, Bolivia, Malaysia
Silver	Communist Countries, USA, Canada, Mexico, Peru
Tungsten	China, USSR, USA
Zinc	USA, USSR, Canada

Figure 13.4. Problem materials by year 2000.

current developed countries. Taking the extreme case of continuation of the present rate of growth in the LDCs, then early in the next century there could be 20 billion people on the planet (compared with only 1½ billion at the beginning of this century) and most of these will be in the LDCs.

In addition to this great increase in population (the so-called population explosion) there is an associated problem that will materially affect the pattern of the distribution of wealth and the migration of technology. This is

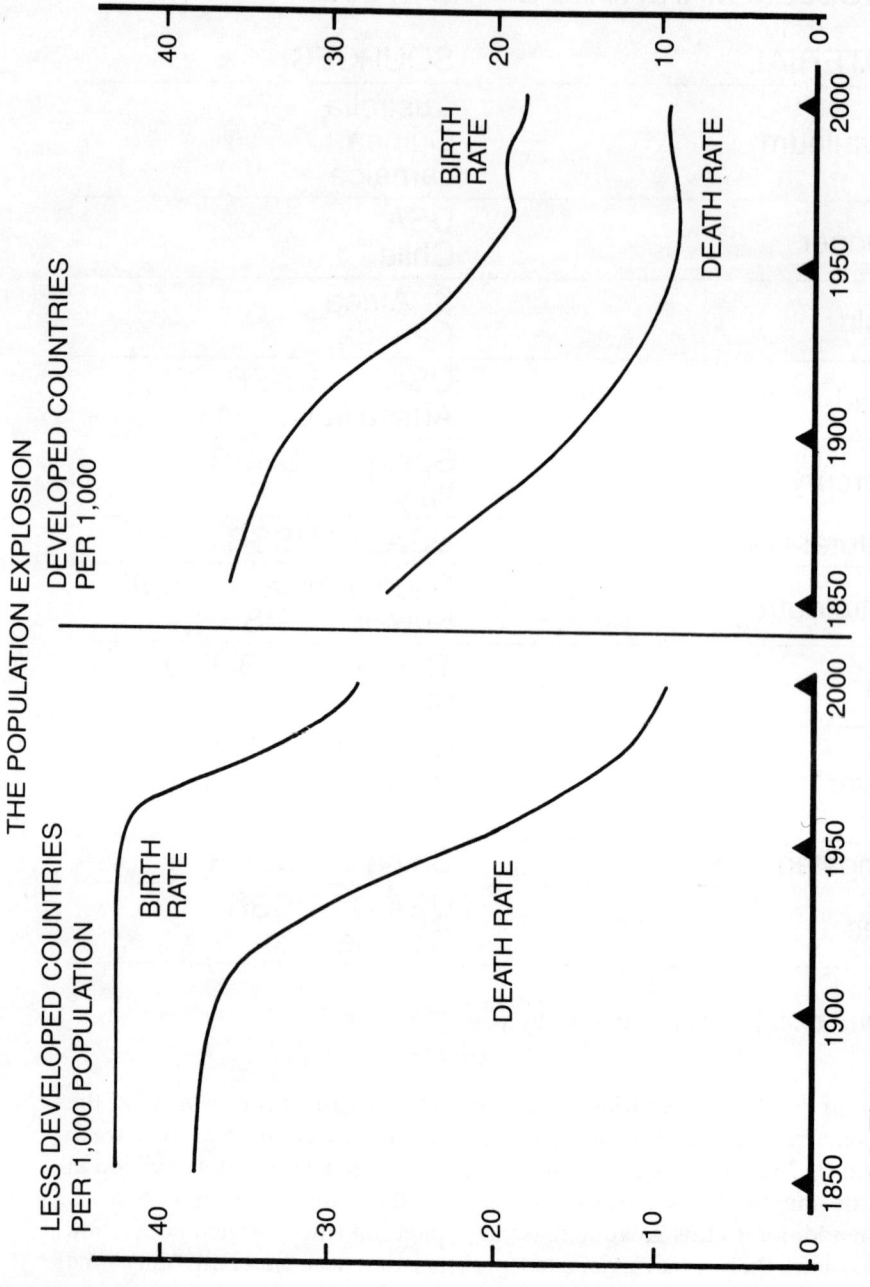

Figure 13.5. The population explosion: rate of growth is set by size of vertical gap (see graphs) between birth rate and death rate.

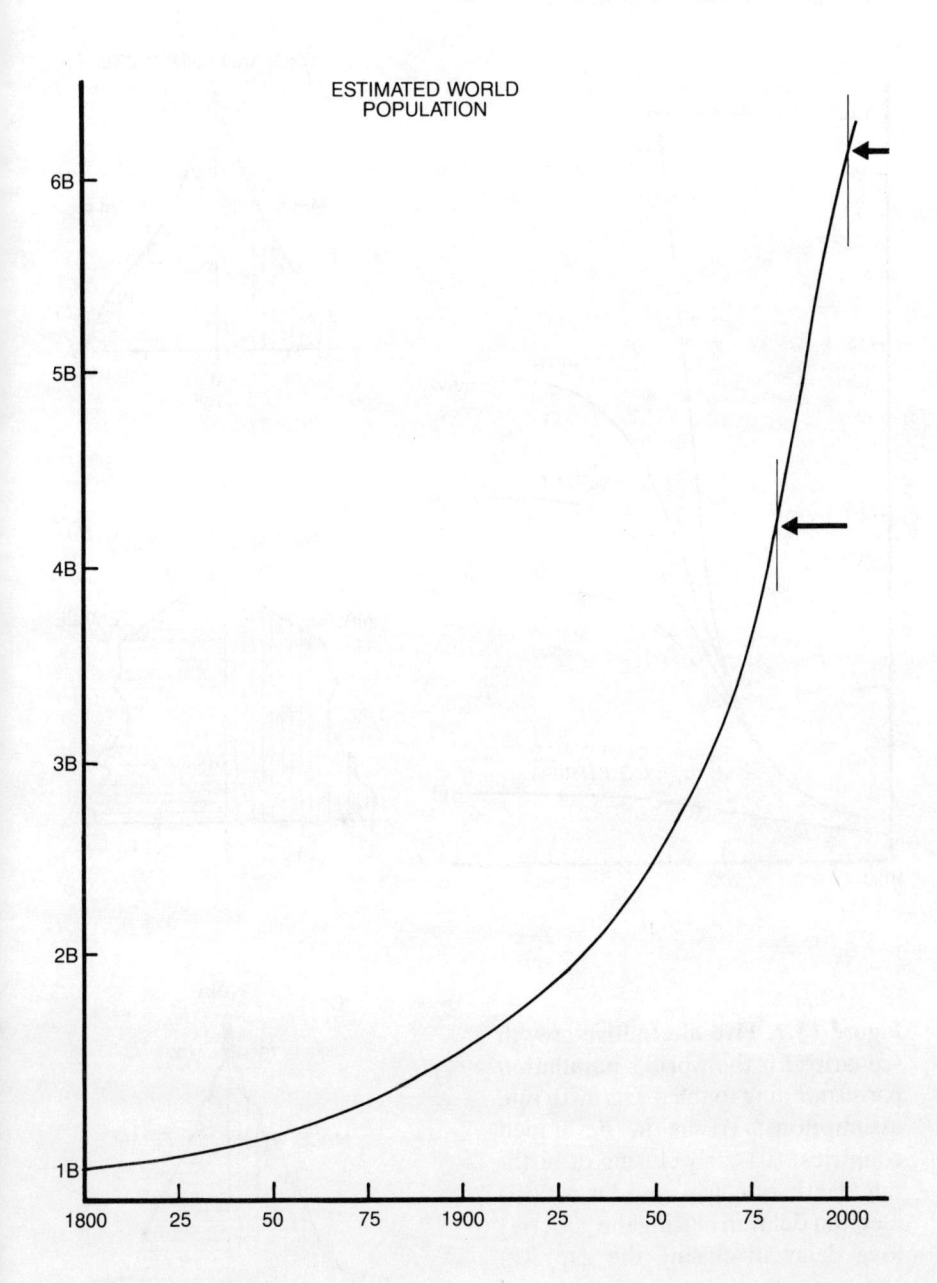

Figure 13.6. Estimated and projected world population.

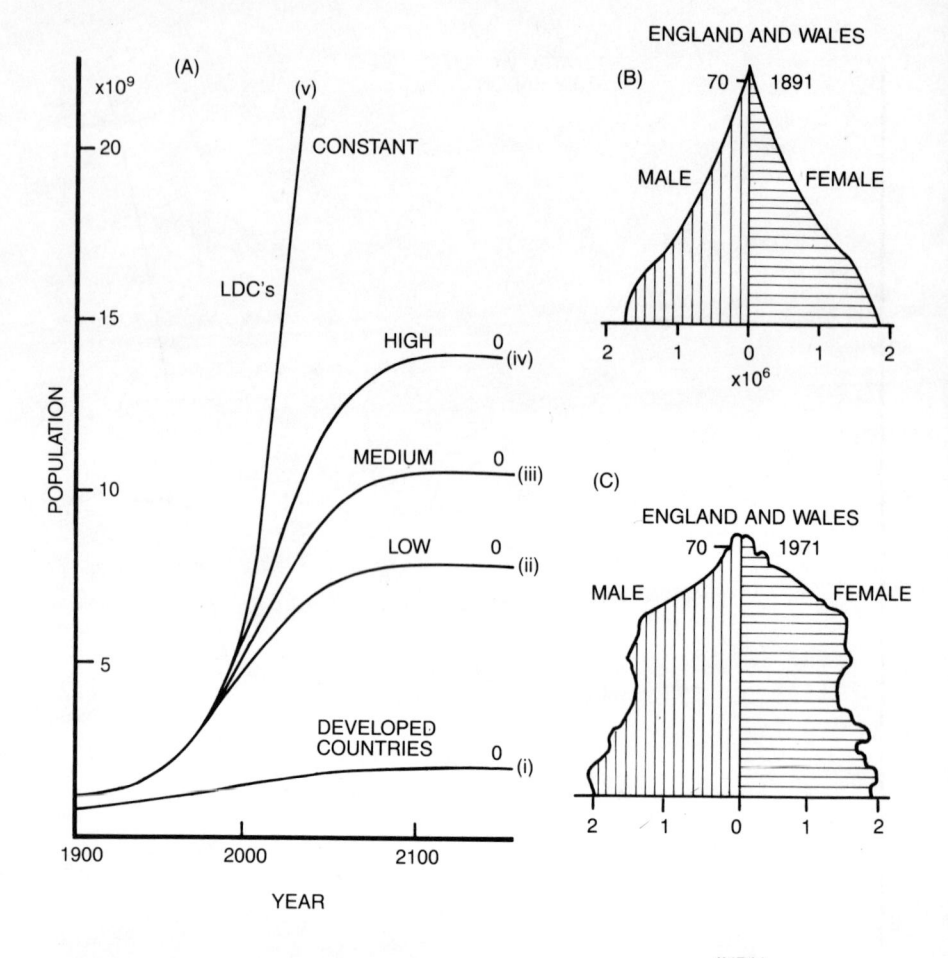

Figure 13.7. Five alternative growth scenarios for the world's population corresponding to the five growth rate assumptions: (i) as in developed countries; (ii) early closing of birthrate/death rate gap in LDC's; (iii) medium delay in closing the gap; (iv) long delay in closing the gap; (v) constant rate of increase (no closing of the gap).

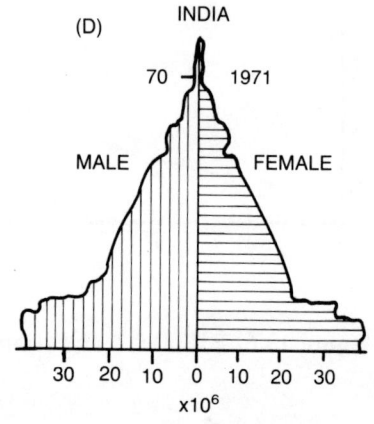

change in the character of the population particularly the age distribution. The probable course of future events can be deduced from charts B, C and D in Fig 13.7. Fig. 13.7B shows the numbers of people in England and Wales against the ages from birth to over 70 years (males on left, females on right) derived from the census of 1891. This shows a steady decline in the numbers as age increases, indicating an almost constant percentage death rate per annum with females showing somewhat better than males.

The 1971 census shows a very different pattern with both males and females surviving to a much greater age (Fig. 13.7C). (The slight inward constriction in the middle region shows the effect of the war years.) With almost zero net population growth the proportion of older people will continue to grow with all the attendant social and economic problems which will ensure. A whole library of literature exists which is devoted to this topic and it would be a mistake to try and pursue this here.

If, however, we look at the corresponding graph for India in 1971 (Fig.13.7D) there is a stark difference. The sharp inward "notch" in the first decade and a half of life indicates the high rate of infant mortality. These are young people who never themselves reach the age where they can become parents. After the age of around 20 the male and female numbers follow the same form as that shown in the 1891 census for England and Wales — steady decline throughout the age range. What then is the future for India (and all of the LDCs)?

The expectation must be that a vastly greater number of juveniles could survive to the age of parenthood and to very much older. That this is likely to be so is indicated by the curves in Fig 13.5. This shows the change of birth rate and death rate in the developed and the developing countries. Whilst in the former the birth rate has been dropping steadily since the middle of the 19th century the death rate has been dropping at roughly the same rate, so the gap between the two curves has remained reasonably constant. It is this gap which determines the net change in the population numbers. In the LDCs, however, the birth rate is dropping faster than in the developed countries but the death rate has dropped even faster. The all-important gap between the two curves has opened up and the populations will grow rapidly for several decades. Fig. 13.7A shows the consequence. Depending on the estimate of the date when the gap converges once more to the zero growth level, it is possible to make an estimate of the total global population. An early equilibrium point would produce a total population of around 8 billion in the second half of the next century, whilst a much longer delay in reaching the equilibrium between the birth and death rates could lead to a global total in the region of 16 to 18 billion, most of which would be in the countries currently classified as LDCs. As this occurs the age/abundance curves will progressively change from that in Fig. 13.7D (India, 1971) to something more akin to that in Chart C (England and Wales, 1971).

Many demographic studies have indicated that the gap only narrows when a relatively high standard of living has been achieved, with a corresponding increase in numeracy/literacy. On this basis the early part of the next century will not only see a global population nearly twice the present size but also a very much higher living standard throughout. What has happened in Japan, Hong Kong, Singapore and Taiwan in recent decades is a precursor of what is going to happen globally well within the working lifetime of the children currently in school.

A continuing increase in consumption and output from the developed nations whilst bringing forward the living standards of the LDCs will stretch the resources of the planet beyond the breaking point. The next 20 years will be crucial and will pose more acute problems than any that have been experienced in any part of history. The historians of the 21st century will look back at this one and be astonished at the irrelevance and irresponsibility of the nuclear confrontations of the second half of the 20th century when viewed side by side with the immense problems of the less developed nations. They will see this wasteful use of material and human resources as just as irrelevant as the perpetual warfares that racked Europe in the past several centuries, only to discover by the second half of the 20th century that there is no option but to settle down in peace and co-operation with each other. It is clear that to have any hope of tackling global problems of the future, it will be impossible (quite apart from being immoral) to continue threatening let alone fighting, mediaeval-type wars with 21st century weapons.

What has been said above indicates the total time available for not only addressing but largely solving the problems of the less developed nations — it must be achieved in the next 20 years or it will be too late. To put things in a more stark perspective, there are *only 1,000 weeks left*. To fail to do so will be to bequeath to the next generation a problem of such magnitude that it will be beyond the wit or the resources of mankind to resolve, except through some cataclysmic event which could spell disaster to the human and many other species.

There are those who prefer to take a cynical view of the LDC problem and who prefer to argue that "the poor are always with us"; that we should just accept that an increasing number of people will continue to live at below the subsistence level, that millions will die of starvation, disease and maladministration. Quite apart from the blatant cynicism and inhumanity of such an approach, it also lacks realism. History is rich in examples where great inequalities in the distribution of wealth and power have led to a catastrophic breakdown of order, leading to revolution, civil wars and the bitterness of revenge. Up until fairly recently the world has been insulated from this type of reaction from the less developed nations by the absence of communication — they were just too isolated to discover how poor their own circumstances were compared with others elsewhere. Now the rapid growth in time and speed of communication in so many ways, the transistor radio, television, filmshows, air travel, motor transport, etc. is removing the age-old insulation. The legitimate demand for a "fair share" is growing rapidly.

An additional factor which argues for a realistic as well as a human approach is the distribution of the world's key resources. Many of these are located in the countries which are currently LDCs and whereas, up to the present, the countries concerned have patiently allowed more developed nations to come in to exploit their indigenous wealth this will certainly change, just as the countries in Arabia, Africa and South America have seized and exploited control over their indigenous oil supplies. It is unrealistic to assume that a few countries can continue to grow ever wealthier whilst plundering the resources of countries much less fortunate than themselves. The OPEC phenomenon is likely to repeat itself manyfold in the next 20 years.

Another factor which has to be taken into account is the increasing mobility of technology which is discussed in the next section.

The Mobility of Technology

The ability to make use of a technology depends in part on its availability and on the capacity of the recipient to make effective use of it. When a country is below a certain minimum level of average literacy and numeracy it is difficult to absorb new and advanced technological skills. Once the educational level passes a certain threshold, the capacity to absorb a wide range of technologies increases rapidly and those fields of industrial technologies which have reached a virtual plateau in their development can be absorbed most readily. Hence the speed in which not only Japan but Taiwan, Hong Kong, Singapore, South Korea, the Philippines and several South American states have been able to absorb such industries as photographic goods, radios, and TV, internal combustion engines, steel making, shipbuilding, domestic durables such as sewing machine, refrigerators and a wide range of office machinery. This rate of absorption is very rapid compared with the original time taken to reach the plateau by the originating countries. Some of the reasons for this are discussed later (learning and forgetting curves).

There is no shortage of examples of this growth of mobility. Table A gives a reminder that many technologies which only two decades ago were regarded as the monopoly of a very few European and North American

TABLE A

TECHNOLOGIES ALREADY MIGRATED
TEXTILES GARMENTS SHOES
PHOTOGRAPHIC EQUIPMENT
CONSUMER ELECTRONICS
ELECTRONIC COMPONENTS
KITCHEN EQUIPMENT
TIME KEEPING
MOTOR CYLCES
CARS
TRUCKS
ELECTRIC MOTORS
CHEMICALS — HEAVY
         POLYMERS
         MEDICAL
         AGRICULTURE

IRON & STEEL
PRODUCTS
SHIPBUILDING
TABLE-WARE
DOMESTIC APPLIANCES

Table A. Technologies once regarded as the monopoly of a few European and North American countries which have "migrated" to rapidly emerging nations.

countries have now been completely dominated by the rapidly emerging LDCs. Because of this it is easy to argue that the developed nations should move to a much higher technology plateau and leave these humbler (but vital) pursuits to the LDCs.

Increasing Entrance Fee

Attractive as it is, this thesis runs into difficulties for the following reasons.
1. Technology is not only advancing within each discipline, it is also advancing through the interplay between disciplines with the result that each new increment in performance involves a much greater number of uncertainties — and therefore costs.
2. There is an inevitable "diminishing return" effect in most technologies where a substantial proportion of the potential performance has already

been achieved and further advances are difficult to win. The rapid advance of railroads up to 1930, of motor vehicles up to 1950 and of telephones up to 1960 are a few examples where although much progress has been made in more recent years, the cost in effort and money to win the extra gains has been very high.

The "entrance fee" to a new generation technology in many industries has now become so high that it goes beyond the resources of even very large companies. This leads them to seek support from government and even this becomes a limited resource in many fields. Either the companies have to grow into multi-national giants or the supporting governments have to seek multi-national alliances. This has already occurred in aircraft, space, pharmaceuticals, telecommunications, nuclear power and computers, and is growing visibly in motor vehicles, electronic components and petrochemicals.

A good illustration of this increase in entrance fee can be found in the polymer industry. Fig. 13.8 shows the cash flow pattern of three polymers launched in the mid-1930s, 1940s and 1950s. Initially the flow was negative until such time that monies began to come back from the marketplace. In the mid-1930s the peak outflow was reached in three to four years and break-even was reached a decade after the launch of the project. In the mid-1940s the peak outflow occurred after about seven years and it took 20 years to reach the break-even point. In the 1950s it took over 10 years to reverse the cash flow and it is likely that break-even point will never be reached, let alone profits generated. An ever-increasing number of companies engaged in advanced chemical manufacture are becoming disenchanted with launching new product lines for this reason and are more likely to cross-trade with existing technologies.

There is therefore a dilemma. More and more of the plateau technologies will become the province of new developing countries, whereas the very advanced technologies will become progressively the special province of giant multi-national corporations or multi-governmental enterprises. It will become increasingly difficult for the smaller members of the advanced nations to find a locus between these two extremes without substantial loss of national identity.

Human Factors

Within the developed nations, the combination of a high standard and availability of education and extensive communications has increased the interaction of each individual with each point of decision. Whereas a century ago most people were isolated by either ignorance or poor communication from knowing about or reacting to potential decisions which

184 IMPACT ON LIFE AND WORK

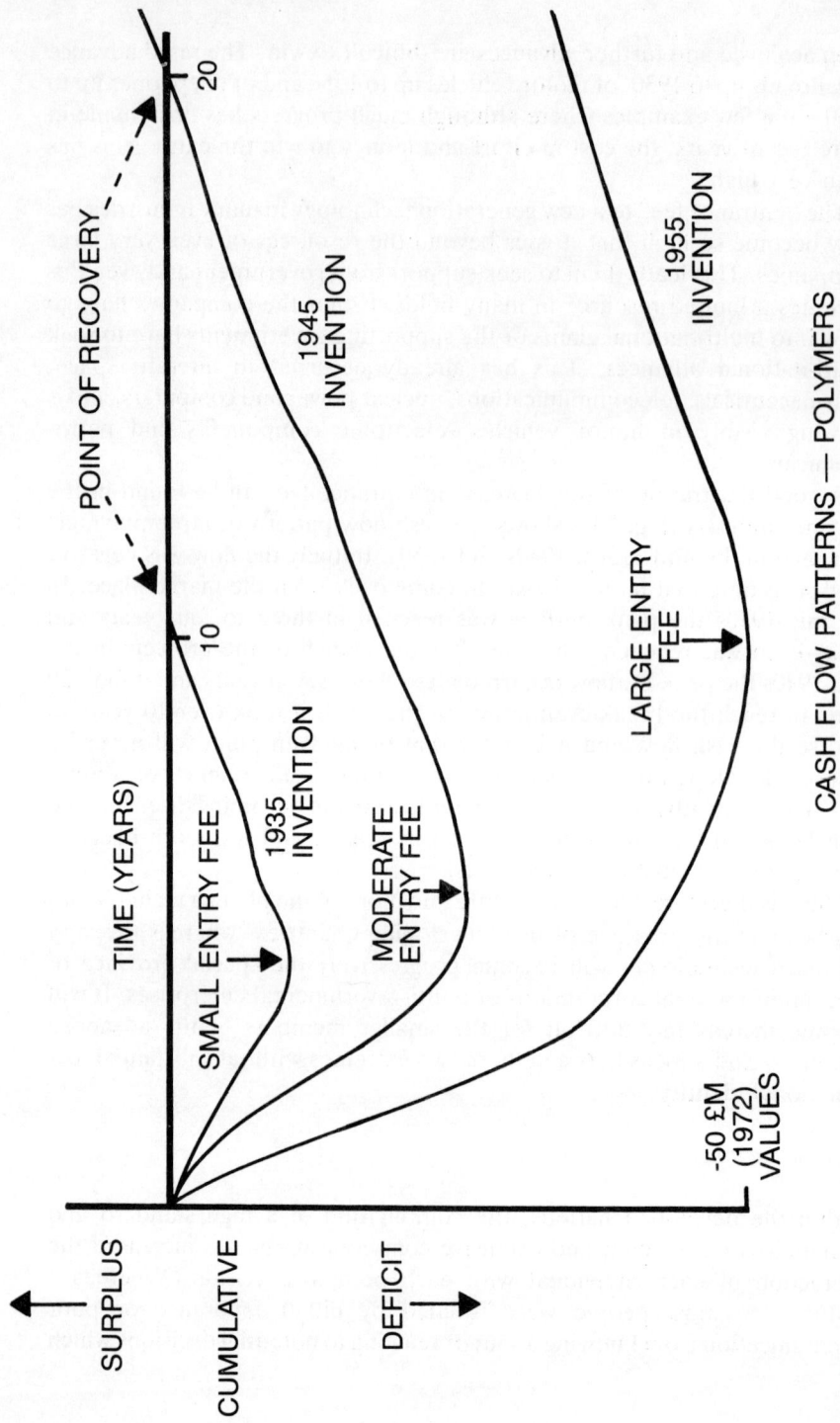

Figure 13.8. "Entry fee" means total amount by which organization must go into the red before the climb back to break-even ("point of recovery").

CASH FLOW PATTERNS — POLYMERS

were likely to affect them, there is now involvement on a massive scale. The public reaction to pollution, nuclear safety, intrusion (airport noise), genetic damage, threat to employment, the dehumanisation of work, outdating of jobs and a legion of other industrial, social, economic and political affairs is powerful, widespread and instant.

It is no longer possible to contemplate building a new airport, chemical plant, or nuclear power station without involving this process of mass consultation, nor is it practicable to rationalise a production facility, change product lines, or introduce new manufacturing methods without bringing in the human factor. To design aircraft in the future without regard to the problem of noise, fuel consumption, or polluting emissions will be just as irresponsible as inadequate application of the laws of aerodynamics, metal fatigue or combustion technology. To conceive elegant and complex methods of numerical (i.e. computer based) control of manufacturing machinery without bringing into consideration the effect on the pattern of employment, of job interest, or the ability of the human operators to adapt to new regimes will no longer be acceptable.

Table B lists some of the activities, all of a very large scale, where decisions by governments or by large commercial undertakings have been challenged, impeded or indeed reversed through the collective influence of

Table B. Activities influenced by human factors.

PUBLIC RESISTANCE TO CHANGE

Siting of Nuclear Plant

Siting of Chemical Plants (Flixborough)

Construction of Motorways

Location of Airports

City Centre Reconstruction

Introduction of Automated Machines (eg printing)

High Productivity Plants (blast furnaces)

Overtime versus Time Off (capital equipment)

Standardization

human factors. All too often those who are trying to promote these projects become very angry, try to brush aside opposition, or search for sinister underlying motives. This widespread and possibly, in some cases, ill-informed opposition will become an ever increasing component of political and industrial life. Entrepreneurs, engineers and policy makers must take this into account right from the outset of a project. To plunge into commitment, consume large resources and raise expectations (at least of some) only to founder at the very last because of human reactions is just bad management.

The Mighty Chip

Reverting to the technological explosion, there is one technology, implicit in what has been written above, which must nevertheless be singled out for special comment. When the historians of the 21st and later centuries look back at this one, they will probably label it as the "Technological Century". But when cataloguing the technological discontinuities which would justify such a title, their first choice will not be the internal combustion engine, jet aircraft, nuclear power or plastics — it will be semi-conductors. Whereas all the other technologies have advanced dramatically they have only given more impetus to things that man was already able to do with the use of machines — travel, shape materials, provide horse-power, construct buildings etc. etc. The impact of the micro-electronics revolution manifests itself in very different ways i.e.:

1. By its ability to extend or even displace man's capacity of thinking, his intuition or his judgement.
2. By its pervasiveness; there is virtually no field in manufacturing, the utilities, the service industries or commerce that can fail to be profoundly influenced by this advance.
3. Replacing many devices which have traditionally been the territory of precision mechanical (or electro-mechanical) devices by purely electronic systems — itself a very substantial revolution. Cash registers, wrist watches, telephone exchanges, etc. have already gone this way. Many more will follow.
4. The speed of advance. Never has a powerful technology advanced so rapidly in such a short time. The performance of a single chip measured in terms of the number of gates it can contain (see Fig. 13.9) has increased ten thousandfold in a period of 15 years. The speed of obsolescence of not only the chips themselves but of all the ways they can be applied is so great that there has hardly been time to get adapted to one regime before another emerges.

TECHNOLOGY AND THE FUTURE OF WORK 187

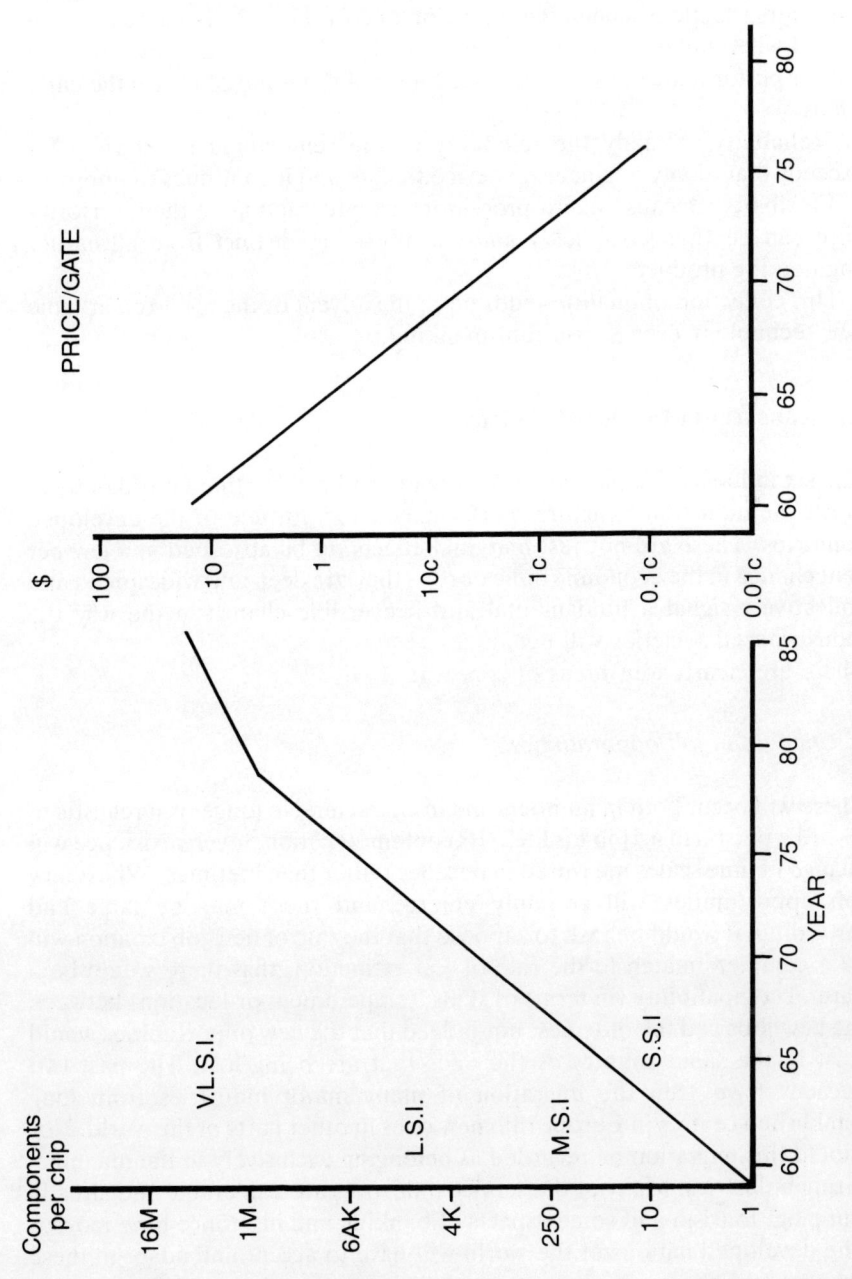

Figure 13.9. Two measures of increased computing power.

5. Reduction of cost. Not only has the performance increased, but even more remarkable has been the reduction of cost. Fig. 13.9B shows that in a period when inflation and escalating costs are the norm, the price of each unit of performance has reduced one hundred thousandfold since the early 1960s.
6. Reliability. Already the reliability of the semi-conductor devices far exceeds that of any engineering device to date and it continues to improve.
7. Flexibility. Because micro-processors are programmable their performance can be changed quickly and cheaply — as distinct from all earlier engineering products.

This collection of qualities adds up to the advent of the most remarkable new technology ever to confront mankind.

Consequences to Developed Nations

The six influences catalogued have already and will continue profoundly to affect the industrial structure, performance and attitude of the developed countries. These are not just marginal effects, to be absorbed in a few per cent change in the economic indicators — they are deep and widespread and collectively signal a fundamental and irreversible change in the way the industrialised societies will live.
There are clearly four areas of concern:

1. *Changes in job opportunities.*

These will occur both in numbers and in character. No longer is it realistic to regard a person in a "job for life". Its content, location or very existence will change in time scales measured in decades rather than lifetimes. Whilst new job opportunities will certainly emerge and these may be large and rewarding, it would be rash to suppose that the rate of new job creation will be a complete match to the rate of job extinction, that there would be a natural compatibility (in terms of skills, temperament or location) between the new jobs and the old ones, nor indeed that the new opportunities would exist in the same country as the ones that are being lost. The past two decades have seen the migration of many major industries from long established centres in Europe into new ones in other parts of the world. Nor should this migration be regarded as belonging exclusively to the manufacturing industries. Many of the service industries are vulnerable and already shipping, tourism and some aspects of banking and insurance have moved. The developed nations of the world will have to accept and adapt to these changes and be prepared to accept their impact on their society.

2. Polarisation of the Work Force.

There is the real likelihood that the workforce will become polarised into a relatively small technological elite, able to move with and enjoy the advancing technologies and to adapt to the changing circumstances and a much larger proportion of work people whose skills have become outmoded and who lack the education or the mental attitudes to adapt to change. A widely based initial education, greater use of further education and re-training and an acknowledgement by society that anyone who has served well for as long as they are able to do, deserves to be well treated in later years, are all matters that will have to be appreciated. If they are not, then unmanageable social stresses are certain to arise and the consequences are likely to be catastrophic.

3. De-industrialisation.

There is the likelihood that whole industries will be rapidly extinguished because of a combination of the influences described above. This has happened before leaving "ghost towns" where the older people cling on; the younger ones migrate to new areas. The textile industries, shipbuilding, farming have seen such changes but the pace was slow enough to allow individuals to adapt. The problem of the future is the speed of change, where flourishing and competitive industries can be liquidated within a few years. Motor cycles in Britain, watch-making in Switzerland and France, photographic goods in Germany are but a few recent examples. The tempo of national planning and redistribution of industries is likely to prove too slow to adapt to the rapid changes and a more responsive system will be needed.

4. De-humanisation

Already many of the manufacturing processes contain very little job interest, leading to lack of commitment and poor morale within the workforce. This trend will increase and accelerate as the developed nations seek to increase their competitiveness against the low labour costs of the emerging countries by an ever greater amount of automation. This is likely to fuel a social problem which is already difficult to resolve. The old technique of disgorging surplus labour or unwanted skills into the unemployment pool will no longer be sufficient. A clear awareness that staff will have to be redeployed and that this will demand not only retraining but also sympathetic handling of the human problems involved will be needed.

These factors in combination pose great problems in the education, training, selection and management of the future workforce in the developed nations and it is doubtful whether the past and existing practices will be even faintly adequate for the future.

The British Case

All of what has been said above applies to all of the developed nations of the world. In the case of Great Britain there is an additional ingredient — that of adapting to the liquidation of the British Empire. Whilst it has now become unfashionable to refer to that long lived institution, and its extinction, the change which occurred has had and continues to have a profound effect on the British economy. Throughout the much acclaimed industrial revolution and the splendour of the Victorian era the British Empire was in full flood. By right of treaty, commercial enterprise or conquest, "Britain" became effectively a vast multi-racial, multi-lingual continent, containing within itself nearly every natural resource that the home economy needed. But in addition to these material resources there was the almost limitless supply of cheap manpower, well adapted to their tasks. For every one British worker at home there were at least 20 workers toiling away overseas. These were busy adding value to their natural resources, but the benefits did not go to them — the major share went to Britain. All too often the Britain of those days is portrayed as productive and prosperous without acknowledging that much of the prosperity came from other people's endeavours and resources. Admittedly there were also some penalties: colonial administration, naval and military patrol work, the periodic wars all added their burden, and consumed the services of some of the ablest people in the country. But the net benefit to the British economy was very large indeed.

This situation existed for many generations yet came to an end quickly within a single generation. The length of the time scale and the suddenness of the end can be seen in Fig. 13.10 which shows in the form of a bar chart the beginning and end of each component of the one-time Empire. Such a rapid change after such a long established regime must inevitably produce a shock effect on the British economy and some of the problems which have appeared in recent times stem from the failure to realise the completeness and irreversibility of this change. Phrases such as "Britain regaining her rightful place in the world once more" not only lack realism but impede the change of attitude which is essential in order to adapt to the changed circumstances.

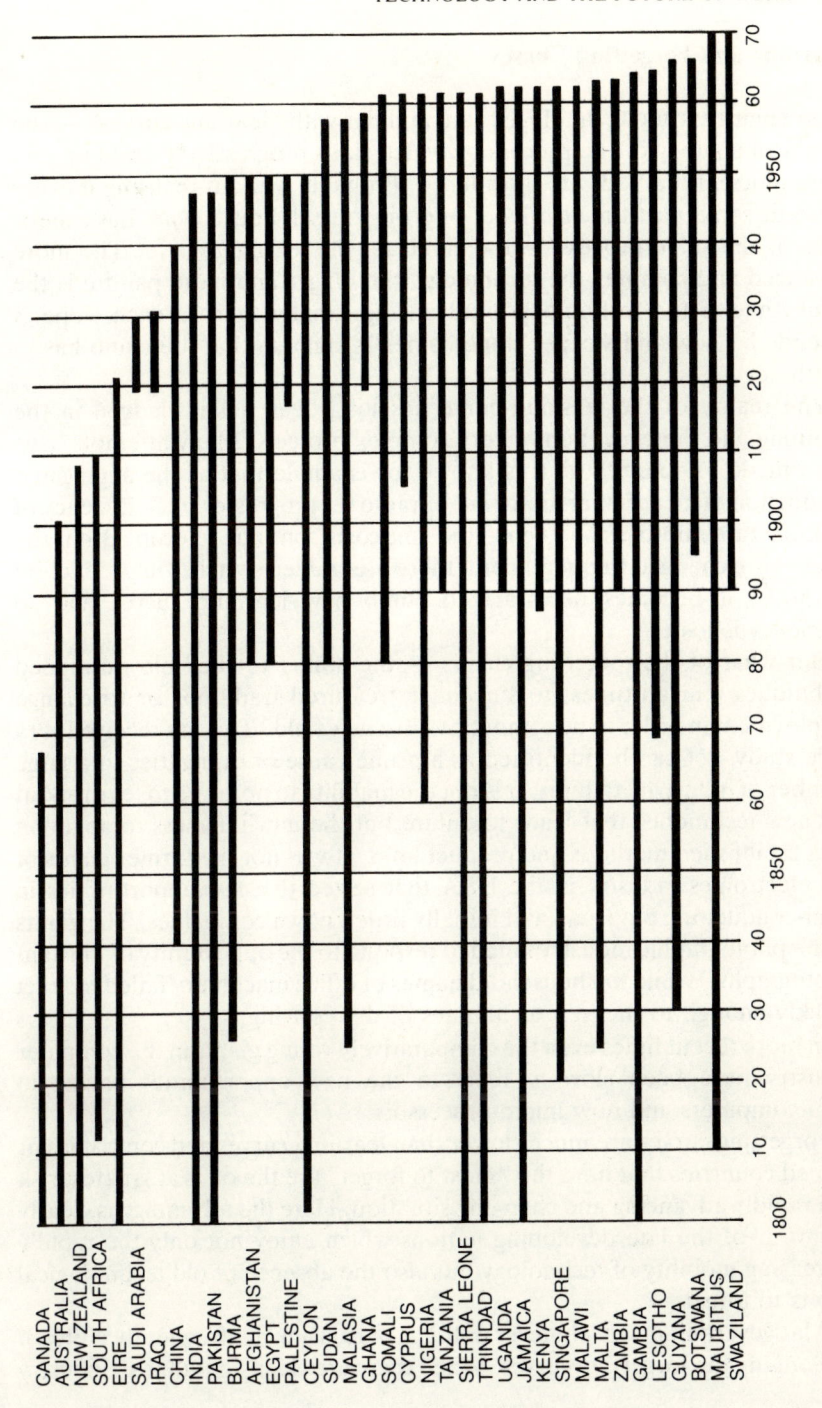

Figure 13.10. Duration of membership of the British Empire for 37 countries.

Learning and Forgetting Curves

Most engineers and technologists are familiar with "learning curves" — the graphical analogy of the process by which skills progressively build up and more efficient methods are introduced. Probably without realising it every amateur cook, part-time gardener or do-it-yourself houseowner has experience of the same process — the climb up the learning curve. The more advanced and complex the technology, the longer and more painful is the climb, and if the technology is advancing rapidly then as each slope is ascended a new and steeper slope comes in sight so that the climb has to continue.

The reality of the learning curve has long been acknowledged in the planning and the execution of very complex projects. Many attempts have been made to quantify it. It is known for example that as the aggregated production of a particular motor car or radio set progresses, the efficiency of manufacture improves and hence the unit costs continue to drop. But if the models are changed frequently or if there are sudden switches in production methods, it becomes necessary to climb new learning curves and so efficiency is lost.

But what of the forgetting curves — the ability to shed old outmoded techniques and attitudes, to surrender treasured traditions or to change employment in order to be competitive in a new field? This has received very little study, yet can be identified as a prime cause of difficulties in a large number of industrial failures. It is not the inability to note and to learn about the new techniques that leads to failure but the unwillingness to abandon long established methods and product lines. It was not the former giants of the electronics industry in the USA that seized the new opportunities in semi-conductors, but small and initially little known companies. The giants of the photographic industry failed to respond to the opportunity of "instant photography" while the household names of office machinery failed to react quickly enough to the new techniques of dry copying.

In more recent times even the comparatively young giants in the computer industry have been slow to react to the new opportunities arising in mini-computers and now micro-processors.

Forgetting curves are much slower than learning curves and companies or indeed countries that have the "most to forget" are the ones at greatest risk in a rapidly advancing and changing situation. Here the advantage is clearly in favour of the late developing nations which enjoy not only the rapidly increasing mobility of technology but also the absence of old technological habits to forget.

Alas governments of whatever political persuasion are frequently guilty of prolonging the forgetting curves. When there are clear signs that an industry or company is in hazard they will rush in and protect it. Rather than note that a radical change in the size and character of the industry is essential and encourage this change, they will postpone and ultimately increase the agony of readjustment. Instead of facing the fact that the disease might be terminal and therefore seek new birth and growth elsewhere, the profitable, dynamic and expanding industries are taxed in order to provide the funds to sustain those that are in final decline.

How is it possible to establish the balance between the undoubted advantage of prolonged learning curves on the one hand and the damaging effects of prolonged forgetting curves on the other? On the one hand one is concerned with the familiar, the confident and quite frequently the affectionate, and there are human, geographical and even cultural factors which will influence the decision maker. On the other hand there is the unknown, the uncertainty of a new technology, a different marketplace, a new amalgam of human skills and a different tempo.

It is very unlikely that the transition from the one to the other can be done by deliberate "planning". Giant organisations whether they are governments, multi-national corporations, nationalised industries or very large companies, are unlikely to have the agility to shorten the forgetting curves. The flexibility and adaptability required comes most readily from the creation and growth of new companies, composed of resources — human and inanimate — matched to the new opportunity and unencumbered by the habits and traditions of large parent organisations. In the presence of a great number of such new enterprises, hungry for labour, the decline of a major company or industry would be less alarming or even a blessing. A situation where the new triumphs over the old by natural extinction is to be preferred to the deliberate policies of fossilisation which have been pursued by governments over many years.

The ability of new companies to emerge, to expand and to adventure is substantially determined by the economic and social climate. Creating a new enterprise is immensely hard work and there is a high likelihood of failure. To encourage such enterprises they must be easy to start, success must be well rewarded, and failure should not be regarded as a social disgrace. None of these ingredients exists in Britain at this time. Capital is difficult to raise and is very costly, employment of labour is hazardous, success is meagrely rewarded whilst failure and bankruptcy is treated as a scandal.

Not only are these social and economic factors of great significance, the very structure of industry can be a powerful disincentive to innovation. As companies and organisations (be they private or publicly owned) become larger, they become more introvert, they cross-trade within themselves, defining requirements very specifically to their own needs, and become ever less prepared to look beyond their own perimeters for goods, services or even utilities. This inhibits the ability of the entrepreneur to enter the field with a new idea.

Here the habits of the European companies and organisations differ from those of the USA. In America, sub-contracting is an acknowledged way of life. A high percentage of the very successful small and medium sized companies in the USA thrive because they established themselves as specialised sub-contractors to a number of competing larger companies. In this way it is possible to have within the one country both giant companies that can afford the very large costs of designing, producing and marketing large complexes, whilst still permitting the emergence of a constant flow of new dynamic companies.

Alas, in Europe and particularly in Britain this attitude is less evident. All too often a high measure of vertical integration exists making it difficult to break into an established field with innovative ideas. Industries such as computers, semi-conductors, instrumentation, telecommunications, electrical equipment, software etc. have been inhibited by the fact that so much is already contained within the maw of the giant organisations in both private and public sectors.

One way of overcoming this structural impediment is illustrated in a schematic way in Fig. 13.11. In Europe there may be four companies, A, B, C and D, each with specialist internal divisions producing components X, special processes Y, and services Z. Any innovative drive in these divisions will have to fight its way through the decision making of a large company and be constrained by this.

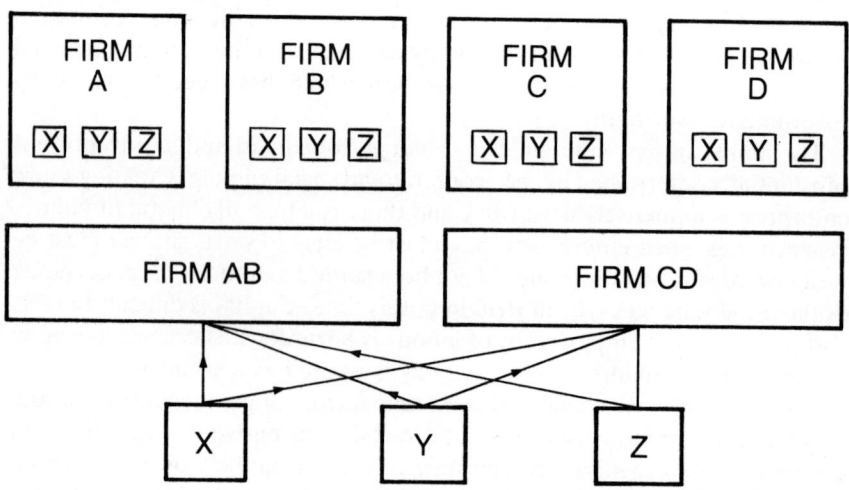

Figure 13.11. Initially there are four companies each relying on three functions which are duplicated by all four. After re-organization there is no duplication.

To adapt to the rapidly changing hazards and opportunities of the future a move to a far less rigid and inhibited structure is urgent. Sub-contracting and complete "hiving off" should be the aim rather than the deliberate creation of giant monoliths. Here the trend of the past two decades has been in the wrong direction.

The Pattern of Employment

That all of the changes described above will affect the pattern of employment is self evident, but it must be possible to do more than just to speculate about the way this is likely to occur.

The distribution of the labour force in the UK as it stood in 1976 is shown in Fig. 13.12. Nearly all of the activities to the right of the chart are "production" in some form or another, whilst all of those on the left are service industries involving person to person encounter. It should be noted that manufacturing — which receives most of the attention when the future of employment is being discussed — employs no more than one third of the total and it should also be noted what a small proportion of the workforce is now engaged in the vital and successful industries of agriculture, mining and quarrying, and the utilities (gas, electricity and water). The prominence of professional and scientific services (lawyers, doctors, architects, accountants etc.) and insurance and banking are noteworthy, which together with catering employ more labour than the whole of manufacturing.

What will happen to this distribution in the future? An indication can be gained by looking at the change in the pattern of employment since 1800 (Fig. 13.13). On that date the distribution between the primary (agriculture, fishing, forestry etc.) secondary (manufacturing and other production industries) and tertiary (service — mostly domestic) was divided into approximately equal thirds. Employment in the primary industries declined steeply throughout the 19th and early 20th century until now only about 3% of total employment lies in this sector. Yet both volume and quality of output has increased by orders of magnitude during this period. For a while the secondary and tertiary industries grew at roughly equal pace until the beginning of the century when the proportion going into the secondary industries stopped growing and this has remained constant for the past half century or so. The tertiary industries continued to grow, as the higher professions expanded (banking, insurance, lawyers, doctors, entertainment, etc.). There are now strong signs that the secondary industries are beginning to follow the pattern of the primary industries as technology displaces labour. Until recently the cost of capital equipment was high and therefore the equilibrium between the use of capital and labour still favoured a high labour content.

PATTERN OF EMPLOYMENT 1976

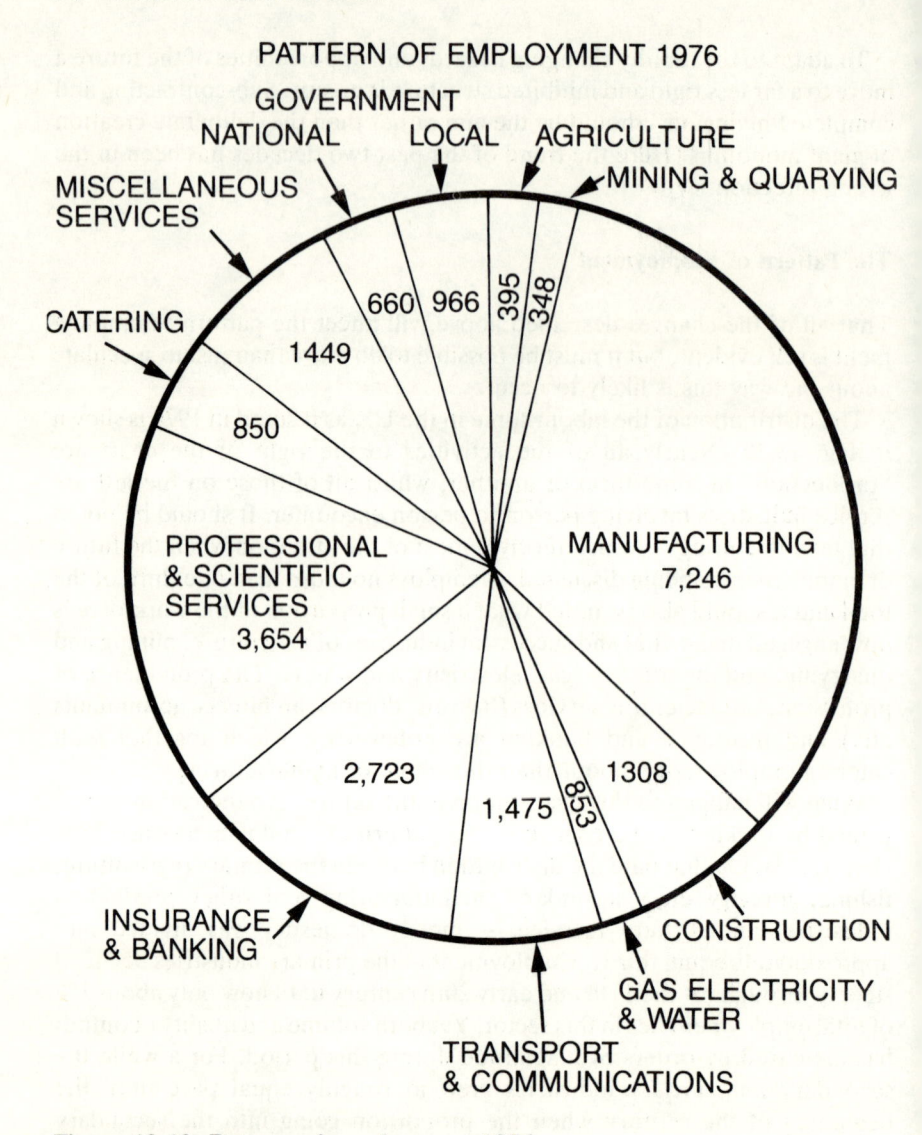

- GOVERNMENT NATIONAL: 660
- GOVERNMENT LOCAL: 966
- AGRICULTURE: 395
- MINING & QUARYING: 348
- MISCELLANEOUS SERVICES: 1449
- CATERING: 850
- PROFESSIONAL & SCIENTIFIC SERVICES: 3,654
- MANUFACTURING: 7,246
- INSURANCE & BANKING: 2,723
- TRANSPORT & COMMUNICATIONS: 1,475
- GAS ELECTRICITY & WATER: 853
- CONSTRUCTION: 1308

Figure 13.12. Pattern of employment 1976.

Now, both due to the advent of the micro-processors and new methods of production, the cost of capital per unit of output is becoming low compared to the cost of labour and the move to capital intensity is accelerating. Whilst the harmful effects of this on employment will be offset to some extent by the creation of new manufacturing activities, it is very doubtful whether these will be as demanding of labour or will expand fast enough to absorb

Figure 13.13. Changing pattern of employment, from 1800.

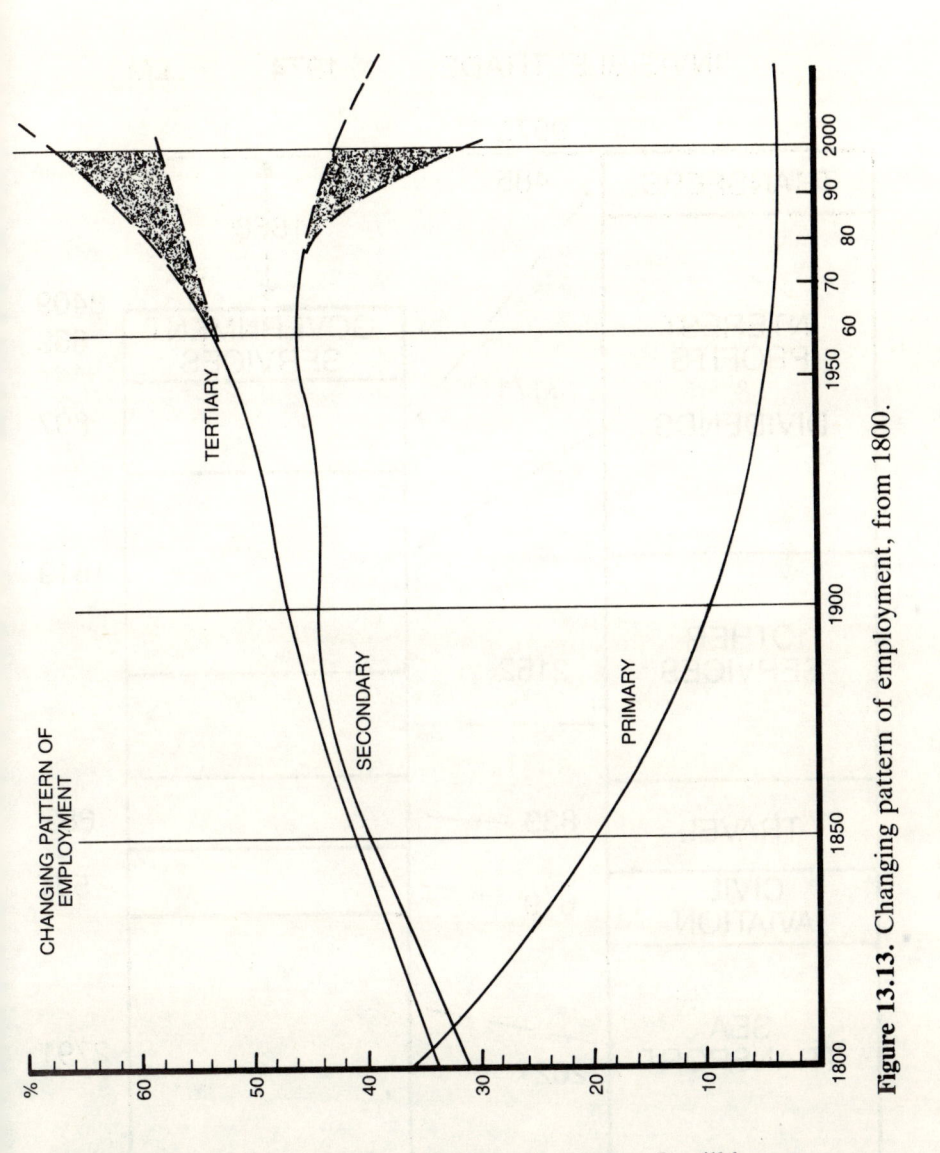

the growing surpluses from the manufacturing sector. It will be even more unlikely that the type of labour required and the location where the needs arise will be compatible with the surpluses that are generated and this implies that extensive retraining of people and relocation of industries will become necessary. Even so the proportion of the workforce engaged on manufacturing will continue to drop, possibly to no more than half of its present value.

198 IMPACT ON LIFE AND WORK

'INVISIBLE' TRADE 1974 £M.

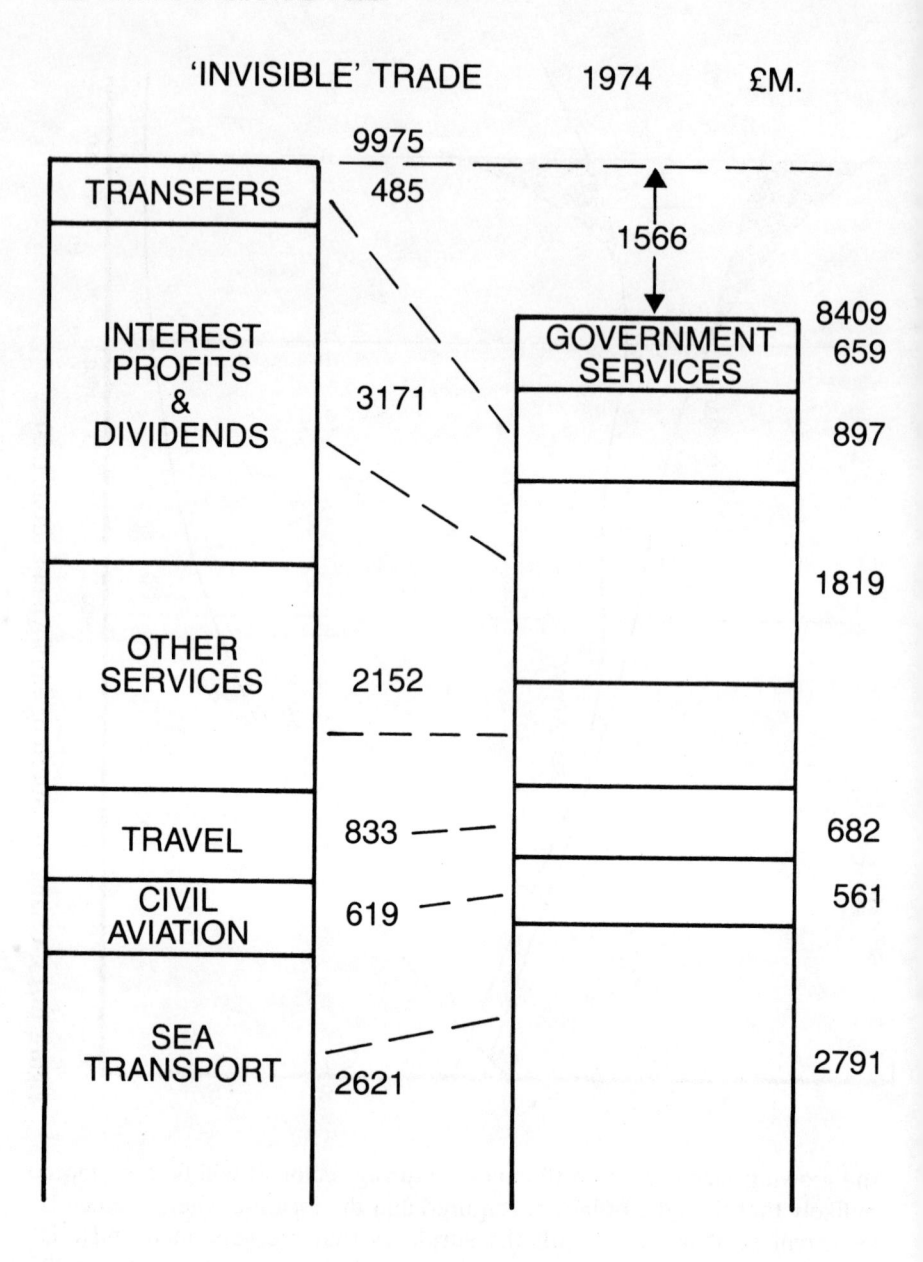

	Inflow	Outflow
	9975	8409
TRANSFERS	485	659
		1566
INTEREST PROFITS & DIVIDENDS	3171	897
GOVERNMENT SERVICES		1819
OTHER SERVICES	2152	
TRAVEL	833	682
CIVIL AVIATION	619	561
SEA TRANSPORT	2621	2791

Figure 13.14. Inflow and outflow of cash into Britain as a result of "invisible trade".

The question therefore is whether the service industries on the left of the chart can expand with sufficient speed to absorb the labour displaced from the right. It has to be faced that in some cases the service industries will also be adversely affected by technological change, but here there is more likely to be an offset by natural expansion. The growth of tourism in Britain, the expansion of the (very successful) retailing businesses, the growth of the leisure industries, entertainment, publishing and financial services have all profited from advancing technologies.

The future pattern is therefore likely to be a steep decline in the proportion of the workforce engaged in the manufacturing industries and a corresponding increase in employment in the tertiary industries, both by natural growth in the service industries and also by the creation of new ones.

This should not be regarded as a disaster but be welcomed and encouraged: the ability of the tertiary industries to contribute to the economy is high. Fig. 13.14 shows the inflow and outflow of cash into Britain in 1974 as a result of invisible trade and the figures are comparable (about one half) to those of visible exports and imports. But not only is there an economic benefit in the tertiary industries, there are even more important social gains to be made. By any measure it can be seen that more, better trained and equipped (and rewarded) people are needed in nursing, the police force, the emergency and health services, welfare, sports, tourism, retailing, entertainment and the arts. There is already the need for more teachers, smaller classrooms, whilst the demand for further education and retraining will increase for the reasons given above.

But there is an important corollary to this desirable switch in human resources. The production industries must be positively encouraged to achieve the very maximum efficiency. The best plant, the most modern methods must be introduced and exploited to the full. Obsession with the short term advantage gained by retaining unwanted labour in inefficient industries will only postpone, possibly disastrously, the inevitable redistribution of the workforce, and the much desired social improvements.

Conclusion

The growing pressures on the pattern of work, on the structure of industries in all of the developed nations cannot be ignored. Both the likely magnitude and the speed of change will exceed anything experienced by these nations outside major warfare and the governmental, social, industrial and commercial institutions must be alive to, and equipped for these changes. A brooding resentment of the changes and a reluctance to adapt will only produce disaster in due course. Acceptance of the challenge and a willingness to seize the opportunities can lead to a better society.

Author Index
(italic numbers refer to bibliography entries)

Appel and Haken, 13
Bennett, J. S., and Engelmore, R. S., 43, *54*
Bobrow, D. G., and Winograd, T., *54*
Bratko, I., 58, *68*
Bratko, I., and Mulec, P., 61, *68*
Buchanan, B. G., and Feigenbaum, E. A., 44, *54*, 60, *68*
Buchanan, B. G., et al, 46 *54*, 60, *69*

Church, 6,12
Clancey, W. J., 44, *55*
Colmerauer et al, 33, *35*

Dantzig, 15
Davis, M., and Putnam, H., 19, *35*

Feigenbaum, E. A., 22, 23, 44, 48, *54*, *55*, 60, *68*, 102
Fraenkel, 6
Frege, 6

Gabrielli and von Karman, 96, 97
Gilmore, P. C., 17, 19, 20, 21, 28, *35*
Godel, 6, 12, 17, 19, 20, 21, 24, 28, 32
Godel and Herbrand, 17, 19, 20, 21, 24, 28, 32
Goldbach, 7, 12

Hilbert, 6
Hunt, E. B., et al, 60, *69*

de Jouvenal, Bertrand, 147, 148, 152

Khachian, 15
Kowalski, R. A., 33, *35*

Leibnitz, 5
Lenat, D. B., 46, *55*

Mc'Dermott, J., 61, *69*
Michaulski, R. S., and Chilauski, R. L., 59, *69*
Michie, D., *69*
Mostow, D. J., and Hayes-Roth, F., *55*

Nii, H. P., and Aiello, N., 51, 55
Nii, H. P., and Feigenbaum, E. A., 48, 55

Osborn, J., et al, 42, 55

Paterson, A., and Niblet, T. B., 69
Peano, 6
Plato, 159
Plutarch, 5
Pople, H. E., et al, 59, 69

Quinlan, J. R., 60, 69

Robinson, J. A., 35
Robinson, J. A., and Sibert, E. E., 35
Roussel, P., 35
Russell and Whitehead, 6, 17
Russell, Bertrand, 6, 17

Shepherdson, J. C., 19, 20, 26, 33, 34, 35
Shortcliffe, E. H., 39, 55, 58, 69
Skolem, 19
Stefik, M., 44, 55

Turing, 6, 10, 11, 12

Van Melle, W., 42, 55

Wang, H. J., 17, 19, 35
Warren, D. H. D., 33, 34, 35, 36
Whitehead, 6, 17
Wippke, W. T., 59, 69

Zermelo, 6

Subject And Name Index

AGE system,   44, 51
aircraft, automatic control in,   83, 84
Albert, Prince,   154
Aldiss, Brian,   139
ALGOL,   7, 8, 9, 33, 34
ALGOL compiler,   8
algorithms, complexity of,   14, 15
AM program,   46, 47
AQ program,   60
Archytas,   5
Aristotle, on syllogisms,   4, 5, 20
ARPANET,   54
artificial limbs, automatic control in,   84–100

Balfour, Lord,   67
BASIC,   7
BCPL,   45
Bodmer, Julia,   101, 104
Boolean Processor,   78–80
Brandt Report,   146
Bratko, Ivan,   58, 60
Braverman, Chuck,   136, 137

calculus, the Calculus of Reasoning,   CH.1
cancer, diagnosis of,   103, 106, 123
    Imperial Cancer Research Fund,   101, 104
    lymphatic cancers,   60, 61
    research,   106, 109
cellular logic arrays,   74–81
'cellular logic image processor',   78–81, 110, 123, 125
Cetus,   65, 66
chess,   27, 58, 60
CLIP 4, *see* 'cellular logic image processor'
CLS,   60
clustering algorithms,   106
Completeness Theorem, of Godel,   19, 20, 28
computers, DEC PDP 10,   33, 34, 45, 50, 51, 54
    DEC PDP 11,   42
    DEC 2060,   54
    DEC VAX 11/780,   54
    Edsac 11,   103

SUBJECT AND NAME INDEX 203

    IBM 360/185, 118
    IBM 370/168, 13
    IBM 704, 19
    IBM 3032, 118
Cosira, 68
cryptographic coding methods, 15

DENDRAL, 44–50, 60
diophantine equations, solvability of, 10
A Distant Mirror, 146
DNA, the analysis of, 102, 103, 107–110
Down's syndrome, 102
Duff, Michael, 67, 93, 110, 123

educational system, role of in the past, 154, 155
    future skill requirements in, 155–165
electrophoresis, 2D gel, 103
Electron Beam Lithography Facility, 119, 121
electronic mail, 104, 105
employment, age-related careers, CH.12
    effect of new technology on, CH.9
    future of work, CH.13
EMYCIN, 42–45
'ethnotronics', 131
Euclid, 4, 5
Eudoxus, 5
EURISKO, 4, 7
expert systems, goals of, 38

Farley, Dr. Pete, 65
Feigenbaum, Ed, 58, 101, 106
Fleischer, Dick, 137
Ford, President, 137
FORTRAN, 7, 33
Frank, Dr. Andrew, 90
Frege's system, 6

General Electric Quadruped Vehicle, 90, 91
The General Sciences, 5
genetics, computer-aided work in, CH.7
Godel-Herbrand algorithm, 19, 20, 21, 24, 28, 32
Goldbach program, 7, 9, 10
Greenberg, Stanley, 136, 137
group theory, 10, 21
GUIDON package, 34
GAELIC program, 119

halting problem, unsolvability of, 6–12
HEARSAY-2 speech understanding project, 44
Herer, Dr. Ewald, 87
Heston, Chuck, 136

204 SUBJECT AND NAME INDEX

Hirose, Professor, 95
HLA system, 106
Hunt, Earl, 60

ID3, 60
inference engine, 22–35
    in MYCIN, 41–44
instantiation, 28
Interactive Computing Facility, 115, 118, 122
INTERLISP, 54, 61
Ion Implementation Research Facility, 121

Jacobsen, Dr., 59, 60
Japan, industrial efficiency of, 131, 150–152, 155, 164, 165
Jevons' logical piano, 13
Johnson, President, 139

Kajiyah, Professor Jim, 33
Khachian-type algorithms, 15
knowledge base, in logical reasoning, 22–39, 47, 48
    in DENDRAL, 44–46
    in MYCIN, 39–44, 58
knowledge engineering, the applied side of, CH.3
    problems of, 50–53
    promise of, 48–50
    two major principles of, 47–48
knowledge refinery, a prototype, CH.4
KRL, 44

Laski, 146
Leibnitz's dream, 5–6, 12, 13
Life of Marcellus, 5
'limits of growth' controversy, 149, 150, 170–174
Limits to Growth, 170
linear programming, 15
LISP, 7, 34, 39, 45, 50, 51
Lloyd, Ian, 64, 67, 68, 151
logic, first order predicate logic, 11–15, 26
    Integrated Injection Logic, 120
    logic cells, 73–81
    'logic programming', 33
    propositional logic, 11, 15, 26, 27
logical reasoning in machines, CH.1–3
    history of, 4–21

Maddock, Sir Ieuan, 63, 68
maps, four colour conjecture of, 13
MARC, 42–44
Marx, 141, 146
mass spectrometry, 44–46

mass spectroscopy, 60, *see also* DENDRAL, Meta-DENDRAL
Mc'Gee, Dr., 67
mechanisation of reasoning, *see* logical reasoning in machines
medical bio-technology, computers in, CH.7
Menzi Muck machine, 89, 95, 96
Meta-DENDRAL, 44–46, 52, 60
Michalski, 58, 59
Michie, Donald, 5, 63, 64, 67, 68
MYCIN, 39–44, 58
MYCIN-like systems, 43–44
Myers, Jack, 59
Myers-Pople knowledge base, 59
Morgan, Henry, 141

NASA, 85, 87, 88, 99
Newton, 84
NMOS process, 120

oil platform fault diagnosis, 59
Orbital Test Satellite, 124
organic chemical synthesis, 59
OSU hexapod, 93–95, 96

PASCAL, 5
pattern recognition in machines, CH.5, 125
Pearce, John, 140
'Phony Pony', 90, 92
Plato, 5
Polya, George, 37
Pople, Harry, 59
population, over-population, 135
 population explosion, 174–181
Principia Mathematica, 17
Project UNIVERSE, 116, 123, 124, 125
PROLOG, 33, 34
PROLOG compiler, 33, 34
PROLOG interpreter, 33
proof-finding, in logical reasoning, CH.1–2
proteins and their shapes, 103, 104
PUFF, 42, 53

Read, Bill, 57, 62, 64, 67, 68
resolution, 15, 27, 28
Robinson, Edward G., 139, 140
robot motion, CH.6
robots of the future, CH.9
ROSIE, 51
Rossum's Universal Robots, 130
Rutherford Appleton Laboratory, 115–121

SACON,   43, 53
Sahl, Mort,   151
Science and Engineering Research Council,   114–125
Selzer, Walter,   136
semantic questions about programs,   8, 48
silicon processing facilities, in universities,   115, 120–121
simplex algorithm,   15
simulation, in computer-aided education,   156, 163
Soylent Green,   135
SPICE program,   119
symbolic computation and inference,   37–39, 48
syntactic questions about programs,   8, 30

Tawney,   146
technology, and the future of work,   CH.9, 12, 13
    and the universities,   CH.8
       disparities in technological capacity,   146–152
       mobility of,   181, 182
       technological explosion,   168–170, 186–188
tessellation,   74–76
tomography scanner,   102, 103
truth table method,   6
Tuchman, Barbara,   146
Turing machine,   10
TYMNET,   45, 54

UK 5000 project,   121, 122
unification algorithm,   32, 33
unifier,   29–32
UNITS package,   44
UNIX,   61

Van Vogt,   138
Vetut, Jean,   85

walking machines, *see* robot motion
Warren, David,   33, 34
Whittle,   64
Williams, Rolf Dudley,   64
Wilson, Harold,   68
Wippke knowledge base,   59

Xerox, marketing of,   64
x-ray diffraction,   104
    replication,   120
x-ray photos, analysis of,   102–103